PLOUGHSHARES

Winter 1996–97 · Vol. 22, No. 4

GUEST EDITORS
Robert Boswell & Ellen Bryant Voigt

EDITOR
Don Lee

POETRY EDITOR
David Daniel

ASSISTANT EDITORS
Susan Conley & Jodee Stanley

ASSISTANT FICTION EDITOR
Maryanne O'Hara

FOUNDING EDITOR
DeWitt Henry

FOUNDING PUBLISHER
Peter O'Malley

PLOUGHSHARES, a journal of new writing, is guest-edited serially by prominent writers who explore different and personal visions, aesthetics, and literary circles. PLOUGHSHARES is published in April, August, and December at Emerson College, 100 Beacon Street, Boston, MA 02116-1596. Telephone: (617) 824-8753. Web address: http://www.emerson.edu/ploughshares/.

EDITORIAL ASSISTANTS: Matt Stark, Jessica Olin, Heidi Pitlor, and Nathaniel Bellows. FICTION READERS: Billie Lydia Porter, Craig Salters, Monique Hamzé, Michael Rainho, John Rubins, Tammy Zambo, Joseph Connolly, Todd Cooper, Emily Doherty, Holly LeCraw Howe, Barbara Lewis, David Rowell, Kevin Supples, and Karen Wise. POETRY READERS: R. J. Lavallee, Richard Morris, Renee Rooks, Michael Henry, Jessica Purdy, Brijit Brown, Bethany Daniel, Tom Laughlin, Lori Novick, Ellen Scharfenberg, and Lisa Sewell.

SUBSCRIPTIONS (ISSN 0048-4474): $19 for one year (3 issues), $36 for two years (6 issues); $22 a year for institutions. Add $5 a year for international.

UPCOMING: Spring 1997, a poetry and fiction issue edited by Yusef Komunyakaa, will appear in April 1997. Fall 1997, a fiction issue edited by Mary Gordon, will appear in Aug. 1997. Winter 1997–98, a fiction and poetry issue edited by Howard Norman & Jane Shore, will appear in Dec. 1997.

SUBMISSIONS: Reading period is from August 1 to March 31 postmark dates. Please see page 241 for detailed submission policies.

Classroom-adoption, back-issue, and bulk orders may be placed directly through PLOUGHSHARES. Microfilms of back issues may be obtained from University Microfilms. PLOUGHSHARES is also available as CD-ROM and full-text products from EBSCO, H.W. Wilson, Information Access, and UMI. Indexed in M.L.A. Bibliography, American Humanities Index, Index of American Periodical Verse, Book Review Index. Self-index through Volume 6 available from the publisher; annual supplements appear in the fourth number of each subsequent volume. The views and opinions expressed in this journal are solely those of the authors. All rights for individual works revert to the authors upon publication.

PLOUGHSHARES receives additional support from the Lannan Foundation and the Massachusetts Cultural Council. Marketing initiatives are funded by the Lila Wallace–Reader's Digest Literary Publishers Marketing Development Program, administered by the Council of Literary Magazines and Presses.

Distributed by Bernhard DeBoer (Nutley, NJ), Fine Print Distributors (Austin, TX), Ingram Periodicals (La Vergne, TN), Koen Book Distributors (Moorestown, NJ), and L-S Distributors (S. San Francisco, CA).

Printed in the U.S.A. on recycled paper by Edwards Brothers.

© 1996 by Emerson College

CONTENTS

Winter 1996–97

INTRODUCTIONS

Robert Boswell 5
Ellen Bryant Voigt 10

FICTION

Andrea Barrett, *The Forest* 12
Christopher McIlroy, *Medicine* 34
Kevin McIlvoy, *Green House* 173
Steven Schwartz, *Skeleton* 184
Elizabeth Searle, *Why We're Here* 197
Kathleene West, *Those Poor Devils* 213

POETRY

Dick Allen, *Cassandra in Connecticut* 73
Claudia Emerson Andrews, *Bait Man* 74
Sally Ball, *Gymnasium* 78
Dinah Berland, *Angeline* 79
Steven Cramer, *A Brief History of the Enclosure Movement* 80
Chard deNiord, *The Invisible Body* 81
Carl Dennis, *Writing at Night* 82
   Distinctions 84
Stuart Dischell, *Evening II* 86
   End of the Century 87
   Psalm 88
Stephen Dobyns, *The Cunning One* 89
   Artist 90
   Discord 91
   Icarus's Flight 92
   Blemished and Unblemished 93
   Last Wisdom 95
Lynn Emanuel, *Self-Portrait as a Small Town* 97
   Poem About a Landscape in the Country 98
   Painting the Town 100
Caroline Finkelstein, *My Little Esperanto* 101
Carol Frost, *Bliss* 103
   Companion Of 104
   Self 106
Greg Grummer, *End of the Road* 107
   This Has Happened Before 108

Donald Hall, *Letter with No Address* 109
Paul Jenkins, *Headboard and Footboard* 113
Alice Jones, *Tap* 115
Sue Kwock Kim, *Flight* 116
Laurie Kutchins, *New Moon, End of October* 118
Thomas Lux, *Pismire Rising* 119
Campbell McGrath, *Praia dos Orixas* 121
Leslie Adrienne Miller, *A Connect-the-Dots Picture* 124
Steve Orlen, *Poem Against Ideas* 127
Gregory Orr, from *Orpheus and Eurydice* 132
Lucia Perillo, *Air Guitar* 139
   Trees 142
   Pomegranate 143
Joyce Peseroff, *Birthday* 146
   Wind 147
Clenn Reed, *Catatonia: In a Classroom for the Slow-to-Learn* 148
Martha Rhodes, *Oh, Luminous* 149
Kenneth Rosen, *Browntail* 151
   The Little Lie 152
   The Dying Gull 154
Alan Shapiro, *The Coat* 155
   What 156
Faith Shearin, *Ruins* 157
Gary Short, *Sway* 158
Ralph Sneeden, *Off Little Misery Island* 160
Lisa Russ Spaar, *Rapunzel's Exile* 162
Nance Van Winckel, *The Company We Keep* 163
Ellen Doré Watson, *Liza* 166
   Now that the Fields 167
Renate Wood, from *German Chronicle* 168
Jody Zorgdrager, *Lunacy* 172

ABOUT ROBERT BOSWELL *A Profile by Don Lee* 216

ABOUT ELLEN BRYANT VOIGT *A Profile by Tony Hoagland* 222

BOOKSHELF/EDITORS' SHELF 226

POSTSCRIPTS *Zacharis Award Winner Kevin Young* 234

CONTRIBUTORS' NOTES 236

DONOR ACKNOWLEDGEMENTS 242

INDEX TO VOLUME XXII 244

Introduction

According to the stories my mother tells, I refused to speak a word until I was almost four. She became so worried that she took me to a doctor—an extreme act in the rural Kentucky region where I was raised; in fact, for the remainder of my Kentucky youth, I would never see another M.D. but go to the local chiropractor when I was ill. The doctor advised her that there was nothing wrong with me physically, that I was merely stubborn and preferred grunting over speech out of some willful streak of perversity. In all of my mother's future stories, the adjectives "stubborn" and "willful" would serve as euphemisms for "stupid," a term she was too polite to use. I embraced stupidity for a long time, refusing to talk although I was capable of it.

When I finally did speak, my words were arranged in sentences. Sometimes my mother says my first utterance was "Daddy made a boo-boo." In unguarded moments, she confesses that my actual first words might have been "Smoke Kools." There is something in both sentences, it seems to me, that is quintessentially American, which is in some circles, I know, yet another euphemism for "stupid."

My own children could not have been more different from me. They were eager and brilliant in their adoption of language. They mimicked sounds early and often, and then, around the age of two, they suddenly realized they didn't have to wade through words. They discovered they could swim. Each unhesitantly took the plunge, and their ability to comprehend and use language became abruptly more complex.

As I understand it, virtually every child goes through this developmental stage at roughly the same age, regardless of intelligence, race, sex, class, or nationality. The acquisition of language follows a pattern that has little to do with the particular dialect or culture or even the individual child, and everything to do with the evolutionary status of homo sapiens. Even children who refuse to speak, as I did, acquire language at the same age as the others. The syntax necessary for language is an integral part of humans at birth. The folks who seriously study this business argue that language is "hard-wired" in the brain, and a child need only be exposed to speech at the right developmental stages for the acquisition to occur, which is then followed by the ability to embrace increasingly abstract concepts.

I've known a number of people, though, whose ability to think in the abstract seemed somewhat below the low end of the normal range. Some were, in fact, retarded, and I worked with them as a counselor (my job before becoming a writer). Others were more or less normally functioning people, those humorless and persistent types who corner you at parties (without understanding the meaning of "to corner") and relentlessly count away at the events of their lives (or their afternoon) without coming to what we might impolitely call "a point," or to that other, more desirable type of conclusion that signifies one has heard a story. Often they are conspiracy buffs, the notion of conspiracy denoting the apogee of their ability to think abstractly. They can provide a multitude of facts about the Trilateral Commission, but terms such as "opinion," "joke," and "coincidence" baffle them; which is to say, make them suspicious. Ultimately they must be told, "The party is over. Go home." In their defense, they take no affront from being told to leave. Why should they?

I think of popular conspiracy stories as rudimentary narratives because all effects have a single cause. While this has a certain kind of appeal—that of tidiness, if nothing else—it lacks the power of more sophisticated narratives. The ability to comprehend and create complex narratives requires one to conceive of abstractions and sequences, and to connect events in terms of cause and effect. Typically, it requires something like compassion, and often, I would argue, the ability to hold contradictory ideas simultaneously.

Some of the most complex narratives, of course, are those involved in successful works of fiction. Such narratives, for both the speaker and the listener, become a way of thinking, a means of discovering what one already knows but had been unable to otherwise express. It is this sense of discovery that writers often talk about at great length, saying how the whole story seemed to exist in their head before they ever put pen to paper. It fits, to my way of thinking, with the model of pre-wired ability; that is, if one's capacity to comprehend and create narrative is hard-wired, then it would make sense that the experience of creating a narrative would feel like discovering something you, in some way, already knew.

As I said, for my children, it was at about the age of two when their use of language passed into a more complex realm. They began to rely on it more heavily, and, perhaps more significant, they began to sense its possibilities. But it was no match for their desires. Temper tantrums ensued as they tried and failed, again and again, to explain what it was that they wanted. I can remember my son in the kitchen, stomping his feet and demanding, over and over, "The other one," while my wife and I hurried about looking for the elusive other. The "terrible twos," as the age is known in toddler vernacular, has, I think, lexical origins. What children of that age wish to convey may be as simple as the desire to be held and comforted, but their vocabularies betray them.

Little do they know that this problem will stay with them for the remainder of their lives. Their ability to express themselves will be constantly outstripped by their increasingly mysterious and fugitive desires. Just the other day, my son, now five, asked me, "How does Mother Nature get a Band-Aid?" He was frustrated by my inability to figure out just what it was he wanted to know, and he could formulate no better description of his desire. He tells me that he knows what he wants to be when he grows up, but he doesn't know the name for it. He's not sure there is a name for it.

To attempt to fully name one's desires is, I think, one of the primary reasons that people write stories. *This is the story of a man whose heart is breaking,* the author writes. There is no need to add, *And I desperately need you to hear it.* Great stories are measured not only by the eloquence and accuracy of desire's expression, but by the magnitude of the desire. It is often this magnitude that separates literature from entertainments, that determines what is serious and what is fluff. There are many beautifully written entertainments, as well as awkward masterpieces of literature. D. H. Lawrence, for all his embarrassing moments, is a literary writer who will endure because of the magnitude of his desire. Mark Twain is another. Intellectually speaking, one may point to Flannery O'Connor's narrowness of scope, but the greatness of her stories makes such criticism seem petty; they seek, after all, to save the reader's soul.

Of course, one cannot really label the desires of the great writers without diminishing them, although it's fair, I think, to say that John Updike's has something to do with human sexuality, and Alice Munro's has to do with personal and collective history, and Toni Morrison's has to do with freedom and responsibility, and so on. To pin them down too much is to deny the stories themselves.

A few years back, at the house of friends, my wife and I watched with our hosts while our daughter, who was five, played with an assortment of blocks and toys. She created a community of buildings, people, and animals. Her play was intense and entirely absorbing. For hours, she played in the dining room doorway while we adults talked and observed. Then our son, just two years old at that time, came bolting through the doorway and knocked everything over. Our daughter burst into tears. Because we adults had been studying her play, we were able to reconstruct the community for her very precisely, but she was not satisfied with it. "It's not the same," she cried. Of course she was right. She had been creating a story and inhabiting its world. In place of that world, we could offer only blocks and toys, a reconstruction of what was merely correct.

Children who are taken away by their play are almost always deep in a narrative, and that narrative, too, grows from the expression of desire. For my daughter, it was then and is now a desire that has to do with harmony and something like equality between humans and animals. She daily works to construct and reconstruct its telling.

One could argue that the ability to tell complex stories and appreciate them has given humans a significant edge over other animals. A tiny portion of the human population lacks this talent. I am told there is a type of autism that has as a central characteristic the inability to comprehend narratives. This rare disorder is thoroughly devastating, as one might well imagine.

That the narrative knack can be separated from other activities of the mind suggests—to me, anyway—that it has indeed been selected for, that it is the product of countless years of evolution. This may help explain the pleasure one takes from good fiction, a pleasure that is much more than merely intellectual, a pleasure that connects with the hard-wired instinct for story. The human spirit, if it does not originate from a god, may well reside in this generational longing that is both the product and residue of natural selection.

All of which is to say, a good story is the best way I know to touch upon the spiritual, to ride the elusive circuitry of the soul. The extent to which stories connected for me with that deep and satisfying yearning has been my fundamental criterion of selection for this issue.

Introduction

It had been twenty years since I'd taken a turn in the editorial trenches, so the invitation to return to *Ploughshares* for one of its anniversary issues seemed an irresistible symmetry, a chance to observe directly some of the changes in the magazine and perhaps, by extension, in American poetry.

Three differences are clear. First, the increased efficiency at the journal with its system of screeners, overseen by the poetry editor, David Daniel; detailed guidelines (and deadlines) for the guest editors; and attentive staff. Second, the higher quality of work submitted—I could have easily filled twice the number of allotted pages. Third, the ambition of the poems I read. If there has emerged a common element which characterizes this issue, and differentiates its pages from those I assembled as a guest editor in 1976, it is a greater inclusiveness, a greater amplitude, within the poems.

Notable in this regard is the number of strong and varied poems of substantial length (corresponding, quite accidentally, to the proportion of longer stories and novellas that Robert Boswell found on the fiction side): the "vivid and continuous dreams" of Hall and Orlen, Miller and Perillo; the shrewd cuts and juxtapositions by Andrews, McGrath, and Van Winckel; the interlocking parables of the Dobyns sequence, included here in its entirety; and the provocative mosaics by Orr and Wood, excerpted from longer works. I also recognized some of the same impulse and intent in what I might call circumstantial sequences by Dischell, Emanuel, Frost, and Rosen, whose manuscripts rang with interesting echoes among discrete poems linked by theme and style. In addition, I was gratified to find a similar inclusiveness accomplished in shorter pieces through lyric means: i.e., the "fine excess" in the textures of Finkelstein, Lux, and Spaar, the meditative leisure of Ball and Dennis, Berland's controlled ambiguity, Jenkins's patterned momentum.

As is usual, however, the issue seems finally marked more by its lively variety than by anything else. Balancing the evocative, straightforward narratives of Short and Sneeden are the shimmering lyrics of Kutchins and Zorgdrager; and while Grummer and Rhodes prove the exhilaration of voice, bird on the branch, Jones compels with muscular restraint, Watson with urgent figurative language. I did not see, in the forwarded submissions, insistent practitioners of particular (and warring) "schools" or camps, although I did read an inordinate number of poems that handle myth—the deft single pieces by deNiord and Allen survived tough competition. Also: a plethora of sestinas.

As is usual, readers will have both the pleasure of discovery, with distinctive new makers like Kim, Reed, and Shearin, and the pleasure of recognition, with poets who have faithfully sent *Ploughshares* their best work over the years. I'm especially pleased to have strong poems by Cramer and Shapiro, whose early publications I sponsored two decades ago, and by Joyce Peseroff, who worked so diligently, alongside DeWitt Henry and Don Lee, to develop the magazine and its deserved reputation for eclectic excellence.

In memory: Larry Levis

The Forest

Later the squat white cylinders with their delicate indentations would be revealed as a species of lantern. But when Krzysztof Wojciechowicz first glimpsed them, dotted among the azaleas and rhododendrons and magnolias surrounding Constance Humboldt's kidney-shaped swimming pool, he saw them as dolls. The indentations cut the frosted tubes like waists, a third of the way down; the swellings above and below reminded him of bodices and rounded skirts. Perhaps he viewed the lanterns this way because the girls guiding him down the flagstone steps and across the patio were themselves so doll-like. Amazingly young, amazingly smooth-skinned. They were sisters, they'd said. The tiny dark-haired one who'd appeared in the hotel lobby was Rose; the round-cheeked one driving the battered van, with her blond hair frizzing in all directions, was Bianca. Already he'd been clumsy with them.

"You are...are you Dr. Humboldt's daughters?" he'd asked. The sun was so bright, his eyes were so tired, the jumble of buildings and traffic so confusing. The step up to the van's back seat was too high for him, but neither girl noticed him struggling.

The small one, Rose, had laughed at his question. "We're not related to Constance," she'd said. "I'm a postdoctoral fellow at the institute." The blond one, who called to mind his own mother sixty years earlier, pulled out of the hotel driveway too fast and said nothing during the short drive to the Humboldts' house. He feared he'd hurt her feelings. For the last decade or so, he'd been subject to these embarrassing misidentifications, taking young scientists for children or servants when he met them out of context. They all dressed so casually, especially in this country; their faces were so unmarked—how could anyone tell them from the young people who chauffeured him about or offered trays of canapés at parties? But of course he should have known these girls, he'd probably met them earlier. And now, as he stepped down into the enormous back garden and moved toward the long table spread with food and drink, the girl called after a flower veered toward a crowd gathered by the pool and left him with the girl he'd affronted.

"Dr. Wojciechowicz?" she said, mangling his name as she steered him closer to the table. "Would you like a drink, or something?"

Reflexively he corrected her pronunciation; then he shook his head and said, "Please. Call me Krzysztof. And you are Bianca, yes?" He could not help noticing that she had lovely breasts.

"That's me," she agreed dryly. "Bianca the chauffeur; Bianca, Rose's sister; *not* related to the famous Dr. Constance Humboldt. No one you need to pay attention to at all."

"It's not...," he said. Of course he had insulted her. "It's just that I'm so tired, and I'm still jet-lagged, and..."

Could he ask her where he was, without sounding senile? Somewhere north of Philadelphia, he thought; but he knew this generally, not specifically. When he'd arrived two days ago, his body still on London time, he had fallen asleep during the long, noisy drive from the airport. Since then he'd had no clear sense of his location. He woke in a room that looked like any other; each morning a different stranger appeared and drove him to the institute. Other strangers shuttled him from laboratory to laboratory, talking at length about their research projects; then from laboratory to cafeteria to auditorium to laboratory; from lobby to restaurant and back to his hotel. He had given a talk, but it was the same talk he'd been giving for years. He had met perhaps thirty fellow scientists and could remember only a handful of their names. All of them seemed to be gathered here, baring too much skin to the early July sun. It was Saturday, he thought. Also some holiday seemed to be looming.

"Do forgive me," he said. "The foibles of the elderly."

"How old *are* you?"

Her smile was charming, and he forgave her rude question. "I am seventy-nine years of age," he said. "Easy to remember—I was born in 1900, I am always as old as the century."

"Foibles forgiven." She—*Bianca,* he thought, *Bianca*—held out her hand in that strange boyish way of American women. Meanwhile she was looking over his shoulders, as if hoping to find someone to rescue her. "Bianca Marburg, not quite twenty-two, but I'm very old for my age."

"You would be in college, then?"

She tossed her hair impatiently. "Not *hardly*. My sister and I were dreadful little prodigies—in college at sixteen, out at nineteen, right into graduate school. Rose already has her Ph.D.—how else do you think she'd have a postdoc here?"

Would he never say the right thing to this bristly girl? "So, then, you...what is the project you are working on?" Americans, he'd been reminded these last two days, were always eager to talk about themselves.

"So, then, *I—I* should be in graduate school, and I was until two months ago, but I just dropped out, it was seeming stupid to me. Unlike my so-successful sister, Rose, *I* am at loose ends."

She moved a bowl of salad closer to a platter of sliced bread draped with a cloth, then moved it back again. "Which is why I'm driving you around. Why I'm here. I'm sort of between places, you know? Between lives? I got a temp job typing for this Iraqi biophysicist here—see that short guy over by the volleyball net? He hired me because I can spell 'vacuum' and he can't spell anything in English. Eight weeks, typing some grant applications. I'm staying with my sister until I get enough money together to move. I might go to Alaska."

"That's nice," Krzysztof said helplessly.

"Oh, please," she said. "You don't have to pretend to be interested. I'm low on the conversational totem pole here, and you're this big famous scientist, and I know you've got better things to do than talk to me. Go talk to the other famous people. Constance collects them, they're everywhere."

She huffed off—furious, he saw. At him? In the battered leather bag that hung from his shoulder, he felt the bottle he'd carried across the ocean as a special gift for his hostess. But his hostess was nowhere to be seen, and no one moved toward him from the pool or the round tables with their mushroom-like umbrellas. Already the top of his head was burning; and he was all alone and wished he had a hat. Was it possible these people meant to stay in the sun all afternoon?

Bianca made a brisk circuit through the backyard, looking for someplace to settle down. There was Rose, leaning attentively toward Constance's husband, Roger, and listening to him talk about Norway as if she were actually interested. Entirely typical, Bianca thought; Rose submitted herself to Roger's boring monologues as a way of pleasing Constance, who was her advisor. But Rose had forbidden Bianca to go anywhere near Roger, since he'd overheard her in the cafeteria comparing his droopy, fleshy face to that of a camel. Constance herself was holding court from an elegant lawn chair beneath an umbrella, surrounded by graduate students and postdocs and talking about the session she'd chaired at a Gordon Conference two weeks earlier—but Bianca could not bear the way Constance patronized her, and she steered wide of this group. Almost she joined the two girls Constance employed from the small women's college down the road, who were trotting up and down the steps bearing pitchers of iced tea and lemonade; she would have felt at home with them, but Constance had rebuked her, at last week's reception, for distracting the help. The knot of protein chemists at the volleyball net beckoned, Rick and Wen-li and Diego stripped of their shirts and gleaming in the sun, but she had slept with Diego after that reception, and things were still awkward between them. Vivek and Anisha, easing themselves into the shallow end of the pool just as Jocelyn, already cannonball-shaped, curled her arms around her legs and launched herself into the deep end with a splash? No, no, no. Vivek was charming, but Jocelyn was impossible, and she was already whaling down on her young squire. Everywhere Bianca looked there was laughter, chatter, the display of flesh—much of it, Bianca thought, better left hidden—flirtation and bragging and boredom. A standard holiday weekend party, except that all of these people were scientists and many of them were famous; and she was neither. And had, as Rose reminded her constantly, no one to blame for this but herself.

Off by the fragrant mock-orange tree, she spotted the institute's two resident Nobel laureates side by side, in dark pants and long-sleeved shirts, overseeing the scene like trolls. She drifted their way, curious to see if they were clashing yet. Arnold puffed and plucked at his waistband; Herb snorted and rolled his eyes. But the serious drinking had not yet begun, and these were only false charges, still made in fun. Last week she had sat next to Arnold during Winifred's seminar on the isozymes of alpha-amylase, and watched him and Herb shred Winifred in their boastful cross-fire. Arnold had smiled at her.

"Nice to see you gentlemen again," Bianca said, when she reached their circle of shade.

The men stared at her blankly. On the smooth green grass, Arnold's left foot tapped.

"Bianca Marburg," she reminded them. He *had* smiled at her, hadn't he? When she asked that question about the electrophoretic bands?

"You're—in Jocelyn's lab?" Arnold said now.

"Rose Marburg's sister," she said, grinning stupidly.

Herb frowned, still unable to place her. "Don't you . . . didn't I see you . . . were you *typing*? For Fu'ad?"

She held her hands up like claws and typed the air. *"C'est moi,"* she said. What was she doing here?

"Ah," Arnold said, with his most condescending smile. "You must be helping Constance out. It's a lovely party, isn't it? So well-organized. Constance really amazes me, the way she can do this sort of thing and still keep that big lab churning out those papers."

"Well," Herb said. "But that last pair of papers, really . . ."

Bianca fled. From the corner of her eye, she saw the man she'd driven here, that Polish émigré, physical chemist turned theoretical structural biologist, Cambridge-based multiply-medaled old guy, standing all alone by the bamboo fountain, watching the water arc from the stem to the pool. Pleasing Constance inadvertently, she thought; Constance fancied her home as a place conducive to contemplation and great ideas. Krzysztof raised his right hand and held it over his head, either feeling for hair that was no longer present or attempting to shade his gruesome array of freckles and liver spots from the burning sun.

Quickly Bianca traversed the yard and the patio, slipped through the glass doors and across the kitchen, and ran upstairs to the third and smallest bathroom. The door closed behind her with expensive precision: a Mercedes door, a jewel box door. On the vanity was a vase with a Zen-like twist of grapevine and a single yellow orchid. She opened the window and lit up a joint. Entirely typical, she thought, gazing down at Krzysztof's sweaty pate. That Constance and Arnold and Herb and the others should fly this man across the ocean to hear about his work, then get so caught up in institute politics that they'd forget to talk to him at their party. Had it not been for the lizard-like graze of his eyes across her chest, she might have felt sorry for him.

* * *

Of course Constance did not let Krzysztof languish long by the fountain; that would have been rude, she was never rude. After a few minutes he crouched down by the rock-rimmed basin and began touching a blade of grass to the water, dimpling the surface and thinking about van der Waals forces. Perhaps Constance caught the movement and thought he was feeling ill. She rushed to his side, she burbled and babbled. She asked him about common acquaintances at Cambridge. Did he want to swim?— but of course not, he should come sit here; he knew everyone, didn't he? She helped him into a long, low, elaborately curved chair, webbed with canvas that trapped him as securely as a fishnet. She seemed unaware that he could not rise from it unaided. And how could he say, as the faces bent toward him politely for one brief moment, then turned back to each other and their animated conversations about meetings he hadn't attended, squabbles among colleagues he didn't know, that in fact he'd forgotten almost all their names and was incapable of attaching those he did remember to the appropriate faces and research problems?

The sun had moved, was moving, so that first his knees then his thighs and crotch were uncomfortably roasted. Constance had brought him to the throne room, he saw. This cluster of chairs, perched where an adrenal gland would be if the pool were really a kidney, held her and him, Arnold and Herb, Jocelyn and Sundralingam. All the senior scientists. Directly across the pool the junior researchers stood in tight circles, occasionally glancing his way; the postdocs and students were gathered at the farthest end of the pool, where a group of bare-torsoed, highly muscled young men had set fire to a long grill. The smoke rose in disturbing columns. He made columns in his mind: faces, names, research projects. Then he tried and failed to match up the lists. The girl named Rose walked by and smiled at him, and he smiled back eagerly but she continued to walk, past him and between a pair of those low white cylinders standing among the glossy mounds of hosta like dolls in a dark wood. He knew he'd fallen asleep only when his own sudden, deep-throated snore woke him.

It was not dark yet, not nearly, but the sun had dropped and the sky was the most remarkable violet-blue. Perhaps it was six o'clock. A few people still swam in the pool, but most were out, and mostly dressed, and the smell of roasting fowl filled the air. Across the water, on the patio, people milled around the grill and the table with paper plates in their hands. Bottles of wine, bottles of beer, dripping glasses, ice; he was, he realized, very thirsty. And past embarrassment, although the chairs near him were empty now, as if he'd driven everyone away. Somehow he was not surprised, when he rolled sideways in an unsuccessful attempt to pull himself from his lounge chair, to see Bianca, cross-legged on the grass, smiling ironically as she watched over him.

"Have a nice nap?" she asked.

"Lovely," he said. She seemed happy now; what had he missed? "But you know I *cannot* get up from this thing."

She held out a hand, but it was not enough. "If you would," he said, "just put your hands under my arms and lift . . ."

Effortlessly she hauled him to his feet. "You want to go over toward the tables?"

"Not just yet. Perhaps I'll just sit here for a minute." This time he chose a straight metal chair with a scallop-shell back. He sat gingerly, then more firmly. A fine chair, he'd be able to get up himself.

"How about I go get you some food?"

He sniffed the air. He had no appetite yet, and the smell of singeing flesh was strangely revolting. "Get something for yourself," he said. "Maybe I'll eat later. But I'm terribly thirsty—do you suppose you could bring me a glass of something cold? Just some water?" He remembered, then, the bottle in his bag. "And if you could find two small empty glasses as well," he said. "I have a treat to share with you."

When she returned he gulped gratefully at his glass of cold water. "Do you like vodka?" he asked.

"Me? I'll drink anything."

He reached into his leather satchel and took out the bottle he'd meant to give Constance. "You brought glasses?"

She held out two little paper cups, printed with blue and green daisies. "The best I could do."

"Good enough." He held up the heavy bottle, so that she could see the blade of grass floating blissfully inside. "*Zubrowka,*" he said. "Bison vodka, very special. It is flavored with the grass upon which the bison feed in the Bialowieza forest, where my family is from. A friend brings it to me from Poland when he visits, and I brought it here from Cambridge."

"Cool," she said. "Should I get some ice?"

"Never," he said, shuddering. "We drink this neat, always." He poured two shots and handed one to her. "You must drink it all in one gulp—*do dna*. To the bottom."

"Bottoms up," Bianca said. Together they tossed the shots down. Almost immediately he felt better. Bianca choked and shook her head, her pale hair flying in all directions. He forbade himself to look at her smooth neck or the legs emerging, like horses from the gate, from her white shorts. He focused on her nose and reminded himself that women her age saw men like him as trolls. Even ten years ago, the occasional women with whom he'd forgotten himself had let him know this, and cruelly. How was it he still felt these impulses, then? That the picture of himself he carried inside had not caught up to his crumpled body?

"Take a sip of water," he said.

"It *burns!*"

"Of course. But isn't it delicious?" He refilled the ridiculous cups, and they drank again. She had spirit, he thought. This time she hardly choked at all. He tried to imagine her as the grand-daughter of one of his oldest friends, himself as an elderly uncle.

"Delicious," she agreed. "It's like drinking a meadow. Again?"

"Why not?"

Around the left lobe of the kidney came Rose, a platter of charred chicken in her hand. Simultaneously, Krzysztof thought, she seemed to smile at him and glare at her sister, who was caught with the paper cup still at her lips. Was that a glare? He could not figure out what was going on between these sisters.

"Welcome," he said. And then, reluctantly—he could not help basking in Bianca's undivided attention—"Will you join us?"

"I can't just now," Rose said. "But Constance wants to know if you'd like to come over to the patio and have something to eat." She thrust the platter toward his face. "The chicken's great."

"Maybe later."

"Bianca? You want to come eat?"

"No," Bianca said firmly; she seemed to be rejecting more than just the food. For a minute the sisters glared at each other—*Children*, Krzysztof thought; then remembered Bianca's earlier word.

No, prodigies. All grown up—then Rose made a clicking sound with her tongue and walked away.

Her mouth tasted of meadows and trees, Bianca thought. As if she had been turned into a creature with hooves, suavely grazing in a dappled glade. The joint she'd smoked earlier was still with her, but barely, palely; this warmth in her veins, this taste in her mouth, were from the splendid bison vodka. And this man, whom at first she'd felt saddled with, and longed to escape, was some sort of magician. Now it was beginning to seem like good fortune that everyone else had abandoned him to her care. The two of them rose from their chairs, on their way to join the crowd and examine the platters of food. But the voices on the patio seemed terribly loud, and someone over by the table was shrieking with laughter, a sound like metal beating metal. They drifted toward the Japanese fountain tucked in the shrubbery; the same place she'd seen Krzysztof standing earlier, all alone. He was smiling now, he had a wonderful smile. It distracted her from the odd way his lower lids sagged, exposing their pale pink inner membranes.

"Isn't this a pretty thing?" he asked, and she agreed. There were ferns surrounding one side of the fountain, lacy and strongly scented. She peered down into the stony basin and said, "We could just sit here for a bit."

"We could," he agreed. "If you would not mind lowering me down on this rock."

This time she knew just how to fit her hands into his armpits, and she got him seated with no fuss at all. "So what is it you do, exactly?" she asked. When he hesitated, she said, "You know, I did do a couple years of graduate work in biochemistry. Remember? It's not like I can't understand."

"I know that," he said. "I know. It's just that no one this whole visit has actually *asked* me anything. And I'm more or less retired now."

"So what did you used to do?"

His whole long life as a scientist stretched behind him, and he could hardly imagine how to tell it quickly. "In Krakow," he said, "where I went to university, I was trained as a physical chemist specializing in polymers. I went to England, just before the Second World War"—he looked at her open, earnest face, and skipped over all that painful history, all those desperate choices—"and after I'd been there a little while, I was recruited to work on a secret project to develop artificial rubber. Then I studied alpha helices and similar structures in polymers, and then did some fiber-diffraction work on proteins. Once I gave up running a lab, I started doing more theoretical things. Thought-experiments. Do you know much thermodynamics?"

"Enough to get by," she said. "But that kind of heavy math was never my strong point."

"I like to think about the thermodynamics of surfaces, and its relationship to the folding of globular proteins. You know, the buried residues inside the assembly and all that. There is a set of equations..."

But Bianca shook her head. "Your bad luck," she said. "I'm probably the only person here who can't follow your math."

"I can show you something," he said. "Something that will make you understand at once."

"Yes?" she said. She was, she realized, wonderfully, happily drunk. Her companion, who was at least elated, reached into his magic bag once more.

"More vodka?" she said. "I could do another shot."

"Absolutely." The paper cups were soft-edged now, and partly crumpled, but he straightened their edges and filled them one more time. "There's something else in here, though," he said.

He delved around in the capacious bag, searching for the toys he always carried. Sometimes, when he traveled to foreign countries, his audiences were so diverse that he had to bring the level of his standard lecture down a notch, use visual aids so the biologists could grasp what he was saying as well as the biochemists and biophysicists. He had not had to use those aids here at the institute, where the staff prided themselves on their mathematical sophistication. But now his hand found the coil of copper wire, and the little plastic bottle.

"Perhaps," he said, "if there was a way we could get a bowl of water?"

Bianca pointed at the basin just below them. "Water's right here."

Had he not had so much *zubrowka* he might have considered more closely the relationship between the limpid water in the basin and the tiny stream trickling from the hollow bamboo. But he looked at the small pool and the eager, beautiful girl beside him, and without further thought he opened the bottle and poured several ounces of solution into the basin. From the wire he quickly fashioned several simple polygons. "Watch," he said.

She watched. The voices from the patio faded, the ferns waved gently, her vision narrowed until she saw only his hands, the basin, the rocks where they sat. He dipped a wire shape in the basin and blew a large bubble; then another, which he fastened to the first. More wire forms, more bubbles, more joinings—and before her, trembling gently in the air, rose a complicated structure supported by almost nothing.

"See where the faces join?" he said. "Those shapes the film makes as the faces join other faces?" He launched into an explanation of molecular interactions that seemed simplistic to him, incomprehensible to her. "You see," he said, "what a clear visual demonstration this is of the nature of surface tension. I stumbled on this some years ago, blowing regular old soap bubbles for the grandchildren of some friends of mine."

"That wasn't soap?" she said. "What you put in the water?"

"Not exactly—the film it makes isn't sturdy enough. There's glycerine in here, some other things..." He added two more bubbles to his airy construction.

There was a theory behind all this, Bianca knew. An idea that this growing structure of soap film and wire exemplified; and she was the only person at this rarefied gathering incapable of grasping what he was trying to explain. Yet as she sat there in the blue air, that bubble-structure elongating while he expounded on his ideas, she felt almost purely happy. Soon she would have to leave this place. Although she was closer to Rose than to anyone else in the world, so close they sometimes seemed to share a soul, she and Rose could not seem to get along now. At night, lying on the couch in Rose's tiny apartment, she could feel the fierceness of Rose's desire that she go back to school and continue the work they'd shared since their father gave them their first chemistry set. Or, if she refused to do that, that she would go away and leave Rose to her own life. It had been a mistake, she knew, to follow Rose here to Philadelphia, graft herself even temporarily into Rose's new world. But her job had only a few weeks to go, and she felt the pull of other places and lives, the same pull that had, in part, made her drop out of graduate school so suddenly.

Soon her whole life would change. But at that moment, sitting on the rocks with Krzysztof, she felt as if he'd led her to a castle from which she'd been barred, opened the front door with a flourish, and then gaily flung open other doors one by one. The rooms were filled with sunlight and treasure. And although they were rooms she'd given up, rooms that from now on would belong to Rose and not her, this moment of remembering that they existed comforted her like balm.

She said, "I had a grandfather who did wonderful tricks. Maybe not as good as this, but still, you would have liked him. He was from your part of the world, I think. I mean the part where you came from originally."

"He was Polish?" Krzysztof said eagerly. That she equated him with her grandfather was something he wouldn't think about now. "You have Polish blood?"

"Sort of," she said. "Not exactly. I'm not sure. Our grandfather's name was Leo Marburg, and the story in our family goes that he had a German name but was born and raised in Poland, near some big forest somewhere. Or maybe it was Lithuania. But somehow he ended up in the Soviet Union, trying to establish vineyards in the Ukraine for the Communists, not long after the revolution. And then—this is all confused, my mother told me these stories when I was little—he came to America, and he worked as a janitor for a while, but then he found a job with one of the big wineries on the Finger Lakes."

"Finger Lakes? What are those?"

She held up her right hand with the fingers outstretched. "Some long skinny lakes all next to each other, out in western New York, where I grew up. The glaciers made them. It's a good place to grow grapes. When he'd saved enough money, he bought some land of his own, and established the winery that my father still runs. I know a lot about making wine. Grandpa Leo was still alive when Rose and I were tiny, and he used to bring us down into the corner of the cellar where he had his lab and show us all sorts of apparatus. The smells—it was like an alchemist's cave. No bubbles, though."

It was astounding, Krzysztof thought. What she left out, what she didn't seem to know. That Leo might have been hardly older than him, if he were still alive; what did it mean, that he'd worked once for the Soviets? That he'd escaped, made his way here, worked as a laborer, but then reestablished himself and his real life? "So was he German, really?" he asked. "Or Russian, or Polish?"

"I don't know," she admitted. "He died when I was five or so, before I could ask him anything. Most of what I know about him my mother told me, and she died when Rose and I were still girls. I don't know much history, I guess. My own or anyone else's."

How could she tell him about her mother, whom she still missed every day? And talked with, sometimes, although this was another point over which she and Rose quarreled bitterly. She felt a sudden sharp longing for her sister and craned her head toward the crowd behind her, but Rose had her back to them, she was talking with Vivek. She belonged with these people, as Bianca herself never would. "It's because of Grandpa Leo," she said, "that I studied biochemistry in the first place. Because of him and my father and the winery..."

"But you stopped," Krzysztof said. "Why was that?"

She could not explain this to Rose, or even to herself: how could she explain it to him? The argument she and Rose had had, when they were working together on one of the papers that grew out of Rose's thesis—how bitter that had been. At its root had been one small kinetics experiment that Rose interpreted one way, she herself another.

"It's so ... *pushy*," she said. The easy excuse, and at least partially true. "Science, I mean. At least at this level. When I started I thought it was something people did communally. Everyone digging their own small corner of the field, so that in the end the field would flower—I didn't know it got so vicious. So competitive. I hate all this hustling for money and priority and space and equipment. Actually," she said, "I hate these *people*. A lot of them. I really do."

"We're not very inspiring in groups," Krzysztof said. "That's true." He pulled his hands apart and dropped his wire forms, disrupting the bubbles so that suddenly he held nothing, only air. Science was a business now, and sometimes he could hardly bear it himself. Yet he could remember the excitement of his youth, that sense of clarity and vision; it was this, in part, that had pulled him from Krakow to Cambridge. But not only this.

"Your grandfather," he said. "If what you remember about his youth was true, our families might have come from the same place. In northeastern Poland is this huge forest—the forest where the bison live, where this vodka comes from. That might have been the forest your mother meant in her stories."

"Do you think?"

"It's possible," he said, and he repeated the name he'd told her earlier: Bialowieza. Bianca tried to say it herself. "It's a beautiful place," he said.

"And there are bison there? Real ones, I mean. Now?"

"There are," he said. "It is partly because of my own mother that they still exist." The whole story swirled before him, beautiful and shapely and sad, but just as it came together in his mind, Bianca leapt up from her seat and held out her hands.

"I could show you something," she said. "Something really beautiful, that you'll never see if we stay here. You probably think this country is ugly, all you ever see are airports and highways and scientists. Do you want to get out of here for a while? We'd only be gone less than an hour, and you could tell me about the bison on the way."

"I don't want to be rude," he said.

"I promise you, no one will notice. I'll have you back so soon they'll never know you're gone."

No one had approached them this last half hour; the other guests had taken root, on the grass and the steps and the chairs, and were eating and drinking busily, arguing and laughing and thrusting their chins at each other. But a threat loomed, in the person of the woman—the wife of Arnold?—standing closest to them. Although she was chattering with a postdoc about her work with adhesives, she was sending glances Krzysztof's way, and these made him shudder. At dinner, the previous night, he'd been stuck with her for an hour while she explained the chemistry of what made things sticky, but not too sticky. As if he didn't know. She worked for some huge corporation; the net result of her work, if he remembered it right, had something to do with those small yellow slips of paper that now littered all other sheets of paper, and on which his colleagues scribbled curt notes. How vulgar she was. If he and Bianca continued to sit by this fountain, the woman would eventually sidle over to them. The possibility was unbearable.

He held out his arms to Bianca. "If you would?" Just then the low cylinders in the shrubberies lit up all at once, casting a warm light on the paths and the pool and the patio—yes, of course they were lanterns, not dolls. Expensive, tasteful lanterns, meant to look faintly Oriental.

"My pleasure," she said. She raised him and held her finger to her lips in a gesture of silence. Then, to his delight, she led him through the ferns and azaleas until they disappeared around the side of the house, unseen by anyone. Krzysztof was too pleased by their cunning escape to tell Bianca how badly he needed to urinate.

They drove toward the glorious red horizon, as if chasing the vanished sun. Although the road was narrow and twisted and sunken, almost like an English road, Bianca drove very fast. Krzysztof clutched the dash at first, but then relaxed; what was left of his hair lifted and fanned in the wind, tugging at his scalp like a lover's hands and distracting him from the pressure in his bladder.

"Is there any of that vodka left?" Bianca asked.

He handed her the bottle and watched as she held it to her lips. "So," she said. "Tell me about those bison."

He stuck one hand through the open window, letting it cut into the rushing breeze like a knife; then tilted it slightly and let the air push his arm up. "I was born and raised in Krakow," he said. Had he told her that already? "But my mother grew up in the country, in this forest where perhaps your grandfather was from. It is so beautiful, you can't imagine—it is the last bit of primeval forest in Europe, the trees have never been cut. There are owls there, and roe deer and storks and bears. And it was the last place where the wild bison, the *zubre*, lived. When my mother was young the Russians controlled that part of Poland and the forest was the tsar's private hunting preserve."

"Your mother was Russian?"

"No—*Polish*. Defiantly, absolutely Polish." He almost stopped here, overwhelmed by the complexities of Polish history. But it wasn't important, he skipped it all; it was not her fault that she knew nothing and that, if he were to hand her a map, she could not place

Poland more than vaguely. "After she married my father they moved to Krakow—he was an organic chemist, he taught at the university there. During the First World War he was conscripted into the Austrian Army and disappeared. We don't even know where he died. So it was just my mother and me after that. When the war was over and I started university myself, we heard stories about how the German armies trapped in the forest during the war's last winter started eating the *zubre* after they'd finished off the lynx and wild boars and weasels. There were only a thousand or so of them left in the world. The forests had been cleared everywhere else in Europe, and rich people had been hunting them for centuries. Then those German soldiers ate all the rest. What could they do? They were freezing, and starving, and they butchered the *zubre* with their artillery. This made my mother very bitter. Her father had been a forester, and she'd grown up watching the bison grazing on buttercups under the oaks."

Bianca interrupted him—suddenly he seemed old again, he was wandering. And crossing and uncrossing his legs like a little boy who had to pee. Was a bison the same as a buffalo? In graduate school she had once met a man, a philosopher, who raised buffalo with his wife not far from Ithaca and peddled the meat. Lean, dark, a little tough.

"This is Meadowbrook," she said, gesturing at the gigantic houses and formal gardens tucked back from the road they whizzed along; hoping to pull him back to the present. "Isn't that a ridiculous name? All the rich people live here. And so do Rose and I, sort of—she has a little apartment above the garage of one of these estates. It used to be the gardener's quarters—over there, see that big stone house?"

She gestured vaguely, and he ducked his head to see over her shoulder. Whatever house she'd pointed out had vanished. Suddenly she slowed and turned the van down a narrow lane between two stone pillars. "Almost here," she said.

He hurried on with his story, sensing that time was short. He skipped everything personal, all his struggles between the two great wars. He skipped the strange evolution of his mother's heart, the way she had left him alone in Krakow and returned to the forest of her youth, burning with a desire to rebuild what had been destroyed. The way she had turned in disgust from his work, from every kind of science but forestry.

"The bison were gone by the end of the war," he said. "Almost extinct. But near the end of the twenties, a Polish forester started trying to reestablish a breeding stock—and my mother moved back to the Bialowieza, to help him. There were a few in a zoo in Stockholm, and some in zoos in Hamburg and Berlin. A few more had survived the war in the south of Poland. And my mother and this man, they brought some females from that little group to the forest, and borrowed bulls from the zoos, and they started a breeding program. From them come all the European bison left in the world. There are several thousand of them now—because of my mother, you see? My own mother."

They were in a forest of sorts right now—the lane grew narrower and turned into a dirt track, and trees brushed the side of the van. When they emerged into a small clearing, Bianca stopped the van without saying a word in response to his tale.

"I run here," she said. "Almost every night. It's a park, this place. But no one comes here, I never see any people. I like to run just before dark." For a second he pictured her, pounding down the dirt paths; perhaps this explained her extraordinary legs. She came around to his side of the van and helped him down the awkward step.

"It's beautiful," he said. Why had he been telling her that story? The forest, his mother, the starving soldiers; the bison, so huge and wild, just barely rescued from oblivion. That part ended happily. The rest, which he would never tell Bianca, did not: during the Blitzkrieg the German army had overrun the forest in a matter of weeks. Then it had passed to the Russians, then back to the Germans; swastikas had flown from the roofs. The resident Jews had been slaughtered under those ancient oaks, and the farmers and foresters had been deported. His mother had disappeared. And all the while he had been safe in England, unable to persuade her to join him. Unable to save her, or anyone. In test tubes he had grown chains of molecules, searching for something that might be turned into tires for planes and jeeps.

"It's a national park now, that forest," he said, unable to let the story go. Then the pressure in his bladder grew unbearable, and he said, "Would you excuse me for a minute?" He stepped behind an oak and into a thorny tangle, disappearing in the brambles.

Behind him, Bianca was puzzled and then amused as she heard the long splatter of liquid on leaves, a pause, more splatter, a sigh. The sigh was one of pleasure; even this simple act was no longer reliable, and Krzysztof felt such relief as his urine flowed over the greenery that he was hardly embarrassed when he emerged and Bianca gently pointed out the bit of shirttail emerging from his fly like a tongue.

After he tidied himself, Bianca led him across a muddy field and into the trees at the far edge of the clearing. The sky had turned a smoky violet gray, truly dusk, all traces of red disappeared and with it the color of the leaves and Bianca's hair.

"No bison here," she said cheerfully. "But I think we made it just in time. This whole area—I hate this area, it's one giant suburb. This is the only bit of real woods left for miles. But something kept eating everything Rose planted in her garden, and when I started jogging here I found out what it was. Be quiet now."

He was. He was exhausted, remarkably drained, the vodka swirling through his veins. The marzipan-like taste of the bison grass; was it that flavor the secretive, lumbering creatures had craved as they grazed? The only time he had visited his mother in the forest, just before he left for England, she had fed him a dish of wild mushrooms, wild garlic, and reindeer, washed down with this vodka. He had tried to persuade her that war was inevitable. Her hair was gray by then, she no longer looked anything like Bianca. She lived in a low dark hut by herself and said she would rather die than leave her home again.

A deer appeared in the clearing. He blinked his eyes; it had not been there, and then it was. Bianca inhaled sharply. "Oh," she whispered. "We made it just in time." He blinked again: four deer, then eleven, then seventeen. They came out of the trees and stood in the gathering darkness, looking calmly at each other and at the sky. How beautiful they were. He squeezed Bianca's hand, which was unaccountably folded within his own.

She stood very still. Night after night, during these long strange weeks, she had left Rose's cramped apartment and their difficult quarrels, slipped on her running shoes, and sped down the long driveway, past the houses of the wealthy, across the busy suburban road, and into this park. And almost every night she was rewarded with this vision. She could hear her mother's voice then, as if the deer were transmitting it; they seemed unafraid of her and often stayed for half an hour. Tonight they were edgy, though. Their tails twitched and their ears rotated like tiny radar dishes; their heads came up suddenly and pointed toward the place where Bianca and Krzysztof were hidden. They were nothing like bison. They were dainty and delicate-footed, completely at home here and yet so out of place beyond the confines of this small haven. Still she could not figure out either how or when they crossed the bustling road between the park and Rose's apartment to browse on the lettuce and peas.

She did not have to tell Krzysztof not to speak; he stood like a tree, wonderfully still and silent. But his face gleamed, she saw. As if he'd been sprayed with water; was he crying? Suddenly one doe leapt straight up, turned in the air, and then bounded away. The others quickly followed. It was dark, the show was over.

"You okay?" she whispered.

"Fine," he said. "That was *lovely*. Thank you."

"My pleasure."

She slipped an arm beneath his elbow to guide him back through the muddy part of the field, but he shook her off. He was restored, he was himself. He strode firmly over the ruts and ridges. "It's hard to believe there's a place like this so close to the congestion," he said.

She was behind him, unable to make out his words. "What?" she said.

He turned his head over his shoulder to repeat his comment. As he did so, his right foot plunged into a deep hole. For a moment he tottered between safety and harm, almost in balance, almost all right. Then he tipped and tilted and was down in the mud, looking up at the first stars.

In the emergency room, the nurses and residents were very impatient with them. No one seemed able to sort out Krzysztof's health insurance situation: what were these British papers and cards, this little folder marked *Traveler's Insurance*? Then there was the vodka on his breath, and Bianca's storm of hysterical tears; for some minutes the possibility of calling the police was raised. X-rays, blood tests, embarrassing questions: "Are you his girlfriend?" one nurse said. From Bianca's shocked rebuttal, Krzysztof understood that, just as he'd feared, she had never seen him, not for one moment, as an actual man. Almost he was tempted to tell her how clearly, and in what detail, he'd imagined her naked. She sat in an orange plastic chair and sobbed while he was wheeled in and out of rooms, his veiny white legs exposed in the most humiliating fashion. And this exposure was what distressed him most, although more friends than he could count had met their deaths through just such casual falls. Somehow the possibility of actual bodily harm had not occurred to him as he lay calmly regarding the stars from the muddy field.

"The ankle's not broken," a young doctor finally said. "But it's badly sprained."

"So he's all right?" Bianca kept saying. "He's all *right*?" She could not seem to calm herself and sat, as if paralyzed, while the doctors drew a curtain around Krzysztof and went to work.

An hour later Krzysztof emerged with his lower leg encased in two rigid plastic forms, each lined with a green plastic air-filled pod. Velcro straps clamped the shells around him, as if his ankle were an oyster. A boy young enough to be his grandson had given him two large white pills in a white pleated cup, which resembled in miniature the nurse's cap worn by a woman he'd loved during the war; the woman's name had vanished, as had the pain, and his entire body felt blissful. Bianca carried the crutches, and a sheaf of instructions and bills. She opened the van's side door and tried to help as two men lifted Krzysztof from the wheelchair and draped him along the back seat.

All the way back to Constance's house, Bianca drove slowly, avoiding potholes and sudden swerves. "Are you all right?" she asked every few minutes. "Is this hurting you?"

Drowsily he said, "I have not felt so good in years." Actually this long narrow seat was more comfortable than the vast bed in his hotel. The jacket Bianca had folded into a pillow beneath his head smelled of her; the whole van was scented with her presence. On the floor, just below his face, he saw nylon shoes with flared lumpy soles and socks and shirts and reeds and a bird's nest, a canvas sack and a withered orange. Behind his seat was a mat and a sleeping bag. "Do you sleep in here?" he asked.

"I have—but not these last weeks. I'm so sorry, I never meant—I can't *believe* this happened."

"My fault," he said. "Entirely. You mustn't blame yourself."

"Everyone else will," she said bitterly. "Everyone."

Should she bring him straight back to his hotel? But she had to stop at Constance's house, let Constance and the others decide what was best for him. Perhaps Constance would want to have him stay with her. It was past eleven, they'd been gone for hours; and although Bianca had had plenty of time to call from the hospital, the phone booth had seemed impossibly far away, and malignant. Now the only honest thing to do was to show up, with her guilty burden, and admit to everyone what had happened. Behind her, Krzysztof was humming. Stoned out of his gourd, she thought; she would have given anything for their positions to be reversed.

"Talk to me," he said. "It's lonely back here. All I can see is the back of your head."

"Those bison," she said. "Are they anything like our buffalo?"

"Similar," he said. "But bigger. Shaggy in the same way, though."

"I heard this thing once," she said. "From a friend of my mother's, who used to visit the winery when Rose and I were little girls. He was some kind of naturalist, I think he studied beetles. Once he said, I think he said, that the buffalo out west had almost gone extinct, but then some guy made a buffalo refuge in Montana, and stocked it with animals from the Bronx Zoo. Like your mother did, you see?" For a minute her own mother's face hovered in the air lit by her headlights.

The van slowed and made a broad gentle curve—Constance's circular driveway, Krzysztof guessed. "In Polish," he said dreamily, "the word for beetle is *chrzaszcz*." Bianca tried to repeat the word, mashing together the string of consonants in a way he found very sweet. How pleasing that after all she'd paid attention to his stories. Their slow progress through the afternoon and evening had culminated properly among the deer, not here, and all of it had been worthwhile.

"We're here," she said. "Boy, this is going to be *awful*—just wait for a minute, I'll tell everyone what's going on, and we'll see what to do."

She turned and touched his head, preparing to face her sister.

"Don't worry," he said gently. "I'll tell everyone I asked you to take me for a drive. I had a lovely evening, you know. I'm very glad to have met you."

Neither of them knew that out back, beyond the rubble of the party, large sturdy bubbles had been forming for hours at the lip of the bamboo fountain, to the mystification of everyone. They did not see the bubbles, nor the inside of the house, because Rose and Constance came flying out the front door to greet the van. Terrified, Bianca saw. And then, as she prepared the first of many explanations, the first clumsy attempt at the story she'd tell for years, with increasing humor and a kind of self-deprecation actually meant to charm in the most shameful way, she saw their faces change: that was rage she saw, they were enraged.

In an instant she had thrown the van into gear again and stomped on the gas. Krzysztof said, "Where...?" and as they lurched back onto the road, leaving behind Constance and Rose and the fountain and the lanterns, the squabbling scientists, the whole world of science, she said, "Back to your hotel, you need to be in your own bed."

Back, Krzysztof thought. Back to the airport, back to England, back across the ocean and Europe toward home; back to the groves of Bialowieza, where his mother might once have crossed paths with Bianca's grandfather. Might have escaped, like him; might have survived and adopted another name and life during all the years when, in the absence of family or friends, her only son shuttled between his laboratory and his little flat and the rooms of the women who one by one had tried and failed to comfort him. Back and back and back and back. Where had his life gone?

He thought, *Back,* but Bianca—her foot heavy on the accelerator—thought, *Away.* She had her wallet and her sleeping bag and her running shoes and her van; and she drove as if this were the point from which the rest of her life might begin.

Medicine

The Buffalo Vision

Late on the third night of the Sun Dance, most of the hundred Crow people within the Big Lodge had fallen asleep. The fire was low, the singers' voices hoarse over the drumbeat.

Only John Sees the Hill still danced in place, his back to the circular wall of upright aspen boughs. Shrilling his eagle-bone whistle, John weaved toward the Center Pole, a white cottonwood limb. From beneath its forked crest a mounted buffalo head stared at him blindly, firelight seething across its brown wool and steely horns. John's legs wobbled, though an eagle plume stood stiff upright in each of his fists; like the other dancers, he had neither eaten nor drunk in over two days. John ran at the animal, daring it to turn its anger on him and release its power. But when the buffalo's lifeless eyes ignored him, John retreated to the shadows. Mouth parched, drained of sweat, he felt like a column of dust. The round moon shone down, so bright it could break.

Twice more John shuffled, stumbling, to the white tree, only to fall back. Panting, he saw the night as a tilted, spinning wash of light and dark.

The drum and singers kept a steady murmur. Beside the fire John's father, Clayton, one of the two Sun Dance chiefs, sang along, wrapped in a red Pendleton. He raised first one bare foot, then the other over the embers, spreading his toes like a hawk grasping its prey. Those talons seemed to enter John's body, invigorating him with the knife-like pain. Again John advanced toward the buffalo, bouncing on his feet. The singers' voices surged, lifting and strengthening him, carrying him like the wind. The buffalo's nostrils flared, puffing steam, and its eyes reddened and hardened with fury. John flew joyously. The animal hunched its shoulders, its bulk filling John's sight. He danced into its face. Lowering its head, the buffalo charged. The thunder of its hooves threw the ground sideways. Red eyes hated John, then the horns hooked him, tossing him skyward.

John's body lay on the dirt beneath the stuffed head. The drummers pounded and sang. Clayton strolled back and forth beside the fire.

John looked up at the moon shining through humps of clouds, which were like buffalo lying down. The silver disc sliced an animal's neck, separating the head from the body. Whistling, the head soared into space, a fiery comet among the stars. John entered the buffalo body and instantly felt both its earthbound mass and the head's free, swooping flight among stars that were chunks of crystal. He woke laughing with joy and crawled to his bed of cool reeds.

On the final morning, the more than one hundred Crow men and women whistled up the sun with their eagle bones, their hands symbolically washing the first rays over their bodies. Songs were sung, the blessings of Akbaatatdia, the divine spirit, invoked by the Sun Dance chiefs. In his turn, John approached the Center Pole for the last time. Leaning his hand against it, he lit a cigarette, letting his prayers of thanks rise with the smoke to his friend the buffalo, up the fluttering cottonwood branches, and beyond.

Four chosen women entered barefoot, carrying water to each dancer. Just before the people formed two lines to pass from the Big Lodge, John caught Clayton looking at him, eyes filled with tears, and couldn't help smiling back. Then Clayton turned and led the procession through banks of spectators to a table heaped with fresh fruit and drinks. John's wife, Millie, stood proudly, on either side their son and daughter. Their hands reached for him and wrapped around his body. Millie cried on his shoulder. John closed his eyes, and the images pitched in his head, the buffalo, the moon, coals pulsing with the drum, green leaves waving against the blue sky. When he opened them, a very tall blond woman was staring across the swirl of dark heads between them, pretending to watch the last worshippers leave the lodge. John grinned at her before quickly averting his face.

Medicine

As daybreak had fired the colors within the Big Lodge—the varied greens of aspen and cottonwood leaves, brushy lodgepole needles, grass, the multihued Pendleton blankets draping the seated dancers—Clayton had raised his arms in prayer. It was the first morning's sunrise service, thirty-six hours before John would confront the buffalo. First Clayton gave thanks for the return of sacred Crow relics, after an eighty-year exile, by the Smithsonian Institute. That had been the occasion for the Sun Dance. Then he prayed for the dancers, their families and tribe, the well-being of Indian people, and the rest of humanity. He prayed for the whites who, lured by the notoriety of the Smithsonian case, had journeyed hundreds of miles, hoping to "go in"; no room, he'd had to tell them. "Let our sacred Sun Dance," he beseeched in Crow, "find its way into their lives, too. Aho." In his heart he was praying hard for John, that at least this one of his sons would keep true to Crow way.

Saturday afternoon, the second full day of the Sun Dance, a line of barefoot supplicants passed into the Big Lodge to be doctored by Clayton or the other Sun Dance chief. While the patient placed both hands on the Center Pole, Clayton prayed, touched his medicine feathers to the trunk, and whisked them over the person, concentrating on the source of the ailment. Many improved on the spot, a limp straightening or emphysemic wheeze subsiding. A man only middle-aged but vacant and dribbling with Alzheimer's was led by his daughter to the cottonwood. With the feathers close alongside the man's head, Clayton drew out the sickness and scattered it to the east. "I've never seen so many going into a Sun Dance," the man remarked. "Rain coming, though."

The temperature had dropped twenty degrees under low black clouds, and wind swirled dust into the people's eyes. Still the line stretched far beyond the lodge's aspen enclosure. Thunder crashed on them, lightning ripping the clouds. A tree on the nearby ridge exploded, and minutes later a siren wailed from the BIA fire station, but a wall of rain blotted out the flames. The storm surrounded them, a chill mist gusting sporadically. At the rattle of approaching hail, the dancers drew their blankets over their heads. Above them, though, a circle of sky remained blue, and Clayton kept doctoring. Despite the storm's rumbling, the sun broke through with an unearthly, streaming light that made all look as if they were rising up. Clayton's voice shook with emotion as his prayer brought the healing to an end. Later it was learned that two-and-a-half inches had soaked the Arrow Creek Valley, not a drop in the Big Lodge.

For each petition Clayton spread his palm against the cotton-wood and smoked. Dozens of cigarette butts clumped in the dirt at the base of the pole. He didn't doubt that his prayers would succeed. Whites always were astonished at Indian medicine, calling miraculous or supernatural that which to him was a simple fact of life.

Hours later, among the sleeping dancers in the near dark, Clayton received the final blessing of seeing his son "take a fall" beneath the buffalo head, and of feeling his own heart full to brimming.

Clayton's first son described himself as "cosmopolitan," a word Clayton knew only as the title of the women's tit magazine. He'd lived in San Francisco, Japan, the Virgin Islands, every time losing himself in drink, so that Clayton would have to go after him. "Dad threw out the lasso and drug that dogie home," John would say. A Crow woman had him now, in Billings. He'd helped cook frybread for the Sun Dance buffalo feast, organized by Clayton's wife, Berenice.

The second son, who had dug the pit to roast the meat, worked for the tribe in Crow Agency. "He's sound-headed," Clayton told Berenice, "but spiritually he's along the way of being a dud."

John, the youngest, had shot the two bulls served at the feast. Already this triumph was legendary. After hours of driving, he and his father had tracked the tribal herd to a grassy plateau. By ritual law each hunter was allowed only one shot per animal, which must die from a single bullet. When the Crow game warden had missed at one hundred fifty yards, the herd had stampeded up a hill, two hundred, then two hundred fifty yards away. John fired, and a buffalo dropped. "Hit him just over the shoulder. I could see that bullet going the whole way," he said, and shot again. "Neck," he said as the second beast fell. Jumping up, he ran to the kill, leaping a stream along the way, waving his arms. Clayton knew that only spirit could have made those buffalo give their lives to him.

With the Sun Dance at an end, Clayton "smudged" his fan of medicine feathers in sweet, holy cedar smoke, preparatory to wrapping and stowing them. The feathers, bequeathed to him by his father, had belonged to generations of powerful medicine men. After he'd received them, it was five years before Clayton felt deserving to use them. He'd gone in two, three Sun Dances a season, traveling state to state. The muscles of his chest had been torn by the Lakotas' ritual piercing. Through vision quests he had scourged his body and spirit with hunger and cold to let the knowledge in. When this life left him and the feathers dropped from his hands, Clayton thought, only John's hands could open to take them.

The Tutor

Clayton ladled water from the metal bucket onto the glowing rocks. Steam hissed, and John breathed deep, searing his lungs. He grunted with satisfaction. In the dark of the sweat lodge Clayton's voice began its incantatory praying, reciting a litany of ills and sorrows endured by people that he never would meet. Three weeks after the Sun Dance, correspondence was so overwhelming that a burlap sack served as Clayton's P.O. box. "It's like to being Elvis," Clayton said. Most consisted of touching, even heartbreaking pleas—for a dying child's recovery, the return of a husband's love. Stories of alcoholism and drug abuse. Clayton struggled through the English to get the gist. A New Mexico man asked for victory in his upcoming campaign for constable. People wanted help with their bad cars and backstabbing relatives. "Dear Abby," Clayton said, but he prayed for them all, including the Rhode Island lady suffering from shingles; the images puzzled him, of roofing materials buzzing her like angry insects, or her groaning face above gables protruding from her ribs. Maybe she was insane.

In thanks, some letters enclosed cigarettes or even small bills—welcome, as the Sun Dance had left the family in debt despite their selling off land. Clayton begged for the worthiness to carry these people's hopes.

John switched his own back with willow twigs, driving the heat into his body. Only the second pouring, and he felt incandescent. After the prayer, meditating and drifting, Clayton and John would say whatever came into their heads. "I need the truck for Billings tomorrow," John said.

"Pick me up a case of them motor oil," Clayton said. "What are you doing in Billings?"

"Finding a job. I need a place while I'm taking classes."

After a pause Clayton said, "I didn't think you were really going to go ahead for that college."

"I need them teaching me. I see plenty in my mind, but my hands... The kids do better drawings." John laughed. Anger was impossible in the sweat, even at himself. The reason he'd gone in the Sun Dance—"You got to have a reason, the Big Lodge ain't the mall," Clayton said—was his acceptance by Montana State–Billings, eleven years after high school, bad grades and all, thanks to four landscapes rendered in Wal-Mart poster paints. A neighbor had helped him decipher the applications. The same man not only had praised the pictures, but bought one for twenty-five dollars. John could only shake his head in amazement.

"You can't leave Millie and the children all year," Clayton said.

"I'll bring 'em."

"Your kids in a white school?" Already, while comprehending Crow, the boy and girl responded in English.

With no reply John felt tight, closed in. The idea of obtaining his own income had excited him. All he earned from firefighting or repairing cars went straight to the family. He and Millie had lived with his parents for their entire marriage, eleven years.

"You have a place. With us," Clayton said.

Be a cold winter, hitching fifty miles from Arrow Creek to Billings and back every day, John didn't say.

"We'll fix the old Toyota for you, have it to kicking up its heels," Clayton said.

At first, as John had trusted, the buffalo vision touched with grace his experience of college. He found all his classes. The white students would pause and explain to him in detail the campus layout, drawing maps. He was a sunny being, he felt, whose brief company pleased them. The way he moved exhilarated him, light, loose, kind of crooked like a dragonfly's flight compared to their beeline marching.

Home, he painted boldly, uninhibited by his lack of skill. The tubes of acrylic released bombs of color, things not seen in this world. He might set a blue-faced warrior, mounted on a red horse, beside a yellow boomerang-like object suspended in the sky. Often, though he never would reproduce the sacred vision directly, buffalo and moons possessed the canvas, inspiring the other elements to follow them. His six-year-old son, Dan, sat at his feet while the pictures formed. "Ho," the boy exclaimed as an orange bolt split a mountain. The family's curious hovering, rather than making John self-conscious, gripped and pushed him so that he felt he was painting with their collective mind.

Only Millie scarcely could take notice. She greeted his late arrivals in Arrow Creek with brusque sarcasm, until they went to bed. The past six years she'd used a diaphragm, but now she teased him by pretending to throw it away. She was lean, with fine bones, pockmarked skin, and a rare, girlish smile. One night he embraced her with the diaphragm still in its case. Initially she went slack—they'd agreed that Dan would be their last—but then she let herself go with him. Her legs scissored around his back as he whispered in her ear, "This baby will be born under good luck. Lucky, lucky baby."

Assessing John's torrid output as "highly promising," the art professor gave him a studio key.

Academic courses, however, the English, math, history, were a nightmarish blindness. Lectures, textbooks—John comprehended nothing. Fluent in Crow, he barely read English and spoke it either haltingly or in desperate, helter-skelter bursts. While Millie, who kept the family's account book, guided him through math homework, she couldn't take his tests. The longer he waited for the blankness to lift, the worse it was. Three weeks into the semester he called Teresa Gundersen, the tall blond woman, in her forties, who had waited to glimpse him outside the Big Lodge.

The year before, after watching him fancy-dancing at Crow Fair, she'd slipped him her phone number on her husband's business card. His lobbying for the Montana timber industry generally kept him in Washington, D.C., she said.

Less than an hour after he phoned, Teresa joined him in the studio where he was painting a green disembodied head. A horn grew beside one ear, balanced asymmetrically by a curly forelock. Powwow music thumped from a tape recorder.

"Stunning," Teresa said, flinging up her arms. Her bosom

strained against the buttons of her red silk blouse, just as her tummy bulged out her jeans.

"My professor told me I'm running away from the field. So I look at him: Wha'?" John cocked his head. "It's good. It's good." He laughed.

Teresa cased the studio, examining the various student pieces. "No competition," she confirmed. John smiled in response to her small talk. "You sang at Crow Fair with your dad," she said. "What are they saying?" She indicated the tape player.

"It's a forty-nine, love song, you know. Indian blues."

"Sing me one."

John clicked off the machine. Pounding a heavy cadence with his palm on his knee, he chanted two stately, loping verses.

Teresa's hands folded in her lap. "What does it mean?" she asked humbly.

"Aha, don't you want to know," John said.

"I'm serious."

John laughed, his long ponytail shaking.

"Well, let's play this, then. I bought it at the mall." She popped in the cassette. "Bulgarian women's chorus."

At the first ethereal a cappella notes, John was transfixed. The crystalline dissonances went straight to his groin. The voices were naked angels, like a cottonwood stripped of its bark, more, a purer white than Earth could allow. He looked up at Teresa. Shy to betray desire, she leaned fidgety against the wall, a one-hundred-dred-eighty-pound waif.

John danced her to the floor. The music took him away even while his body feasted. In thanks he kissed the woman's breasts over and over. They were big enough to hide in.

It was while Teresa dressed that he said, "I had a question." Opening his composition book, he pointed to "thesis." "Is it more than one of 'these'?"

"Poor boy," she said. "We're going to have to hold a regular study hall."

Within a few weeks John was passing all his courses but American history. Like many traditional Crows, he was unconcerned with strict chronology; his father might state a given duration as "two month, maybe three years." John couldn't say if Lincoln freed the slaves before or after Martin Luther King.

Teresa drilled him in grammar, spelling, and math, besides negotiating extensions with his professors. She dictated his reports, and when that proved agony, typed them or wrote them out for him to copy.

Education pelted him like a gale with broken sticks and tossed leaves of knowledge. "Picasso, ah yes, Picasso," he told Teresa. "The sad blue people, and bulls, analytic cubism made the illusion of the depth, synthetic cubism the picture is flat...ran, has run, will have been running..."

Millie said, "When we were trying for the baby? It was the wrong time of the month. I knew, but I was still hoping, until today."

John squeezed her hand and pursed his mouth as if he hadn't forgotten. Then he felt a sharp regret, remembering how he loved the calmness in her face as she held a newborn to her breast.

But as the semester progressed and he returned later and later, the kids dozing in front of videos, waiting, Millie withdrew into silent rage. On a morning, actually near noon, when John splashed the sleep out of his head at the kitchen sink, Millie sat brutally beading a pair of deerskin boots, shoving a needle through the leather.

"It's a shame, poor young wife," Berenice said.

"There's a culture festival they're doing down in Wyoming," Clayton said, "and they're wanting us to share our Crow dancing." "Us" obviously included John.

John shook his head. "Midterms are the week after."

"Good," Berenice said.

"But I got to read them books."

"Don't tell me you can't dance with us," Clayton snapped in Crow.

The next day John packed a bedroll. "I'm staying in Billings the next three days. Got to make up all that studying I'm going to lose. Maybe sleep a little on the studio floor." He drove away before anyone could stop him. Teresa rented them a motel room.

"Why do you cover up?" John asked. Teresa had dragged the king-size sheet around her and into the bathroom, affording him only a peek at her snowy avalanche of flesh.

"I'm a grandmother," she said, trailing the sheet back to bed.

"No, you look young. Strong," he said, flexing his arms. "Like one of them." He indicated the track and field on TV.

"A shot-putter?"

John laughed, not understanding. He'd noticed that Teresa always claimed the last comment in any exchange, but that was only fair since apparently she knew everything. Mention Kandinsky, whom John had adopted as his favorite artist, and she discussed the transition from Die Blaue Reiter to the Bauhaus. "Of course the war intervened. Franz Marc dying so young, a tragedy. Or the poets! Brooke, Owen."

"The Vietnam War?"

"Did you know that people actually have been fighting wars since before you were born?"

"Sure. The Crows fought the Lakota a long time. Ten years."

"Try a couple of centuries." She even knew more about the old-time Crows than he did, the society of men's clubs, the ancient linguistic affinity between Crow and Lakota. "But Crow men always were the most beautiful," she said.

In bed, though, she lay stiff and shrinking as if hardly daring hope that he'd touch her. He would straddle her, letting his cock and balls brush her belly, up her breasts to her chin and lips. Then she'd sigh and begin to stroke him, murmuring into his skin, tightening her grip. She was very powerful, and her rolling on top gave him moments of real anxiety before his strength welled up to match her. He'd decided to find nobility in her handsome, broken features, though the sight of her in bright day made him cold.

The culture festival was grim. Under a leaden sky, snow fell steadily. Since John's three-day absence he and Millie hadn't spoken, and the children were cranky, whining and stamping as he tied on their beaded leggings. The entire family, including his brothers and clan relatives, danced or sang with the drum.

John crouched and darted, ruffling his turkey-feather bustle. Against the monochrome afternoon the Crows, vivid in colored fabrics and cut-glass beadwork, plumes wagging, undulated like autumn foliage. Berenice wore an elk-tooth dress, Clayton full headdress and white buckskins. He beckoned the mixed Indian and white audience to join the Round Dance, in friendship. Dipping lightly into the crossover step that rotated the circle, watching the exuberant, giggling whites trip over themselves, John wondered how friendly Clayton would feel when he learned Teresa's request: to participate in a real Crow sweat.

The festival grand marshal presented T-shirts, seventy-five-bucks gas money for the three vehicles, and profuse gratitude.

"Glad to do it," Clayton said. "We know us Crows got something the world needs. World's a pretty tore-apart place, like an old tepee ripped up by the wind, and the snow coming in."

John waited midway through the long drive home to Arrow Creek before proposing Teresa's wish. "She's my tutor," he explained. "I'd be flunking without her."

"This white woman breaking up your home doesn't sweat in our lodge," Clayton said.

"She's my teacher, that's all. She gives me over and over. So I'm just taking and taking, like sucking from a big tit?"

To refuse would be inhospitable, Clayton admitted in Crow, expressionless.

Late on a Saturday afternoon, well past dusk, Teresa drove up in her new Scout. John's footsteps crunched in the snow as he greeted her. Down by the creek a fire blazed, Clayton shoveling in the rocks that would cook the sweat lodge, a dome of blankets and old carpeting draped over bent willow poles.

"Dad's running late," John said. "He was hauling the rocks, and the truck got a flat tire. Oh, he was mad." John shook himself comically like a wet dog, nervous. All day he'd endured, even joined his family's jokes. "Tutor?" his "cosmopolitan" brother, Martin, had said. "The sweat'll blister the toots out of her tooter. She'll be lucky if she can sit on it." But Millie, Berenice, and Martin's woman would sweat with her. Berenice had promised to take care of her, translating the prayers, explaining how to breathe through cupped hands against the cool earth if the heat became too intense.

The family introduced themselves solemnly until Teresa asked Clayton, "Where'd ya get the flat at?" attempting an ingratiating folksy diction.

He gazed at her. "What?"

Teresa repeated the question.

Removing his cap and turning it over in his hands, he said decisively, "My hat's not flat," and walked away. Amid the Crows' roaring mirth, Teresa closed her eyes, face scarlet. Then Clayton got it. Laughing until the tears came, he patted her arm.

The women traipsed off to the sweat lodge. John realized his anxiety was for his friend's pleasure, for the sweat's spiritual benefit to enter her life. The thought of her joy snatched gladness out of him like a startling, gorgeous scarf from a magician's empty sleeve. He couldn't relax, shredding cigarette butts with his fingers while an hour passed. Hearing Teresa's shriek he bolted up, recognizing only from the accompanying laughter that the women were bathing in the icy creek. Soon they burst in the door, ruddy and steaming.

Over steaks and potato salad Teresa expatiated on the differences between the Crow sweat bath and what she'd read of Cree, Salish, and others' practices. She shared gossip, courtesy of her husband, the lumber flack, about congressmen's sexual escapades. She dropped names, a party at Mel Gibson's ranch, an exclusive gala opening for the celebrated Crow artist Shane Two Bears. No one else spoke. "God, what a loudmouth," Teresa said, muzzling herself, and rose to help Berenice clear the table. She joined the women washing the dishes. Though it was past midnight when they finished, neither Berenice nor Clayton invited her to spend the night. She hugged the women in farewell, towering over them.

Scarcely had the Scout's engine turned over when Millie said, "Hulk Hogan." The family cracked up. Berenice's shoulders shook.

"Da Crow sweat...," Martin bellowed, assuming a grappler's stance, chest puffed.

Smiling angrily into his plate, John abruptly shouted, "She's a genius."

"How many times you wrestle her?" Millie said. "Bet she pins you right on your back with your legs in the air."

"I ride her until the sun comes up," John said in Crow. "She's not bony like you. Bony woman! This whole year I'm going to school," he continued in English, "you're just bony. Sticking me any time. You're like a"—he found the word—"skeleton to me." Clayton ordered them quiet. John slept on the couch. The next morning Clayton said Berenice would need John's Toyota for a week or more while he took the truck hunting back in the mountains.

"What do I do?" John said.

"Help me," Clayton said.

John phoned Teresa. He collapsed his easel, rolled up his canvases, and tucked them in a gunnysack.

"You ain't going," Clayton said. John kept packing. Millie took the children to her mother's. Berenice was crying. When Teresa braked in the drive, John flung the sack over his shoulder. Clayton blocked his way, a compact six feet standing slightly bowlegged, hands dangling. Under his shock of black hair, his eyes held John. Like a sleepwalker John swept past him, the sack bumping his father's arm.

Teresa rented him a one-bedroom apartment near the campus. That night John dialed home from a pay booth, asking for Clayton.

"He's hunting," Berenice said.

"I called to say I'm sorry for walking out," John said in a trembling voice. "He's got to understand, I can't leave school."

Berenice sighed. "He ain't feeling well."

John took off walking, hat pulled low against the cold. Up the steep escarpment known as the Rim, he hiked, past the fake day of the luminous but nearly deserted airport. He tramped Billings Heights, downtown, west around the mall. The wind burned his cheeks. In an intersection he saw Clayton, red Pendleton and Sun Dance skirt undisturbed by accelerating cars. Clayton's hand clenched over his heart, thumping his breastbone. Then he vanished. Tears iced John's lashes, fuzzing his vision into bright blobs and wispy shadows. He strode on aching legs, awaiting whatever would happen to him, his heart maybe. He imagined it leaping from his chest, pumping on the sidewalk. When morning came he felt like stone, some strong new stone dug from the earth, yet to be named. He brewed coffee in his new home and went to class.

Just before Christmas break Clayton knocked at the apartment, handing John the keys to a full-ton Ford pickup only two years old. "So you can get home," he said. Millie had moved to her new job in Crow Agency, but the kids visited some weekends and holidays. The evening after his last final, John's new machine was eating up the pavement to Arrow Creek, laughing at ice patches.

Clayton welcomed him at the door. John's drawings and sketches were hung all over the living room. Berenice served roast venison. Clayton hauled out the drum, and the men sang, warmed by the fire, before a midnight sweat. Lying on his back, inhaling the scalding steam, John felt the knots in his muscles— the stress from finals, his incomprehensible textbooks, the whole concrete claustrophobia—melt away into the ground. Before rinsing in the creek, he and his father stood under the cloud-shrouded moon as slow, fat snowflakes dissolved on their steaming bodies.

The children were standoffish at first, and Trina, eleven, conscientiously refrained from calling him Dad. "Take me for ice cream, John."

"Millie's poisoning them against me," John said.

"What do you expect?" Berenice said.

But they played with him, sledding and rodeo, in which he was the bull to be roped, ridden, and tugged to the floor. They helped him stretch canvases.

Millie herself, when she lingered picking them up, was surprisingly deferential. "Still in the ring with old Hulk," she said, but not mean, inviting him to laugh, which he did. She zipped around in a used Taurus and dressed sharp, with padded shoulders and red lipstick. While the family shopped in Billings, they stole an afternoon together in their old room, fucking with the desperate, tittering carnality, and self-pity, of illicit lovers.

"I missed you so much it told me something," Teresa said three weeks later, when he returned to the city. "I'm leaving Captain Clear-cut. After twenty-three years. Goodbye half-million-dollar house on the Rim. Farewell cook and maid. Etc."

"So where you living?"

"In the morning dew," she enthused.

"You can stay here till you find a place."

They upgraded to a two-bedroom. On her middle school teacher's salary, "I think I can swing it," Teresa said. She attempted meals—"Take-out Chinese to the rescue again, I'm afraid"—and vacuumed with gusto. But she scorned John's lack of academic progress. "That's your idea of a sentence?" she exploded. " 'It's becoming Americans be going over doughboys'? And there are no

'Germanians.' Sounds as if flowers are conquering Europe."
Coaching math, she leaned her expanse of face into his, counting
loudly on her parsnip-size fingers.

"If I'm so stupid, why are you bothering with me?" John said.

"Oh, baby." Her hands covered her face. "Oh, John baby." She
rocked back and forth. Kneeling, she pushed her head into his lap
so he scarcely could understand her. "I'm scared," she said. "I've
thrown it all over for you, you know. And you're not like other
people. You're gifted. I'll never be able to count on you. I'll never
know what to expect from you."

In her words John suddenly knew himself. Always something
had divided him from others—Millie, his children, mom, and
brothers, even his dad. Teresa had named it. It was as if he'd been
lost his whole life and now recognized his own woods. He was a
great boulder brilliant with red, orange, green lichen, encircled by
trees whose roots twined around him like veins from a heart. You
were so long finding us, the holy trees said, but now you're here.
Swept by gratitude, John said, "Let's get married."

Teresa lifted her head. "So sweet." She rubbed her knuckles
against his cheekbones. "Of course we're both married already,
but screw the details."

Teresa coaxed a deal with the history prof, permitting John to
focus his term paper on Native American history, specifically that
of the Sees the Hill family. He salvaged a semester D, along with
two C's, a B, and an A.

The spirit told John what to paint, and his hand grew surer. His
beloved acrylics exuded the almost unnatural radiance of Pendleton hues, or the shimmer of cut glass. Strangely, his breakthrough
occurred in watercolor, a Crow in full battle regalia, face black-
ened for a slain enemy, descending from the sun into a tepee.
Composition dynamic, colors bold but harmonious, brushstrokes
deft, the painting was completed in less than an hour, and John
emerged as if from a dream. "That's the painter you'll be a year
from now," his professor said. "And after that—" He spread his
hands wide.

If he were to continue visiting home, John said, Teresa must
come, too. Millie vanished altogether. The family's revenge was to
make Teresa a servant. If Clayton needed a gasket from Billings,

"Send Hulk," and away drove the Scout. After dinner the Sees the Hills would rise abruptly and retire to the living room, abandoning to her the food-and-dish-strewn table and overflowing kitchen.

"And nights I lie with beauty," she said.

The Rendezvous

Almost a year after the Sun Dance, Clayton's celebrity persisted. An item in *The National Enquirer* featured his "transcontinental healing" by mail, referring to the "miracle" of the encircling thunderstorms having spared the Big Lodge. Anthropology students had camped on his lawn the previous week.

But since the moment the past winter when John had brushed past him, sack over his back, to Teresa's waiting Scout, a stone had lodged in Clayton's gut. It blocked his breathing and wouldn't let him shit more than every three or four days.

"I'll run that Hulk out of here," Berenice had threatened more than once.

"We'll lose him," was Clayton's reply. Now, the horses kneedeep in midsummer green pasture, John emerged past eleven every morning, yawning in low-slung cutoffs, to paint. Last night an outrage: a clan uncle staying over, the family was short a room. Teresa volunteered herself and John for the rollaway couch. But after dinner they grabbed and tickled each other into the kids' bedroom. For hours Trina and Dan waited up, bleary and red-eyed in front of the TV, before passing out on the couch. Outside the closed door Clayton would begin to speak, and the stone would paralyze him, stick his mouth open. Picking at his toast and eggs, he felt flaccid with age. Across the table Teresa chainmunched bacon.

"Today whenever he shows his face he makes his own damn breakfast," Berenice said. "Too late for that one, already ate the whole pig." She jerked away Teresa's dish with a peal of cutlery.

Teresa rapped the family's black ledger, which she'd taken over in Millie's absence. "A shambles," she said. Cashing in the last holdings over by Yellowtail Dam would square the Sun Dance debts, but what then? Sell out the land from under their own house? She cited "whopping" payments on John's truck. "In fact the interest rates are extortionary. Racist. We could sue."

"Things have a way of working out," was all Clayton could say.

John bounded in, freshly showered and sleek as an otter. "Surprise," he said, winking at Teresa. "A gallery in Red Lodge is hanging my watercolor, *Creation Myth.* We can go?"

Clayton welcomed the distraction. The entire family, even a resistant Berenice, piled into the pickup.

Red Lodge was an hour away. The painting attracted a knot of viewers. "Look at that," John said, pointing to the price tag, $375. Teresa beaming at his side, he answered questions.

"My Crow way keeps my feet on Mother Earth," he explained. "But my art talent flies all over the universe. But they're both the same."

On their way out of town, they noticed a sign for the Beartooth Mountain Man Rendezvous. The children pleaded to see it.

"Make 'em happy," Clayton told John.

A rutted dirt road led up the plateau, where the mountain-men's encampment of booths, log lean-tos, and tepees spread over several acres. But admission was five dollars apiece.

"Just wait," Clayton said. Claiming to be "one of your Crow dancing performers," he crashed a board of directors dinner, barbecue-chowing, buckskin-clad men glinting with wire-rims and Rolexes.

"I'm looking at your what's-happening on your paper, and I don't see anything about the Crow Indians that live here many tens of hundred years," Clayton said. While he negotiated, his family was invited to browse the exhibits, then share the barbecue. The Mountain Man Society president, topped with a coonskin cap, questioned him with keen, squinting regard.

"The Sun Dance doll that the Smithsonian company was handing over to the Crow tribe," Clayton said, "my great-great-grandfather owned it. That's why it was up to me to be holding the Sun Dance for the people." Originally the Sun Dance was a vengeance ritual, the doll a fetish with the power, if used properly, to help kill one's enemy. White administrators suppressed the ceremony for generations. "This Sun Dance now is thanking the Creator for getting through some hard time, for good luck. It's gathering up a heavy spirit force for the people." Clayton shook his head. "Big, big spirit. Like a tornado!"

"In the old days, then," the president said, "the Big Lodge meant bloodshed."

"Crows killing everybody." Clayton nodded solemnly, then guffawed. "Scared him now!" He drew the edge of his hand across the man's neck. "No, like Chief Plenty Coups told us back in 1910, 1800's something, white is coming, and no one's chasing him off, might as well learn to live with him. What the Crows have, the Creator is giving it to them, and they give it to everybody.

"The thing we're looking at here is heritage," Clayton said. "I know my relatives as long ago as when you Pilgrims back there is getting ready to eat that Indian corn and smoke that Indian tobacco. Some say the mountain lion and the eagle is our relatives. This man—" He patted the president on the shoulder. "What people you from?"

"Polish."

"All right, Polish. You speak Polish? You do your Polish dances at this rendezvous? You and your wife and children wear your Polish clothes to church?"

"I got them mountain men pretty down in the mouth," Clayton said, rejoining the Sees the Hills, who were watching flintlock marksmen blast a stuffed deer. "They look around like they got empty hands. 'Hell, we ain't *got* no heritage.'"

Not only had Clayton been elected to the board of directors, but the Crows were hired to dance every afternoon for the next two weeks, eleven hundred dollars total.

"We're a tourist attraction?" Teresa said.

"Didn't I tell you something would come along, bookkeeper lady? The white wants to give back to us, I don't push it away."

At sundown, the Sees the Hills, honored overnight guests, were shown to their tepee. It was oddly squarish, the fabric stiff, sporting a leering thunderbird.

"Tepee Motel 6," Clayton said.

The Crows were a hit. Admissions nearly doubled for their shows. The dance troupe had shrunk, as Clayton's Arrow Creek neighbors, skeptical of his renown—they called him "the little god"—shied away. But his most profound satisfaction was bringing his own family together again. Drying out after a binge, Martin drummed with shaking hands, grasping the stick as if it were pulling him out of quicksand. Gerald, the son from Crow Agency, sang despite his bad luck. His wife had been hospitalized for a jumping eye, and driving home from visiting her, he'd been rear-ended at a stop sign. Feathers twined in his braids hid the neck brace which had put him on sick leave.

Long before, Teresa had booked what turned out to be the gig's second week for her annual vacation in Colorado, with her daughter's family. Immediately after she left, John fetched Millie, though she had a new boyfriend. She spoke downcast, inaudibly. Afternoons she whipped into her shawl dance with fringe flying, face drawn. John stalked tautly, a stealthy warrior. Otherwise, the most Clayton saw of them was their backs growing tiny as they walked hand in hand toward the surrounding woods.

"So, what happens when Hulk comes back?" Clayton heard in his mind. "Some nights, when the snow piles up over the windows week after week, Berenice and I get mean, sitting across that lonely table, killing each other with our eyes. Still we're together thirty, forty years." But when he faced John his tongue was a dead stone in his mouth.

Throughout their stay the mountain-man president shadowed Clayton, questioning and jotting notes. He was an author of popular regional histories and fictional biographies of personages such as the explorer-priest Father De Smet and trappers Jim Bridger and Old Bill Williams. "One based on Crazy Horse," he said. "*Sioux Marauder.* At least that's how they thought of him at the time." The last day of the rendezvous, he insisted on a tour of the gallery displaying John's watercolor.

An hour later, Berenice tugged Clayton's shoulder, alarmed. John was running full-tilt through the camp, dodging carts and bonneted matrons. "He wants my picture for his book cover," he shouted. The author had assured John that his publisher would pay at least a thousand for the rights to *Creation Myth.* "I can't believe it. Ohhh." John smacked his forehead. He paced the tepee like a lunatic. Millie couldn't calm him. "Jeez." He hit himself again.

John began the fall semester in Arrow Creek, commuting to Billings as did Millie to Crow Agency, an arrangement that lasted until he flunked his first midterm. He moved into Teresa's apartment. Millie packed up again.

On Clayton's answering machine, purchased against the encroachments of fame, a girl's message piped, "Sir? I'm in Mr. John Sees the Hill's art history class? I mean, he doesn't teach the class, but we're in it together. I..." The voice stammered away into nothing and hung up. Clayton erased it.

Calls from New York, a Helen Feld, assistant art director for the mountain man's publisher, were to be saved. The dust jacket illustration was a done deal. Still she phoned both the apartment and the house, even on weekends.

The Sees the Hills and Teresa were seated for dinner when she rang. John settled into an easy chair, leg over the armrest. He chuckled softly into the receiver. "I'm a simple Indian man," he said. Gradually he frowned. "Hello?" He shook the phone.

"She said she had to catch her breath," he told his listeners afterward. "She said, 'I'm melting.'"

The Gift

"Do you have slides of your work?" Helen had managed to continue.

"Oh yes, yes," said John, who didn't, but was certain Teresa could arrange for them.

"I'd like to see them. I have friends who would like to see them."

By March, during his second year of art studies, John would be adding to his book cover a one-man show in New York. Helen scheduled the opening for his spring break.

He was infatuated with her voice, the nasal vowels, their strange liquid music like the buckling of a saw cutting wood. He imagined she might be Chinese.

"You're probably married," she said.

"Separated."

"I'm sorry. I have a boyfriend. He's a restaurateur, fat as a bear."

Wildly jealous, he ransacked his English, retorting with an old TV commercial. "Me? You can't pinch an inch."

"I'll just bet." A gloating silence ensued.

"When we're quiet I can really feel you at the other end," he said.

"Home in Pennsylvania I have a favorite niece who sleeps over with me," she said. "Every morning we do each other's hair. Hers flows halfway down her back. Mine. Ha! Takes two hours, and then if the humidity changes it falls like a soufflé. She's all love for the planet. PBS had a program on vampire bats being poisoned for killing cattle. She cried her little heart out. For the horrible, crawling bats. 'What's your favorite wildlife where you are, Aunt Helen?' 'I saw a squirrel once. Giant rat with a bushy tail. I would've hit it with my purse if it had come any closer.' I wish she could meet you."

As the departure for New York approached, he painted in such a prolific frenzy, the surfaces so large, that he and Teresa would have gone broke replenishing acrylics and oils, not to mention framing, had not Clayton chipped in. He had tapped a steady market for the dance troupe's services, the most lucrative engagement a nearby off-rez town's centennial parade. "Thank you, white people, helping send my boy to college," he announced.

The painting most admired by John's family, the huge *Grandmother Storyteller*, billowed across the canvas brown and red, the whole daubed with the colored handprints of schoolchildren he was teaching as a visiting artist. He also posed Teresa nude in various contortions. Since his brief reconciliation with Millie, Teresa was dull, resigned and dogged in her affections, unrepentant in her contemptuous flicks. "It's okay to speak English, honey," she said of his gnarled attempt to define conceptual art. She indulged his "phone sex," calling Helen "1-900." The Crows referred to Helen as "Melting Woman."

Of course the buildings loomed monstrously above crushing human mobs. But John's dominant sensation, his first hours in New York, was that he couldn't feel the ground. Anywhere. "I'm going to fall off the world," he said.

"Never thought of it that way," Helen said, nodding. She'd met them at the airport. "Figure right under here"—she stamped on the sidewalk—"there's subway." Noise and heat escaped a metal grate. "Two levels. Nothing but concrete and steel and pissy air a long, long way down."

From the publishing house she'd wangled a donation to cover three nights' lodging for the entire family, including Teresa, so they could perform at the opening. In return, the gallery would sell the book featuring John's cover art. "Look," Helen admitted. "The gallery's a basement, can't afford to change the light bulbs. But among the cognoscenti, it's got cachet."

Saturday occupied them uncrating and hanging the artwork. The opening that night was thronged, though overshadowed in the media by a Shane Two Bears show uptown. "Damned luck," Helen said. "Two Crow painters opening the same week? God's an old white bastard who hasn't forgiven you for Custer."

"Crows scouted *for* Custer," Clayton said, but Helen had flitted away, glad-handing newcomers before prodding them back to John. Helen! In moon-white makeup and heavy eyeliner, she turned to John the face of a startled animal. Her coif, candy-apple red, was teased straight up into an inverted flag of pubic hair. Her earrings quivered. Perfume, hairspray. Round hips swiveled her short legs into a voluptuous scurrying. She baffled his senses into a happy swimming.

The conversational hubbub added to his delirium. A blond-maned woman in black, legs planted wide, hands clasped behind her tailbone, stared at his painting while her bearded escort explicated animatedly, hands darting over the surface. Faces surrounded him, opening and closing mouths. He gave out short answers, smiles, and nods. He wore a suit and tie, bought by Teresa, and a hundred-dollar black Stetson, given by his father, which he'd adorned with a single white feather. The other Crows were in traditional costume, Clayton the white buckskins. At a signal from his father, John squatted by the drum and began whacking the heartbeat cadence. Clayton sang, joined by the family, then led the entire assemblage, spilling champagne on their evening clothes, in a snaking dance. The drum ceased; the dancers came to a standstill looking stunned, beatific. Clayton stretched his arms. "Aho."

"Aho," the congregation echoed.

"This is fun," John told his father. "Let's stay some extra days."

"Good," Clayton said in Crow, clasping his shoulder. Teresa and John's brother Gerald would be returning home for work Monday morning, with the rest of the family having booked a flight Wednesday, planning to foot the extra hotel bill. "Hulk will know what to do," Clayton said.

John shook his head vehemently. "You know what she'll think. Pussy. Her." He indicated Helen. "Let her wait and get mean after we're home. Ask Martin." No prob, Martin said, just exchange the tickets.

Helen expertly mediated John's conversations, waiting, as he untangled his incoherencies, with such patient expectancy that his listeners relaxed, not noticing the gaps. He spoke confidently, experimenting with his tie, coiling the silk around his fingers and letting it unfurl like a frog's tongue. When he and Helen drew together, talking, their foreheads almost bumped. Teresa loomed nearby, stolidly sorrowful.

"Who's the roller-derby queen?" Helen said. "She's awfully protective."

"That's Hulk Hogan. Family friend."

Attendance dwindled. Helen tried on his hat. He spun it around her haircrest.

"Where's your man?" John asked.

She shook her head. "He only comes out for Chinese dissidents. Solzhenitsyn. He's a . . . convenience. He takes me places I like to go. He's always badgering me to move in with him." Suddenly she said, "It's over." She smiled and unsmiled. She wiped her eyes, mascara running. John hugged her, stock-still in the emptying basement. "Can you come home with me?" she said.

She hailed a cab for the family.

"Taking me out for dinner," John said.

Helen's West Village apartment betrayed the stylistic dissonance of its four renters, geometric polymer stools abutting a Queen Anne couch, Frida Kahlo sharing the wall with the anguished Han Solo frozen in carbonite. The three roommates lined the couch in their PJs like daughters awaiting a goodnight kiss as Helen swept John past and shut the door behind them.

She kept interrupting their lovemaking. Lifting his hips away, she grabbed randomly a magazine from the nightstand and read him, in a calm tone over hiccuping breaths, critic Arthur Danto on Mantegna. Droplets fell from her nipples. His cock stuck straight out between them. When they began again, he ground his head into the pillow, with pleasure, her pussy closing around him. They moved apart and stood by the window. Below, lives passed slowly in cars. An arm extended from a black sedan, exchanging for a blood-red splash of flowers an eyebrow of folded currency. A youth jumped the bumpers and was honked to the other side of the street. "I wish we had sweetgrass," John said. "I'd like to smell that burning right now." They rocked each other on the bed. He was blacking out. The springs chittered. He slapped at her belly and thighs, not to hurt but to love her both ways, as pure flesh and as Helen, so that he broke free into a despair of wanting. His palms' tingling from the reddened smacked meat of her made him sick to his stomach until he came, washed clean and empty. "Shit, I'm happy," she said again and again.

Led by Martin, the family bussed to the apartment only a half hour late for brunch, Sunday noon. Helen had prepared the spread. The awestruck roommates served the Crows. Clayton was telling an old-time story. "And so it's the wagon coming through the gap, and the children fall out the back. The hoot owls take them children, and it's maybe five, ten year they keep them. The hoot owls raise them babies."

"Hoodows? Is that a tribe?" Helen asked.

"Hoot owls. Hoot. Owls. Loving God, what a simpleton," Teresa exclaimed.

"I beg your pardon. I could swear someone who is eating my food—no small amount of it, I see—just spoke rudely to me. You're welcome to finish your meal on the doorstep."

Instead Teresa walked straight down the hall into Helen's bedroom. Helen followed. While Clayton resumed his story, John strained to hear the women's voices, Teresa's spiraling upwards and downwards in pitch, Helen's interjections increasingly subdued, but he couldn't discern their words.

Teresa emerged and sat at the table. Leaden, John dragged to the bedroom.

"Liar!" Helen said. " 'You're not the first,' she says. 'When you're through he'll be back.' She looked hollow, no person inside. It was horrible. Then she rears over me as if she's going to attack me. Liar." She kicked him. "Your woman came all the way to New York with you. Go take her."

Brunch adjourned hastily. John expected Teresa wouldn't fly, but the next morning she and his brother caught the subway for

Kennedy. "I won't get in your way," she said.

Helen, when he phoned her office, addressed him as Mr. Shah-of-Persia. "I'm all for multiculturalism," she said, "and I don't know what the Crow tribe believes, but in the tribe of Helen the harem stops here. The lying stops here. Is that clear?"

"Yes," John said.

"It's spoiled, but maybe it will come back. I love you, I can't help myself."

"I love you," John said.

She would see him the following night.

Clayton was grave. He had learned the hotel's rates. But he'd found an Indian shop listed in the Yellow Pages, on Fifth Avenue. While Martin exchanged the airline tickets, he and John would pay their respects to the New York Indians.

Sightseeing, Clayton's head swiveled, his large brown hands darting and weaving as if conjuring from thin air the turbaned visages, heaven-seeking glass pinnacles, belching buses, Amazon women furred to the pelvis and naked below, a faraway spider-web bridge dissolving in the foul air. John traipsed in a black mood. Love pulled him down. Everything about Helen mattered, her flushed earlobe, the boyfriend who might be ex, her anger, the bat-loving niece in Pennsylvania. He worried about the fate of bats on the planet. The death of even one would hurt the little girl. It was unbearable. Sheer admiration for Helen oppressed him. He couldn't wait out the hours until her soft push against him, for her disappointment or accusation, anything she might feel towards him. Most, he needed her to want him again.

Moon Lodge was nearly lost in the jumble of signs, the store-fronts and eateries jamming together. Then, through the perva-sive aroma of spicy grilled meats, John detected smoldering sweetgrass. Inside, bins overflowed with sage, cedar, herbs. Stacked powwow cassettes. A buffalo-hide rug. Indian men lounging at the counter half-nodded in greeting.

Introductions followed, with handclasps all around. "Old Muskrat, he lives here off and on, sleeps in the back room," the proprietor said. Old Muskrat and a couple of others seemed pret-ty beat up, clothes filthy and drooping, stinking of sweet wine. The proprietor, a Wyoming Arapaho whose Iroquois wife studied at NYU, opened sodas for the Crows. Clayton uncovered the inevitable links in the Indian network. He had finished second to the Arapaho's uncle in traditional dancing, Rocky Boy Powwow, in 1978. As a fire crew chief in 1981, he had led Old Muskrat from a ravine moments before it vaporized in a clap of flame. "Knew I recognized you," he lied kindly. "Ever since we come off this jet," he said, "I've been thinking, Where do you sweat in this New York?"

"Sauna at the YMCA," a customer said. "Not hot enough, and we can't pour because it shorts out the heater. But I pray. They don't look at me funny anymore."

"My son's rich lady got a little land," Clayton said. "Come over tomorrow night, we build a lodge there." The shopkeeper promised a load of rocks. Clayton left practically skipping. "Indians everywhere," he said.

They separated, John bound for Helen's. She smiled him in the door but gently deflected his hand from her waist. "Best just talk tonight," she said.

"I didn't mean to lie. It was true to me," John said. "I saw you at the airport and...bam! Hulk wasn't my woman. Hulk wasn't even on the world."

"And it slipped your mind to tell her."

Berenice was frantic when John returned to the hotel. Ten p.m., and no word from Martin.

"Cosmopolitan. Knows his way around," Clayton muttered.

"I'm calling the police," Berenice said.

"Do you remember when Martin sold the shotgun for a half gallon of scotch, and you locked him in the toolshed?" John said.

"I'm working not to remember that," Clayton said.

By morning Berenice had satisfied herself that Martin wasn't dead, in jail, or hospitalized. From her office phone Helen confirmed that Martin could have sold the airline tickets, illegally. They could bus home, she suggested, cheaper than new flights at short notice.

"I don't know if you could be lending us the money until John sells some of them paintings," Clayton said.

Helen took personal leave and moved the Sees the Hills into her apartment, giving the parents her bed. "The money. I'm not cheap," she told John privately. "But it's not by preference that I brush my teeth elbow-to-elbow with three others every morning."

The Arapaho's stones arrived on his borrowed flatbed. The Indian men hauled them through the foyer, prompting an appearance by the landlord, who lived in the basement. The fire pit to heat them would be a code violation, he said. That stymied everyone until Helen remembered a potter with an electric kiln across the way.

The common, overlooked by Helen's kitchen window, was a wretched patch of dead grass the size of a boxing ring, edged in dingy concrete, enclosed by apartments' birdlime-smeared backsides. While the Arapaho returned the truck, the stones baked, and the sweat lodge was erected from chairs, broom handles, blankets, and old rugs. Nightfall, the men went in, taking runs pouring and praying, the city Indians in English. Afterward they lolled behind a screen rigged from sheets, singing to where the moon would be if they could have seen it.

Lights went on, heads thrusting from windows.

"Real Indian sweat bath, five dollars," Clayton called. "Fundraiser, send the Indians home."

"You can't get money," John said, looking at his father in disbelief. "This holy thing."

"Collection plate in church," answered Clayton, who like most of the Arrow Creek community attended services as well as practicing native religion.

"It's bogus, brother," the Arapaho said.

"New York takes two hundred, three hundred for a hotel, it can pay," Clayton said.

The Moon Lodge contingent left hurriedly.

Helen's household sweated free, with Berenice. The sheets offered little protection from an overhead view, and by the time the women pranced into the building, wrapped in towels, each face a sundae of streaked makeup, several jostling, cheering men had gathered. Clayton collected five a head. "It will help them more than a movie," he told John. "Do it."

As John's ladle spewed up the first blast of steam, his party wheezed and roared and plunged forward against the ground. He smelled alcohol. Though he was a veteran of a thousand far hotter sweats, these mild vapors burned his lungs and throat, made him want to jump out of his skin. Pressing his head to the questionable earth brought no relief. His voice droned interminably as if it belonged to someone else. He wished it did. Finally freed, he hurled the ladle at Clayton's feet. "No more," he said.

Clayton served past midnight, including the landlord, who demanded and received a cut of the profit.

Meanwhile, John had blundered into the darkened living room, momentarily flicking on the light to locate Helen on their mat. Above the quilt her shoulders were bare, face blinking, rapturous. Even as he shed his clothes, her hand lazily skimmed his leg.

"I'm sick with myself," he said.

Her insinuating fingers became practical, tender. "I didn't understand what the dispute was all about," she said.

"My dad wouldn't tell me to do anything wrong." But the words were wispy, empty as ash. For the first time he noticed that his father had shrunk to a very small man, no higher than John's knee. John wavered as if he had nothing to reach out for, to hold him up. He felt at the ends of his hands for Arrow Creek, for lodgepole pines bent under snow, the sharp reports of branches breaking in the pure cold, but they were taken from him, too. The Big Lodge didn't exist, nor the creek itself, into which Clayton had thrown whole venison steaks and potato salad in thanks for the life-giving water. The skyscrapers were real. A helicopter flew over rooftops, its chop-chop-chop momentarily louder than the din from canyons of traffic. He embraced Helen, who was everything.

Clayton winced throughout the next day and once hopped. "You get Helen to give you medicine for that plug-up bowel," Berenice said. His face was flashing light and dark like neon.

Helen came home elated. The gallery owner would buy the monumental *Grandmother Storyteller* himself and pay immediately. Even minus commission, that clinched the bus. Otherwise, only a lithograph had sold, $175. "Everybody loved the art," she said. "But Two Bears is today's Indian meal ticket. That's the market."

"Please, let us stay for the weekend to find Martin," Berenice said. Of course, the household agreed.

But Martin phoned that night. Helen beckoned John, whispering. " 'Not the old man,' he said."

"You missed your plane," Martin blubbered. He'd awakened that morning in a hotel bed. "Ni-i-ice," he intoned. "Canopy, with fringe." But they'd thrown him out because the money was gone.

Come to Helen's, John directed.

Martin wore a new silk shirt under his jacket. Clayton knocked him to the floor. Shrieking, Berenice rushed between them, pushing Clayton's chest. He waded through her and, as Martin rose from his knees, slugged him down again. "Get that bad spirit out of my sons," he panted, hands clubbed. John and Helen walked him to the couch. Clayton's fist was clammy. Martin's gaping mouth bled into the carpet.

Speaking for the freaked-out roommates, Helen asked the Sees the Hills to leave the next evening. She'd take the day off, for John.

In the morning he showed her the pencil sketch of a Crow woman in childbirth, which he'd titled *Earth Mother*.

"Not my niche, two abortions later," she said, grimacing.

John was stunned. "You killed those little babies?"

"Wait a minute, Almighty Loving Papa, where are your kids?"

"Millie."

"The mother. And how often do you see them?"

John was silent. Then he said, "When Dan was five, he could skin a deer."

"Well, around here the kindergartners just flay each other," she said. "All those kids nobody wanted but were born anyway," she added.

"Together we can put back one of those babies. I want to stay here with you."

Helen smiled and shut her eyes. "Mmm. I just wanted to feel that all over me. You finish school. My lover is no dropout. I'll come to you, I promise."

She offered him the Met, Guggenheim, MOMA. Stubbornly he insisted he wanted only to see the Shane Two Bears show.

Two Bears painted traditional Crow warriors exclusively, in gouache. Through invisible brushstrokes his palette played minute variations on earth tones, then ranging into rose-petal red and the blues of dusk. Pelage and plumage were scratched directly into the paint. Relentlessly energetic, the figures slung themselves beneath galloping ponies, slithered through buffalo grass, pounced from ambush. The hint of caricature in their features made them not comic but *more*—craggier, fiercer.

The artist himself usually dropped by afternoons if they cared to wait, the saleswoman said.

"He's a kind of cousin to me," John said, knowing the exact relationship only in Crow.

"Cousin" is what Two Bears boomed in a magnificent orator's bass a half hour later. "Is this all an illusion?" His wide-flung gesture encompassed at least Manhattan, if not the Atlantic seaboard. "Aren't we really in the Beartooths, horsing our pickup up some two-rut road to hell? Felling lodgepoles for our tepee at Crow Fair?" He was big, in jeans and a Pendleton shirt, with wire-rims and a sparse, silky mustache.

John explained.

"First-rate," Two Bears said, promising to view John's show immediately. "For now, we toast with champagne."

"I don't drink," John said.

"Good for you."

Riding the bus downtown, John said, "I might as well cut my hands off."

"He can paint those in his sleep and probably does," Helen breathed in his ear. Her tongue tip became an absence, the dampness in an empty bed.

In the aftermath of New York, John received a box from Helen weekly. One was a black Italian silk shirt, another a sumptuous volume of Kandinsky, then pine cones from her Pennsylvania hometown.

Clayton shit blood, so that Berenice, who scarcely had spoken to him since the attack on Martin, drove him to a Billings hospital for overnight observation, which determined nothing. He sat outdoors on sunny days, his face paled to granite.

Berenice and Martin treated themselves to margaritas at La Placita in Billings, which featured an enclosed patio with a Spanish-speaking parrot. Once, her right leg stepped hip-deep into the fish pond.

John's home had changed. Spirits had retreated from the mountains' shaggy evergreen brows into the fastness of the range.

Up-thrust sandstone turrets, whose conversations of light with the shifting weather had delighted him, were lumps of geology, another course he was failing. The sun spangling through new spring foliage hurt his eyes with a dazzling pallor that reminded him of death.

He thought only of Helen, who was chopped off from him. He wondered if she could forget him during her job. He imagined her smothered in the arms of the fat, hairy cook or whatever he was, and he ran around half-crazy. He feared she secretly disrespected him because his show had been defeated by Shane Two Bears'. His waking hours were besotted with her pink nakedness, though the nudes of her—all he painted—abandoned the customary fanfare of his palette for grays and sepias bleeding into the umbra of the black background.

During the hour or so on the phone with her, he was eager, happy. He was calling her every day until she told him she couldn't afford it. They tried to plan. "I don't know what I could do in Billings," she said. "I'm an art history major." If he boosted his grades, he could transfer second semester the following year, perhaps to NYU.

But he'd fallen too far behind after the week in New York, then the days bussing across the continent. Having pledged to avoid Teresa completely, he failed all but studio art. He pitied his bad luck loving a doomed abortionist, a love he would follow to its bad end. Come, marry me, he pleaded.

Busting her savings, Helen flew out for a week in July. The Sees the Hills hosted and feasted her. Every outing, even watching a sunset from the backyard, was a family activity. Berenice followed her and John. Gerald brought a venison haunch. Perked up by the obligation to be hospitable, Clayton spun tales of history and legend in his inventive, sometimes guilefully misleading English.

"Your father is brilliant," she told John, "but he's on tighter than my diaphragm. I check under the bed for him." If she moved to Montana, Helen said, they must rent an apartment, which John would split; her earning power would be zero. "I recognize that blank look, Mr. Artist-Chief. You wouldn't fall down dead with a regular job."

"There's women in my classes want to buy me a house," he said. "My English teacher says take her cabin for a studio." He winced saying this, a pain in the cheek as sharp as when he'd hooked himself fishing.

"Nice," she said, then huskily, "Nice."

At the airport they kissed with violent want and played meditatively with each other's hands, as if making up for what they'd forgotten, though they'd had sex many times.

Suffering Helen's absence was like swimming in numbing black water, his limbs heavier and heavier until at times he simply wanted to stop. He got in a fistfight with Gerald, cursed his father. Berenice threw him out for a week. On matchbook covers, he painted parts of his body, nipple, cock, birthmark, and sent them to Helen.

She prevailed on him to enroll for fall semester. He must be tutored, he said. Teresa had agreed to a neutral site, the student union lobby. "Don't worry. I love you," he told Helen.

If her call didn't find him home, Helen became abusive, words he hadn't heard her use. She wept and apologized. "I'm buying something special. Based on your costumes," she said mysteriously.

The package arrived while he was attending class, so he heard secondhand from Berenice. "It's a box. 'Phew,' I say, and the post office holds her nose. 'I thought you'd never pick it up,' post office says, and I say, 'I'm going to bury the stinky thing in the ground.' But before I do, I cut it open, and it knocks me over. Phawgh. It's a rotten dead bird covered with bugs. She's crazy, this girlfriend, sending us this filthy thing."

John didn't recognize Helen's voice, its high-pitched, cracking laughter. She'd ordered feathers for him at Moon Lodge, and when she poked in the sack, "There's a beak. A whole head. I crumple the bag shut and mail it the hell out of here." Moon Lodge assumed she was bringing it home to be plucked that day, she said. "I puked and puked. I'm sick talking about it." She hung up.

Without warning, in early October, she called from Billings Airport. John found her at the baggage terminal, black denim pantsuit already showing the rise in her belly. She threw her arms around his neck. "I don't know what to do," she said. "Marry you, with all your little girls and their real estate?"

"Oh yes, yes." He nestled his face against her ear. "I mean no girls, no. You're really here!" He laughed, carrying her and the luggage to his truck.

"I'll be a secretary. I'll cocktail waitress in a frilly mini. Ranchers will scream and run. Will your dad let you divorce Millie?"

"It's not 'let me.' He don't have a say."

"God, it's beautiful here," she said. "All the autumn leaf dust will make my sinuses explode."

They contacted a Billings lawyer about the divorce. Helen would have to fly back for at least a month to wrap up her job, settle the lease, which was in her name. John announced the engagement at dinner, staring down each of his parents in turn.

"I think Berenice would kill me if she could," Helen said. Later, undressing, she said, "Why can't I get out of my head the suspicion that I'm marrying the slickest dick in the West?" She looked at him searchingly.

"Wo-hoh." With a banshee laugh he tiptoed mincingly, cradling his privates. He kissed her belly, dancing her by the waist with his mouth still stuck to her.

"I'm going to have one this time," Helen said. She sat on the edge of the bed with shoulders rounded and hands clasped between her thighs so that her breasts spread comfortably and ungracefully against her belly.

John looked down at her body, aware in that moment of the body's living for itself without caring about its effect on him. The realization made him feel shunned and powerless, and devoted and happy. Clearly, in the months and even days to come, he often wouldn't recognize himself. Life got bigger and bigger. He wondered if it was that way for everyone.

Aside from her coaching him through a midterm, they took days at a relaxed, spontaneous pace. Initially John complained about her tutoring style; she asked questions but provided no answers beyond further questions. "But I understand it," he said finally, thumping the textbook. "It makes sense."

She tired easily, but her weariness was rosy and euphoric. "Maybe it's the baby," she said. "I don't know, I never carried one this long." He liked to drive one-handed, the other interlocked with hers over her belly. She indulged his tour of Billings malls.

"Very modern," she said. Preferring open spaces, she restored some of his pleasure in the land.

In search of wild horses he eased the truck through a mountain gap and up a tilted tabletop peak. "There," he said. Fifty yards below, the herd grazed along a verdant coulee. Their manes and tails were immensely long. John cut the engine and opened her door.

"Shetland ponies in hats scare me enough, thank you," she said.

He drew her by the hand. The animals shifted in unison like a drill team, first downhill, then, regrouping, toward them, led by a buckskin stallion. John descended the slope alone. "If you need this macho exercise to be good in bed, I don't want to know about it. I'm not looking," she called, looking. The stallion broke into a run, hooves thudding, nearly upon John, who yelled, "Hah," and waved his arm. The horse scrambled to a halt so abruptly he slid on his haunches. John pulled a clump of waist-high grass. The stallion knocked its legs together, skittering sideways. "Here, eat," John said. The horse lips peeled back, teeth nipped away the bundle. Tossing his head, the animal retreated, munching.

John led Helen to the drop, the valley, buff and green, stretching into the haze. "Makes me greedy for quiet," she said. He cupped her neck, and the hard breeze blew her hair against his hand, the first time he'd seen it move; watching her spray and sculpt her hair, and "put my face on," was a daily wonder.

When they reached the house, Teresa's Scout was parked in the driveway. In the living room Teresa stood up, unkempt and jowly, to wait out the awkward formalities. "It's taken me days to get up my nerve," she addressed Helen. "I don't know if I'm telling you this in compassion or revenge. It's the truth, take it or leave it. John lies. He's still fucking me. Millie just had their third kid, for all he cares about it. He has kids by at least two other women on the rez, that I know. And the coeds. Little candy-striper voices phone my apartment. 'Oh, is this Mrs. Sees the Hill?' And they hang up.

"I hit him with all this, and he doesn't even bother to deny it. But you, you picture him waiting for you like a monk in his sweat lodge while you swell up with his baby." Her lip perspired. Finished, she didn't know what to do, looking around as if expecting someone to invite her for dinner.

None of the family met Helen's eyes.

"Sorry," Teresa said. Backing out, she bumped the doorframe jarringly and clutched her shoulder.

"I knew it," Helen said. She jerked her fist against the wall. "Who will drive me to the airport?" Clayton went for his jacket.

John followed her down the hall. "She's lying." His voice rose. "Big fat Hulk bitch jealous to killing us." He couldn't think straight. Frantic, he spread himself against the bedroom door. "It's months and months," he pleaded. "You're here now. You're always here. It's okay." Helen opened the door and crouched for the luggage under the bed. "Please," John cried. She didn't say a word to him, ever again.

When Clayton returned three hours later, John launched himself at his father. "You fuck her?" he shouted. "You have a good time fucking her?" Berenice threw herself between them.

John called New York repeatedly, and they hung up. He left messages on the answering machine. Finally, weeks later, a room-mate said, "She's gone. She got an abortion, she had her tubes tied, and she went home." John asked for her number, and the woman hung up.

He was haunted by a Crow baby in a beaded cradleboard floating down a black river. The baby's eyes were closed.

He couldn't believe Helen had ripped him out of herself and thrown him away, then closed herself against him forever.

But worst was Helen hurting so badly. Her disappearance made her pain terribly large, as if it stretched from her apartment to whatever unknown place in Pennsylvania she had gone. He had torn something from the living Helen. Throughout his days she screamed to him. He felt his whole body as her scream. He had to shut his ears against himself.

The earth and the days became one long silence. He twiddled and fiddled through his time like an idiot.

Only one thought consoled him, imagining Helen giving birth to her niece, the bat girl. Helen stroked the girl's long hair. The bats were ugly and funny.

Amusing Trina and Dan on one of their rare visits, he doodled with watercolors. Materializing on the stout, absorbent paper, in startling detail, was *Winter Warrior*—he knew the title instinctively—moccasined feet padding frozen turf, hunched slightly, an exaggerated curve to the neck. His hands had shown him the virtuosity of Shane Two Bears.

He persisted as a distant, sinking shadow of Two Bears.

The Sun Dance

Short of breath and weak from self-starvation, Clayton went to a healer. "I've got blood coming out both ends," he said.

Stripped, he lay beneath a buffalo robe, doubled up, aching. The healer pushed his knees down. Pale winter light flowed in the window. The healer sang continuously over the sick man, then knelt beside him. Growling in back of his throat, he placed his mouth on Clayton's lower abdomen and sucked forcefully. Pain seared Clayton's gut. Three times more the medicine man made a tube of his lips against Clayton's skin. Rising, he spat out a stone half the diameter of his palm, a fire-red agate veined with green and blue. "Your son is lost," he said. He opened the east door and threw the gem far into the snow.

Clayton walked home light and whole, with the absolute freedom of despair.

Having sarcastically dubbed Clayton "the little god," the Arrow Creek community now reviled him as "the little devil."

On leave of absence from school, John occupied the farthest corner of the Sees the Hills' remaining land with a glamorous white woman of indeterminate age. Identifying herself as Crazy Horse's great-granddaughter, she was reputedly an ex–call girl. She'd established a tepee encampment, the Holy Confluence, to effect upon a wealthy clientele spiritual transformations through traditional Crow sweats and rituals led by Clayton, and feasts hunted by John. For select guests the woman herself conducted private sweats.

Rumor held that Clayton had sold medicine power to her. He'd unwrapped his medicine bundle and temporarily purloined the Sun Dance doll for her viewing.

The mountain-man author was collaborating with him on a book about the Sun Dance, encouraged by a substantial advance. The crux would be the staging of a second Sun Dance, which Clayton had arranged to photograph. The mountain man was squeamish about this breach in tradition, but Clayton argued, "Now the Sun Dance will never die. This book is the Bible for our children's children. Need to know how something's supposed to be, look it up right there." The occasion would be John's grand prize at the Billings Art Fair, awarded for one of his gouache warriors.

With the family dancers starring in festivals from Washington, D.C., to Alabama, Clayton drove a brand-new Bronco and was building a house for each of his three sons, even Martin, who lived with a busboy from the New York hotel where he'd awakened from his spree. Since following Martin west, the man had taught him leatherwork and rudimentary silversmithing, and the two sold well at craft shows. Martin had not drunk alcohol in months. "Still my son," Clayton said. "Put him in a dress, still my son."

John wasn't unhappy with the spirit woman, who treated him graciously and had the body of a movie star. He missed Teresa and Millie. "I'm too fat to fuck," Teresa had said when he called for a chat. At two hundred thirty pounds, she'd been christened "Mt. Hogan" by Martin. Millie's boyfriend was so paranoid about John that he fired his .357 Magnum at pickups that merely resembled his.

During a late spring hunt Clayton and John stalked a deer halfway up a brushy canyon. Rifle cocked, John climbed toward a huckleberry thicket. Rustling froze him. Clayton crept alongside. Both raised their guns and held their breath. A rock cracked.

At that moment the sun broke through the clouds, bathing the hillside in the golden illumination of an ancient age. Into the shimmering the buck ambled unconcernedly, cropping the gilded grasses. Clayton fired, and the deer dropped to its haunches. With John's shot the forelegs crumpled. The men plunged forward through slapping branches, hacking with the rifle butts.

Beyond the bushes they found no deer. The grass was not indented. No huckleberry twigs were broken. There were no blood spots, or hoof prints.

Clayton mumbled a prayer in Crow. John felt his eyes rolling like a terrified animal's. His father poked under the brush. Together they scrambled back down the slope, heads swinging left and right. "Let's go home," John said. They stampeded out of the canyon.

All the drive home they scrutinized a filament of smoke that seemed to exactly mark their destination. Arriving, they found Berenice pacing beside a smoldering pit, what remained of the sweat lodge. "I'm hanging laundry, and right in front of me, pop! like the Fourth of July, and the whole thing's burning up. I'm screaming and yelling, but nobody else is around," she said. "I get the hose, but it's gone, just like that. A big ball of fire."

"When did this happen?" Clayton said.

"Maybe half hour."

The men looked at each other. Clayton told her about the deer. "Same time," he said.

"Oh shit," John said, shuddering from head to foot.

"Don't tell nobody about this," Berenice said.

Clayton shook his head. "It happened. People will know."

"Clayton's lost his medicine." That much was agreed upon, and most awaited the impending Sun Dance with dread, certain calamity would fall on all their heads.

The night Clayton led the procession into the Big Lodge, only twenty-eight went in, half of them white. Many more assembled outside on folding chairs and lounges. If divine retribution were to immolate the Sun Dance, nobody was willing to miss it. Disparagements were traded.

"Never seen that other Sun Dance chief. Where'd Clayton get him?"

"He looks like a teenager. Where'd he get his medicine?"

"Clayton couldn't get a real medicine man for this fake Sun Dance."

Singing and drumming urged worshippers toward the Center Pole, sacred pathway between heaven and earth. His ceremonial skirt trimmed in gold brocade, Clayton looked like an emperor. Under the moonlight John closed his eyes and saw a rain of warriors in the style of Shane Two Bears. For three days band after band leaped and gesticulated, twanged bows and arrows beneath galloping ponies, shook war clubs. Spotted, striped, and daubed, their afterimages crisscrossed in his mind.

For Clayton's doctoring only two came forward, both white. A heart patient too ill to walk left the Big Lodge under his own power but relapsed the next day. The other, despondent over a divorce, claimed to feel better afterward.

Emerging from the Big Lodge on the last afternoon, Clayton faced a line of hills, a gray limestone escarpment that dully returned the sun's light. Beneath the formation were interred hundreds of Crows who had died a century earlier, many wrapped against the winter cold in smallpox-infected blankets issued by the United States government. Others were lost in war against the Lakota and Cheyenne, or in their own feuds and disorders. Clayton stopped, overwhelmed with sorrow and brotherhood for his ancestors. Over the years that sadness would be the one weight in his free flight of despair.

Beside him, John also gazed at the ridge's cold glow. It caught at his heart to wonder how many of the warriors teeming in his head had fallen down there, sleeping.

The much-feared catastrophe did not occur. Though shunned by the Crows, the Sees the Hills continued to prosper. The Sun Dance book sold moderately, John's warriors briskly. As it had for centuries, the community endured. Many who had entered the Big Lodge were succored and uplifted by the hallowed ritual, even for the rest of their lives.

Cassandra in Connecticut

Some read what's left in teacups,
Or soothsay cranium bumps, or Tarot cards.
I read leaf shadows on my neighbor's house
As morning sun brooks down among the poplars
Blown by a strong eastern wind. Here's Count Basie
Playing his piano. Here's a buggy ride.
And there's a wolf devouring a man of God.
But where's the kangaroo I saw two days ago
Leaping the Abyss? Where are the three grape clusters?
No matter. Now, in their repose, the shadows form
A Chinese painting of a cliff and waterfall
Gently serene. I climb among dark boulders
Until my neighbor's shape appears behind the screen
Door of his kitchen—and he walks out
Into a forest glade nine thousand miles from here,
Holding his cup of coffee, scratching his side
As deer cross his patio, flocks of morning larks
Shadow the face he turns up toward the sun.

Bait Man

I was spawned in lost waters. We all were,
but because I can no longer walk, because
this stillness halves me now, I know to hate
why a bass pauses, hovers in still water,
slime-thick and foul, beneath a rotted log.
He is safe, he thinks, at a great distance
from death, though it is death that feeds him, casts
its bait—dull worm and black, panicked beetle—
from the punk of the log, the same as I cast mine.
I, too, struck at what drifted in the womb.

1. Before

The wide, bloodless mouth closes around
the promise and its lie. Some of us learn
to breathe again. I washed my granny's feet,
her tongue—fluent and strange—flying in her mouth.
The preacher lunged, pulled from behind her ear
the cancer like a coin and hurled it down,
ground it with his heel into dust.
I was saved in that clear water where I held
my breath, opened my eyes to white robes rising
and fishes, damned, drifting in the folds.

I was always drawn to what I could
not see. But I could feel the draw of the worm's
cold bloat in muck—the moment of conception
when the cord is sunk in the belly. Water breaks
to a bass flying, his body lost to old
familiar motion. Long into the waning
afternoon, I would wade waist-deep
in all he knew, casting and recasting,

and feel him move against me in the creel—
a backward womb—as if he died inside me.

Before the accident, I painted roofs:
mansard, gable, shed, and hip. Bound burning
waist to cross, I have painted many
a church steeple, the pigeons circling beneath me.
In summer, silver paint would blind. I've seen
above the moon-bored fog a barn roof shine
above no barn—disembodied—hover
like a weightless plane, some new heavenly
body, filled with stolen light that holds
as I did to that pitch, but does not fall.

II. The Fall

I know the dream is nothing but a scar,
healed and pale and nothing like the wound;
still, I live for sleep, for that willful leap
into recurrence. My shirt swells, and I rise,
raptured by the slur of the wind. Below me
in the broom-sedge, a crow lies on its belly—a pupil
shrunken, sunk in its deep, bronze iris.
The breeze teases a black feather; the quill
lifts, flesh-bound but light. The field, blind,
redefines itself, stares backwards, past me.

You have to ask how does it feel? How does it
feel? April-seining, waist-deep in cold so
cold you stand waist-deep in nothing, the net
writhing and heavy, wrestling you down. Or frozen
in hot light, you are gigged; your legs—severed
from you without being severed—suddenly
jump as if on hot iron, your thighs sere-white.
You are your own trophy; you have survived
your own death, your head hung on the wall
that keeps you from the feast that was yourself.

You think you would bear easier a bullet
in your spine, some dark fragment, a deep
unreachable fault lodged there like an axis,
a new equator x-rayed and charted—the point
from which you sail into some other world—
the point from which you are turned back, your legs
ignorant, vain as heavy, braided hair.
You would bear easier an enemy to hate,
and gravity is faceless. And water,
bearing a still face, still won't be walked on.

III. *After*

To make this living, I sell line and hooks,
lures and lies. Mainly I sell bait:
night crawlers and worms—whatever bellies and wears
a hook well—and crickets, black and pale,
massed in a box that stinks of rot and writhing.
They do not use their legs for singing; they are
too desperate, I guess, too crowded. The minnows
complain the same way. Though I am good to them
and change the water in their tank, they still
refuse and leap from it sometimes to deeper

water that is not there. They leap instead
to deepest air, where the current is light,
and won't float them. If I see them fly,
I pick up, one by one, the arcing bodies,
then open my fist to release them in the tank.
If water's what they want, then I am glad,
but if they hesitate, I cast them out
to what they must desire. Death fouls the water
and won't make bait. A bass strikes best at what swims
as if delighted with the hook in its back.

In my time, I have cleaned a multitude
like this. In a fish's belly I have found
the smaller fish, the ragged hook, and once
a brassy ring. I have opened a bass
like a book to its fine-sewn spine and seen myself
in the worm that withers. A reluctant prophet,
I was swallowed up to breathe these days
underwater, where I miss the feel of my heels
beneath me, where I am patient not to die,
but to be vomited at last, whole, upon the shore.

Gymnasium

It's hard to manage privacy while using the machines:
they are so public, and fully half of us are here
wanting to show ourselves, wanting an audience
for this one triumph—sculpted shoulder, sculpted calf.
But to be seen deciding, *Yes, the last repetition,*
to be seen flinching the weights up despite
an amount of pain...

embarrassing. Whatever delight the body wants to feel
is beaten down. Gigantic mirrors everywhere—

reflecting first the surreptitious face, fascinated
by what it only barely lets itself take in:
the governed body lit fluorescently,
inescapable and strong and flawed.

Luckily, it's easiest to be imperfect here;
no dueling with the big-time guys, none of their flirtations,
bald appraisals—just occasional attention.
Always, it seems, to minor struggles.
Often kindly and dismissive all at once.

The problem's rather that this *should* be sexual—
pure enticement for a lover who'd be moved
by a display of urgency, possible displays of pride.
Not so much the arms under construction, but the mind deciding,
the way you meet your own eyes straight ahead and lift the weight.

Angeline

She is not an ordinary
Baby, but a lump of coal.
Grown-ups glance at her
And look away. Only the children
Stare. Their parents tell them
Not to point.

When Angeline's mother
Wheels her stroller
Into the bakery
Everyone falls silent.
When she pushes it
Outside again, raindrops slide
Right off her baby's face.

At night Angeline's mother
Polishes her daughter's
Lustrous skin, then lugs her up
To her bed of gravel, neatly raked
To resemble a trout stream.

She tells her child the story
Of where she came from,
How the trees rose and fell
Like dynasties, first to swamps
Then to the sea.

When Angeline's mother kisses
Her baby good night, she says,
"Sweet dreams, Angeline."
When she turns out the light
Moonlight shatters
Against her daughter's brow.

A Brief History of the Enclosure Movement

"So you see," said Keats, "our English countryside
Was once communal grazing land, before
These fenced-in greens & amber greens
Of private farms." As we continued
Walking arm in arm from bourn to bourn,
He explained Soul-Making & what he really meant
By atoms of intelligence. Snow fell;

We crossed the Heath; he said belief
Came slow to him, like waking up
Came to me this morning, a little sick
But still putting on my boots
For winter errands. It was then
That from a postcard on my wall,

Severn's charcoal of the living Keats
Looked away with the disinterest
He called thought. "When you get back,"
I heard him say, "write something
Without artifice, even without beauty,
Something simple, watchful, true."

Then I felt even sorrier for Severn,
Always the efficient, gallant one
In those two pitiable, foul-aired rooms,
His patient one day begging for the grave,
The next, his books; and below the corner window,
No snow twirled on the Spanish Steps—
All the city's fountains drained & cleaned.

The Invisible Body

I imagined every creature before I spoke
with fatal names.
                    You were the leopard
and goat.
                You were the kestrel
and loon.
                I had the power of speech
because of you.
                        Ten thousand things
came into being from a single form
that was not a form.
                        I made no sense
like this in the after-language to name
the animals.
                    I asked your help with the flowers,
some small relief from too many things,
some purple Latin to quiet their blossoms.
I stared at you at dawn with a look that opened
doors onto a door that had no room, a hardened
glass through which I saw the same new world
where I was dumb and good but not yet strange.

Writing at Night

This empty feeling that makes me fearful
I'll disappear the minute I stop thinking
May only mean that beyond the kitchen window, in the dark,
The minions of the past are gathering,
Waiting for the dishes to be cleared away
So they can hustle supper into oblivion.

This feeling may only mean that supper's done
And night has the house surrounded
And the past is declaring itself the victor.
It doesn't deny that tomorrow I'll wake to find
That the usual bales of light have been unloaded
And distributed equally in every precinct,
That the tree at the corner will be awash in it
And the flaming yellow coats of the crossing guards.

This empty feeling could be a gift
I haven't yet grown used to, a lightness
That means I've shaken off the weight of resentment,
Envy, remorse, and pride that drags the soul down.
A thinness that lets me slip through a needle's eye
Into the here and now of the kitchen
Without losing a button.

An emptiness that betokens a talent for self-forgetting
That lets me welcome the stories of others,
Which even now may be on their way,
Hoping I'll take them in however rumpled they look
And gray-faced as they drag themselves from the car

With their bulky night bags and water jugs.
It's late. Have I gone to bed? they wonder.
And then they see the light in the kitchen
And a figure who could be me at the table
Still up writing.

Distinctions

The world will be no different if the twin sisters
Disputing now in the linen aisle of Kaufman's
Resolve their difference about table napkins,
Whether the color chosen by one is violet
Or lavender or washed-out purple. No different,
But that's no reason to deem the talk insignificant.
It's important for people to make distinctions,
To want their words to fit appearances snugly.
Why wait to get home before they decide if the napkins
Match the plates Grandmother gave them years back
For their twentieth birthday. A pleasure to hear them,
Like the pleasure hearing people in a museum
Discuss how closely the landscape approaches
In their experience the best of the Renaissance
Or would if the paint hadn't cracked in spots
And darkened. Should they deem it fine or very fine
Or remarkable? The world no different but the subject
Not insignificant, the whereabouts of the beautiful,
Just how near it lies to the moment
According to a measurement all can agree on.
That was a beautiful conversation last night
About Vermeer though my friend Ramona
Went off on a tangent, hammering home her theory
As to why he never painted his wife or children.
Could be she was feeling resentful she's only third
On her husband's selective roster of women
Who've left the deepest marks on his character.
But this morning she may be asking herself what right
She has to complain when he's second on hers,
Below the passionate man she walked away from,
Whose curtain lectures on the plight of Cambodia
Bored her silly. No joy for her, back then,
In loving a man whose conscience burdened itself
With the crimes of others, not simply his own.
Now it seems she lost out on a lucky chance

To widen her heart. However painful that thought
It's useful when she finds herself too satisfied
With the life she has, forgetting where it fits exactly
On the spectrum of ripeness. Meanwhile, out in her garden,
It's a beautiful morning. The air is a little gritty,
Granted, and the low clouds in the west
Have lowered its ranking to seven points out of ten
On the scale of likely prospects. But that doesn't mean
She can't make it a ten on the scale of hope,
Ten for her willingness to be proven wrong.

Evening II

Morning let you down like a broken promise.
Noon with its bright clothes stood in your way.
Now it is evening, though, your favorite time,
The kiss of the word feeling good in your mouth.

It is sad to think of people you have failed,
Who thought, early on, you lived up to your word,
Who learned their lesson in bed, at play, or at work.
You were only yourself. You promised them nothing.

Perhaps it was death you were hoping to miss,
Like a pothole or slick in the road at night, the human
Complication that comes with being or being with.
Better a crow or a mutt or the ground you stand on.

But you are not evil on the pavement this evening,
And those you harmed have gotten over you fine.
Improved, in fact, by the wake of your departure,
They do better than you could ever imagine.

End of the Century

I. *Displaced Persons*

Out on the street the children are playing soldier.
It's the end of the century and still they play soldier.
Let's be unfair. Blame them for the toasted corpses,
The orphans, widows, and amputees. One aims
A broomstick, another a plastic missile launcher,
And the little ones on the lawn roll over, "I'm dead,"
They say with joy, "I'm dead," "I'm dead," "I'm dead."

II. *She Stretched Her Young Body and Went Out*

She stretched her young body and went out.
The trolley lines were bright in the sun.
Bees hovered on her dress pattern.
The flowers were of spectral colors.

She was still her parents' girl, living home,
Helping out. She was always the one. She believed
In her soul, in birthday parties, in feathers and drums.
She lived in every neighborhood. You saw her.

III. *Sarajevo Zoo*

With two buckets of water he had gone to the cages.
It was early in the morning, the shelling had stopped.
In a tan windbreaker he had gone to the bears.
He made our target, this old man walking.

Psalm

When the dove of whom there is no memory fell into the sea
We were uncreated, oh yeah, we were speechless before the sky.
There were no words to be sung on the water without edges.
Lord had shown his preference for his serpents and his mosses.

Into depths we drowned, the familial and the animal,
Paired on the deck of our craft going round.
Into depths we drowned and we were lost among us . . .
The opened cages, our bodies starving in the sun.

The Cunning One

It happened like this: he lived in a palace
which was also a prison. You understand
how nothing is ever simple. He had built
a labyrinth for the king's monster son,

a great service, which came with a secret.
One for the king, one in the builder's head.
Be reasonable, could the king ever permit him
to return to the easy conversations of Athens?

But because the king was grateful, no luxury
was spared in this palace which was also
a prison. Wherever one turned, one found
beauty and opulence. Gorgeous wall hangings,

thick rugs, soft cushions. All entertainments
were prepared for him, from the scholarly
to the perverse: the moist flesh of children,
stimulants to engender the sweetest dreams.

Still, the door was locked and after he walked
through the rooms and saw what was to be seen,
he ripped apart the feather cushions and made
himself a pair of wings. By morning he was gone.

How we love these stories. Consider Adam and Eve,
wasn't the Garden for them a similar prison?
And Satan, as he foresaw an eternity of Heaven's
coercive beauty, what could he do but rebel?

Artist

A knot of string, crossed sticks, a dab of ink—
can't any work begin as a passionate doodling?
So here is another of his constructions: a wooden

cow, but so skillful even the bull was tricked.
You see, one must reckon with the jaded boredom
of queens. During the drawn-out days, she lusted

for this bull. What was he? Beef on the hoof,
nothing special. But she stood at the fence
and watched his bull's prick, its muscularity,

its obscene forcefulness, until she couldn't live
without that dazzle within her. So she went
to the artist and he made a cow that the queen

could hide herself within. The bull mounted
the cow, but it was she, her aroused wetness.
And the artist? Can he be blamed for the ends

for which he used his gift? He was the maker.
It was his sickness. It masked what was made.
Consider this, he never heard her brute moaning.

Discord

Never discount what began his wanderings.
In Athens he was the greatest craftsman.
So much work he had to hire his nephew
to help him. But his nephew had his gift

and soon people claimed the nephew's gift
was greater than the uncle's. If the uncle
built with bronze, the nephew built with gold.
So his uncle worried and fussed and at last

he killed him, who also loved him. You see,
he had no other choice. To be outdone meant
to accept his obliteration. For this murder
he was banished from his homeland. But he

had not reckoned on the arguments of the dead,
how they hold the last word on all subjects.
He would make the statue of a god or a bauble
for a queen, then lift it up to the specter

of his nephew. See this? he would say. Could
you ever make this? And of course the nephew
was silent, itself an answer: the better answer.
The uncle worked harder, statues and buildings

became grander, and the uncle's traveling
was ceaseless. He became known as the greatest
of all craftsmen. You understand how fate
can trick you. Without his nephew's murder,

he would never have become famous. Yet what
pleasure could he take in each new marvel,
palace or temple, when in its glossy surfaces
he kept confronting the dead face he loved?

Icarus's Flight

What else could the boy have done? Wasn't
flight both an escape and a great uplifting?
And so he flew. But how could he appreciate
his freedom without knowing the exact point

where freedom stopped? So he flew upward
and the sun dissolved the wax and he fell.
But at last in his anticipated plummeting
he grasped the confines of what had been

his liberty. You say he flew too far?
He flew just far enough. He flew precisely
to the point of wisdom. Would it
have been better to flutter ignorantly

from petal to petal within some garden
forever? As a result, flight for him was not
upward escape, but descent, with his wings
disintegrating around him. Should it matter

that neither shepherd nor farmer with his plow
watched him fall? He now had his answer,
laws to uphold him in his downward plunge.
Cushion enough for what he wanted.

Blemished and Unblemished

Say genius is one side of the mountain,
then is vanity the other? Consider Daedalus
after he escaped from the king's prison.
The king pursued him. He had many jewels

but Daedalus was brightest. Of course
Daedalus concealed himself. The king went
to his lesser kings and set them a task.
He gave each a spiral shell and told them

to run a thread through the spiral, a tiny
labyrinth, much like the one Daedalus
had made for the king. And one after another
the lesser kings failed at this task.

The great king came to Daedalus's protector
and set him the same task. Naturally, he couldn't
unravel it. So he presented it to Daedalus
who guessed the reason for the puzzle,

that he himself was the only person who
could understand it and this was how the king
had determined to trap him. Still, Daedalus
couldn't keep himself from the solution.

He put a tiny hole in one end of the shell
and covered it with a drop of honey. Then he
tied a gossamer thread to the leg of an ant
and the ant wound its way through the labyrinth

to the sweetness. But it wasn't enough simply
to solve the problem, it was also necessary
that the solution be known. So he gave the shell
to his protector who gave it to the king,

who demanded that Daedalus be returned to him.
The protector refused and a fight began in which
many were killed including the king himself
who had once been Daedalus's friend. Is this

what makes art important to us? The paradox
that the flawlessness of the work is fashioned
from the mass of human failings? Here is vanity,
here gluttony, here lust and murder—but polished,

with the sting of our imperfections blunted,
the bloody stain washed out. Art bears witness
to the possibility of perfection. Not for us
but for what is made: white silks from muddy paws.

Last Wisdom

So often in this world what is rejected
creeps back to the heart, what is cast off
again jams the brain. Remember Daedalus,
at the end of his life, gone to Sardinia

as builder for the son of Hercules. But faces
fretted his memory and he began to make
bronze dolls with moveable limbs, forming
their faces into the faces he once loved.

Here was the son who tumbled into the sea,
here was his wife, here was his sister
who hanged herself, the nephew he murdered,
the great king he had betrayed. And others,

their shapes filled his room. He clothed them
and put hair on their heads. He placed small
devices in their hearts so they could walk
and lift their arms. They grouped in a circle

around him, but they remained silent. He tried
to make them talk. He cut the tongues from birds
and made boxes through which the air swirled
to create a wailing but still the creatures

wouldn't speak. So Daedalus disguised his voice,
making it like a woman's, then a boy's. You are
forgiven, he said, and the bronze dolls jittered
their arms. But when people passing on the street

heard him call out, they jeered at him. You see
his gift stopped short of what he wanted most.
You are forgiven, he shrieked to the dumb things.
But he spoke falsely. His trinkets gave no relief.

Was this the wisdom to come to him at last?
That nothing could rid him of his isolation?
His toys no longer hid what was there: himself
and the night and the only entry into night.

Self-Portrait as a Small Town

The creaky rocker, the single boarder
in his billed cap, the three-legged dog,
the sick mother, the endless tasks
that trickle down from the corner
mills and shops. I have been bad.

Even the laundry's angry, I can see it
snapping like big dogs on short leashes.
And my punishment is this gray gruel,
this spindly line of peas (this is a lake,
this a row of trees), and the gluey sauce
of Approaching Storm. *Go to your room,*

the portrait says. All the houses watch me
struggle up the slippery hill that someone
drew for me to struggle with.

Poem About a Landscape in the Country

Mostly it's the same odd obsession with nothing—
the barren verisimilitude, the doggy fidelity to
the natural world. So, this thrust of dark eloquence must be

a yew, a non-deciduous blue-green talon grabbing
attention. It could be that. Or Death. Or Truth. The abstract
nouns stomp around the landscape in their stout boots.

Meanwhile, the yew doesn't care that it is inscrutable.
The crumpled black, the suggestive cleft of shadow, the shape
    itself—all inlet—
is just a harbor of green chop. It is an object. Mute.

The cows are another matter. As we descend the tiny triplets,
rung by rung, to the oceany wash of open meadow,
the cows are there at the bottom to greet us: They are

the lowest stair in this stairway of being. The cows
in their suffocating upholstery of black and white
are landscapes with legs:

wind-swept, rocky coastlines perambulating around the meadow
to remind us of the Pacific Coast Highway or Perth
Amboy, New Jersey, the humble white house perched on
    the black

shore of desolate remembrance.
So it's no wonder the cows stagger under the weight
of their own description. Now, hand over hand,

unclutching each polished rung (line), having to be thrust
from the tiny stanzas, we're going further, until the cows drift
   by us,
stout storm clouds, and it's down, down towards the bottom of
   the page,

the sky scrubbed clean, the blank horizon, that band of
nothingness.

Painting the Town

At the hem of horizon a distant armada of cars
is gnawing its way through the chop of a meadow
going like Columbus toward the end of the world
under banner of no return. I dip my brush into black.
Over a lip I build a black mustache, a small dense
thundercloud, scented with rum, sleek with waxes.
Dad! And now: awash in her pale dresses,
holding her Pomeranians on jeweled leashes: *Mother.*
Under the noses of women I embroider grins, gossiping.
Out of their eyelids grow awnings of lashes.
The spikes of their heels are driven like golf tees
into their lawns. *Every small town I've ever hated...*
And so from the black mouth of the tunnel blooms
the fast black packaging of the car.
I spill a vial of gunfire into the open chest of the dead man
on his shirtfront I plant a lush grotto of blood into which
    my brush,
like the red fox, disappears and reappears as a woman
in a red dress standing under the shaggy aster of a street lamp.

My Little Esperanto

The dirt-and-grease-and-brown-rose-rot-Community-
   Garden-woman-
out-of-the-rice-paddy-with-Toltec-baby-on-the-back
party begins, good morning, like a tiger, a lullaby on the
   dirge-cusp,
and is gorgeous, not ever sitting one minute, not a moment
   insouciant,
and absolutely lagging badly in the calm department, carrying
   life around
in an iron handcart with peony, and a thousand people a
   second attend,
drinking *elixirs,* essence-of-nutrient flavor, no-fat-bubbled-up
   juices,
and all the guests as troubled and as lithe as cats
and as lonely as any human dog. And all of them talking
rare-specimen-of-horticulture talk and sparrow gabble.
They have matches in their pockets and two books: *Faust,*
   translated
by the neighborhood Buddha, the tricky one, and another
   I forget.
They talk love language in couplets, in near-tears, in the soft
   sounds
called love sounds that I love; beautiful sheets they wear,
   beautiful laundry.
There's a child with an old greenish-metal elephant that was
   a valentine;
another child has some marbles shiny with goodbye, but no
   one is thinking
of going yet; it's only afternoon, maybe it's later but *just.*
   Listen, the last time
you kissed me, yesterday, did you think you had me then?
   You had me then.

You had me like this party I'm having, this immaculate tinsel,
    this irony,
this Homeric tradition with salt, this disorder, this groveling,
    this splaying
and rapture; sweetheart, the silence will be awful when we die
    and leave.

Bliss

Hermes, so young, arrives to tell of spring,
a cold wind and a few feathers of snow accompanying him. His
    eloquences
are tinctured with yellow and red—the first colors—
and he warms to his subject, remembering
an earlier year: —of the very sun's first ferment, of coltsfoot on the
    roads' verges,
of newness wherever the gods choose. And we listen, watching
    Hermes's feet
sink ankle-deep in the mud, a dog barking at someone, then a cry
    somewhere down the valley.
If the universe is cruel, then we have grown used to it. Isn't there
    planting to take up,
the bearing and consequences to look forward to? We still might
    feel a precipitant hand
under the collar's nape and, more slowly, the bliss of holding
like all creation, hyacinths, or another's face, up to lips,
    nostrils, eyes.

Companion Of

—And yet this great wink of eternity

October was what it had already become when I entered the
    walled graveyard, the air golden and remote
in the last minutes before evening. A bedstand and springs made
    the gate, pulled aside,
and the stones faced the sunset, all those not overturned, flung
    like cards
from a losing hand. How long the dead had lain listening,
    looking back,
was written on their markers—granite, sandstone, slate—also
    marriages, loves ("companion of"),
homely avowals of affection cut in verse.
As day relented, I could have sworn that there was no more
    reason than before for agony or joy,
that it had been outlived, but for one stone with the barest
    evidence of lettering—a staff with notes
unsounded, but felt. And I knelt to make out what I could and
    ran my hand as if over paper over the cool stone,
and I found under a cache of yellow, crumbling leaves the
    pried-off surface, broken by the years
in nine uneven pieces. What else was meant to do for Mary Hyatt
    but to take home the words for her?
Then it was impossible not to imagine her days and nights,
    especially her nights, when the air seems to suffer most
from all that has come and what is no longer likely to come. She
    enters the rooms I lend her,
humming a melody whose words she's nearly forgotten. How
    significant and strange the badly remembered air.
It gets in her blood, no forget-me-not gayer for the neck and
    face, and the absent lover is everywhere,
in the shadows, frost on the pains, a soliloquy over the piano or
    the card game.
Before bed, she writes him a letter.

The last time we met you had less and less to say, and though I felt
I understood your private musings (oh, joys, memories of past
experiences altogether your own, ghosts, guilts, pains), I felt my
own words falling away from me. One quiet bred another. In the
end, we forgot to say goodbye. Tell me next time we meet you'll
read to me the lines of poetry you are so fond of, that I once heard
you say with all the passion of youth, that so moved us both,
though we are no longer young! Without the trouble of saying a
thing meant, the meaning comes to suspicion. And if nothing is
meant the thing isn't worth recall. I think I know your thoughts but
it is better to hear them from your mouth. I long for you.

He responds, and everything is as it was. Her cheeks burn and her
    hands tremble. For years.
Until chance, seedy and blind, ruins them; in the fresh dark there
    are no words left for this. It is better so.
Worse to hear it from human lips than in the clattering leaves—
    a rancid song—or in the night owl's scream.

Self

They left her alone; it was what she wanted.
The bay waters had not been so secret for a long while, their great
     labor quiet.
She rowed over the calm of the ebb to an island of birds—heron,
     cormorant, egret waiting in
the tall mangroves, placid and self-contained, as if she alone were
     meant to see them
and find some meaning there. She backwatered through the
     down-strewn shallows
until one by one, then faster, all the birds rose, clucking, in some
     tribal crescendo. Immense
cloud heads stood close, above, like the whitened manes of blind
     and venerable gods,
gods, who remembering the fresh lands—now so remote—
     listened hard for the least shout
of anger or amazement. For a moment she felt she had
     pleased them,
though that hadn't been her intention, and no one else knew.
     But it remained in her:
what soared: the fierce rush: the birds crying fear: and herself
     the cause.

End of the Road

A crow settles in at the bar,
and tells one crow story after another,
all hard as his beak.

He scatters out corn, brass cartridges, a penny,
blue glass, a car key, and a ring.

He orders a beer, using it to chase down
shots of dark glances.

Around midnight the crow flies over us,
out of the bar and into all-consuming night.

I take out a match and drag it slowly
over a bed of sulphur, like a scar dragged

over the butt of an old wound.
The match fire could be anyone's self-hesitancy.

"All I need now," I tell her, "is sleep,
and a place to keep it."

"Get away from me," she said.
"Maybe when you're gone I can pray."

This Has Happened Before

That night we drink too many sad stories and go to bed
upset with attempted matrimony.

After undressing and before making love it's necessary
to not speak of the dream where we become so
entangled that I have to get out of bed as her

and go to the mirror, wanting to write a note, but all I
can write is "Dear Sir, Dear Sir . . ." Where I take the black
comb and run it through my missing shoulder-length
hair, then go to the phone and dial, hanging up when her
mother answers, saying "Come get me, I'm freezing."

The dream where I'm hungry and go down to the
basement, and in the corner find wind and let it flow up
my dress.

Where I take down a vine of grapes and eat
everything, including the leaves.

Where, after drinking dust from the floor I look out
through a window and yell, because, although the moon
is burning in a tree, it's my lips that catch fire.

The dream where, while on the steps going back up to
our room, I return to myself slowly, like narrative
tension returning to the short story in the first part of the
twenty-first century.

The dream that by morning is gone and everything's fine
except for the way I'm down in the sheets sick, heaving
grape leaves, flying but unable to rise.

Letter with No Address

Your daffodils rose up
and collapsed in their yellow
bodies on the hillside
garden above the brick patio
you laid out in sand, squatting
with pants pegged and face
masked like a beekeeper's
against the black flies.
Buttercups circle the planks
of the old wellhead, bright
boisterous convergence,
this May while your silken
gardener's body withers or moulds
in the Proctor graveyard.
I drive and talk to you crying,
then come back to this house
to talk to your photographs.

There's news to tell you:
Maggie Fisher's pregnant.
I carried myself like an egg
at Abigail's birthday party
a week after you died,
while three-year-olds bounced
uproarious on a mattress.
Joyce and I met for lunch
at the mall and strolled weepily
through Sears and B. Dalton.

Today it's four weeks
since you lay on our painted bed
and I closed your huge eyes.

Yesterday I cut irises to set
in a pitcher on your grave;
today I brought a carafe
to fill it with fresh water.
I remember bone-pain, vomiting,
delirium. I remember good times.

My routine is established:
coffee; the *Globe;* breakfast;
writing you this letter
at my desk. When I go to bed
to sleep after baseball,
Gus follows me into the bedroom
as he always followed us.
Most of the time he flops
down in the parlor
with his head on his paws.

Once a week I drive to Tilton
to see Dick and Nan
as we used to do.
Nan doesn't understand much
but she knows you're dead;
I feel her fretting. The tune
of Dick and me talking
consoles her.

        You know now
whether the soul survives death.
Or you don't. When you were dying
you said you didn't fear
punishment; but you didn't
dare speak of Paradise.
One moment from the Gospels
repeats itself in my mind: Christ
twists in agony on the hill,
calling in vain to the Father.

At five a.m., when I walk outside,
mist lies thick on hayfields.
By eight, the air is clear,
cool, sunny with the pale yellow
light of mid-May. Kearsarge
rises huge and distinct,
each birch and balsam visible.
To the west the waters
of Eagle Pond waver
and flash through poppies just
leafing out.

        Always the weather,
writing its book of the world,
returns you to me.
Ordinary days were best,
when we worked together and apart
in our common enterprise.
I remember watching you gaze
out the January window
into the garden of snow
and ice, your face rapt
as you imagined Burgundy Lilies.

Your presence in this house
is almost as enormous
and painful as your absence.
Driving home from Tilton,
I remember how you cherished
that vista with its center
the red door of a farmhouse
against green fields.
Are you past pity?
If you have consciousness now,
if something I can call
"you" has something
like "consciousness," I doubt
you remember the last days.

I play them over and over:
I lift your wasted body
onto the commode, your arms
looped around my neck, aiming
your bony bottom so that
it will not bruise on a rail.
Faintly your repeat,
"Momma, Momma."

                        Three times
I drove to your grave today.
Sometimes, coming back to the house,
I imagine you've gone
to Cricenti's shopping
and might have returned before me,
bags of groceries upright
in the back of the Saab,
its trunk lid delicately raised
as if proposing an encounter,
dog-fashion, with the Honda.

Headboard and Footboard

I call my father on the phone it's twenty years today
My mother died and his life turned sorry
And he's filing his fishing hooks smoothing down the barbs
He's going to throw back every bass in Minnesota

When Grandfather died death stood way over there
In a gray sharkskin suit directing the mourners
When the cars arrived back at the house
The cousins hid in the toolshed and dared each other to look

Death don't come any closer as it is
I'm having enough trouble separating things
Milk blooming across the floor where the child spilled it
My father's voice rising inside mine

As the two-way radio calls all EMTs
Subject with a gunshot wound to the head
And Ellen tosses on the first sweatshirt she can find
HEAVEN across her chest in raised letters

They describe a rushing a dark spiral then light
A dolphin in a net that springs a lucky hole
Or the recruit in real battle cradling his bad lap
Until his eyes widen whoops whoops there I go

Death who used to be so obvious the butcher and the blade
Who shaved the corpse a second time then poured another round
As subtle now as a stray thought
Or a slug melting in a slow pail of salt

In my mind as the marigolds blaze like new pennies
In my hands stacking cordwood in neat rows
In the heart that opens one pink valve at a time
In these words that are not words but stifled shouts

In the bed's carved headboard in the bare footboard too
In Ellen's sexual groans no never inside Ellen
In all that's too solid all that dissolves
Fear has always guided me to the things I love

Tap

I love to find a door. Like the spinal tap—
above the draped fetal curve, you work
the trocar inwards. Dowser, boatman,
auger, bore. Every surface has its opening,
even bone. Steel finds fossa, penetrates.
That give, as the needle enters dura.
Slide out the central metal filament,
it rings, and the invisible emerges, drop
by drop, caught in transparent tubes. So

much fineness—glass and silver, the white
field, crystalline fluid. Seek and you find.
How it comes, the brain's clear bath.

Flight

for my great-grandfather

We ran from a home
          we never saw again.

Saw nothing
          remain ours.

My arm shot
          from my body. My wife's broken

neck. Our son burned
          into a wing of smoke.

A peeled face boiling with flies.
          A man tearing

his gangrened leg off
          with his hands. A girl with her eyes

blown away. She was still
          screaming.

I know you
          cannot help us.

We will die before you
          are born.

Things flee
          their names—

Ash. Bone-salt. Charred embers
          of skull

Remember
how lonely the dead are.

The soot is
mute.

Once
it was human.

New Moon, End of October

Morning met the grass in whiteness
white sparks, chalk and
bone.

Noon was a gristle of crickets.

Dusk was black leaf smoke, quick, then dark,
star-still, darker
still.

Pismire Rising

Mealy-bugs, shootflies in squadrons, mites.
A leech sucks your ankle.
A slug slides up your leg; curdled ooze, the glue
in the globs of it, leaky muck
and swamp water, a lacy scree
of green laid upon its surface, *glug,*
glug, mush and slough, bug manure.
Each step
each leg lugged
from its last footprint: you lean
back and pull a leg
from the sucking black
and haul it forward
and it becomes your front leg,
sinking. . . . Monkey scat,
snake scat, rat scat, fish.
Blackwater, blackwater, runnels of oil,
the marrow, the pith
of grasses, of reeds, of spines: foetid
and fangs and fear—but, *and,* too, *as well as*
the heat and breathing
of a billion writhing
and alive things,
a food chain, cell chain, (little) heart chain
from microbe to Yahweh,
from quicksand to elevator,
from the greased pneumatic tube to hell
to the placid glacial lake.
The mud hums with its mud-loving beetles,

and their cousins once removed,
the waterpenny beetles,
moored in their riffles,
the waterpenny beetles
love where they live.

Praia dos Orixas

1.

Farther north we came to a place of white sand and coconut palms, a tumbledown government research station, seemingly abandoned, no one in sight but sea turtles lolled in holding tanks along the edge of the beach. The ocean was rough, riptides beyond a shelf of underlying rock, water a deep equatorial green. We swam. Rested. Hid from the sun in the shade of the palms. A few miles on we found the fishing village by the inlet, the small restaurant with platters of squid and giant prawns on a terrace overlooking the harbor, manioc, sweet plantains, beans and rice in the lee of the cork-bobbed nets and the tiny cerulean and blood-orange boats sheltered in the crook of the breakwater's elbow. A boy selling sugar cane rode past on a donkey; white-turbaned women bent like egrets to the salt marsh. "There is no word for this in English," said Elizabeth,

meaning, by *this,* everything.

Later: goats and dogs on barbed-wire tethers; children laughing beneath banana-leaf umbrellas;

women hanging laundry on a red dirt hillside in a stately ballet with the wind.

2.

The next day we headed back to the city, following the rutted dirt road along the coast until forced to a halt with the engine of our rented Volkswagen thumping and billowing a fatal tornado of smoke.

Fan belt, snapped in two.

It was difficult making ourselves understood in that place; they seemed to speak some backwoods dialect, or else the language failed us completely; neither Anna's schoolbook Portuguese nor Joshua's iffy *favela* slang brought any clear response. People beneath trees ignored us in the darkness, or watched with an air of unhappy distrust, or disdain, or possibly compassion.

Although we couldn't see the beach, a sign by the road read *Praia dos Orixas.*

Eventually, one man took pity upon us, running home and returning with a fine black fan belt fresh in its package, a fan belt big enough for a tractor, impossible to jury-rig to that clockwork machine, and yet no matter how we contrived to explain ourselves, no matter what gesticulations we employed, what shadow play, what pantomime, we could not make him see that his gift would not suffice. *No good! Too big!* We held the broken belt against his, to display their comic disparity, but the man only smiled and nodded more eagerly, urged us to our task of fitting the new piece, happy to be of assistance, uncomprehending. *Won't fit! Too big! Thank you, friend!*

Hopeless.

In the end, money was our undoing, those vivid and ethereal Brazilian bills stamped with the figures of undiscovered butterflies and Amazonian hydroelectric dams. I forget whose idea it was to pay the man for his kindness, but no sooner had the cash appeared in our hands than he at last gave vent to his anger and frustration, insulted by our mistaken generosity, hurling epithets that needed no translation, and so, as the crowd approached, menacingly, from the shadows,

or perhaps merely curious, or possibly protective,

we jumped in the car, still smiling, waving our arms like visiting dignitaries, desperate to display the depths of our goodwill but unwilling to risk the cost of further miscommunication,

and drove away with a gut-wrenching racket into the chartless and invincible night.

3.

What follows is untranslatable: the power of the darkness at the center of the jungle; cries of parrots mistaken for monkeys; the car giving up the ghost some miles down the road; a crowd of men with machetes and submachine guns materializing from the bush, turning out to be guards from a luxury resort less than a mile away; our arrival at Club Med; the rapidity of our eviction; our hike to the *fazenda* on the grounds of the old mango plantation where we smoked cigars and waited for a ride; the fisherman who transported us home with a truckload of lobsters bound for market.

By then another day had passed.

It was evening when we came upon the lights of the city like pearls unwound along the Atlantic, dark ferries crossing the bay, the patio at the Van Gogh restaurant where we talked over cold beer for uncounted hours. That night was the festival of Saõ João, and the streets snaked with samba dancers and the dazzling music of Trios Elektrikos, the smell of roasting corn and peanuts, fresh oranges, firecrackers, sweet *ginepapo*, veins of gold on the hillsides above the city where flames ran shoeless in the fields among the shanties, a fine ash sifting down upon our table, tiny pyres assembled around seashell ashtrays and empty bottles as the poor rained down their fury upon the rich. That night the smoke spelled out the characters of secret words and shadows were the marrow of the ribs of the dark. That night the stars fell down,

or perhaps it was another.

That night we yielded to the moon like migrating sea turtles given over to the tide-pull.

That night we clung together in the heat until dawn as the cries of the revelers ferried us beyond language.

That night we spoke in tears, in touches, in tongues.

for Robert Hass

A Connect-the-Dots Picture

The pine tree at the corner of the lot
where my childhood home, a ranch house,
sits like a snapped sugar wafer on a slope.
Tents in Upton's field collapsed and pushed
aside for a game of kickball or just tumbling.
The oldest Upton girl whom I adore,
nearer adulthood than I, her head in a sky
I cannot but wish to see. *Follow me,*
she says, *I will show you something really neat.*
And I go up the stone path and stairs
among the lolling day lilies and ivy
behind the marvelous girl to a place
nested in trees where a garden hose
uncoils in her hand. *There,* she says,
holding the metal rimmed end to my face.
I must be nine, possibly ten. I love Christy.
She taught me to make ice cream in a bucket.
She combed my hair as if I were a doll.
She took my hand and led me away from the gang
of boys in the field where I tried so hard
to be good and strong. *There,* she says tenderly,
look in there, and I cast my whole being
into her command. Some wonder is about
to happen in the dark hole of the hose.
Sputter of laughter, and more laughter,
and I realize I cannot see her, or anything.
There has been a blast of air, water. I think
I am crying and hope not. In this world
tears have never been good. Once, when Casey cried,
his sister forbade me to tell anyone, ever,
and she smacked him till he stopped.
But now my face is wet, my hair, my loose
summer shirt which I like more than all the others

in my drawer because it has two girls on it,
hand in hand, and they wear shirts exactly
like this one. No, I am not sobbing. Good.
But I am cold, and my eyes sting.
I try to look where Christy was and may
still be when the smarting stops. She is trying
to teach me something adult. Complicated.
How it feels to be stung by the force
of your own desire turned back on you,
and the possible responses: regret or fury.
One day I will understand that one is antidote
to the other. Years later in the darkening room
of a country not my own, real history heaped
in the corners, I stand next to a man
who has just begun to be weary of my hopefulness,
unwavering desire that simply asks for it.
His is a small travesty, a forgotten promise
that left me waiting all of an afternoon.
Smell of wet stones, gnats hovering
around the spigot dribble. My shirt has not
been ruined, Christy clucks, unnerved at this kid
who stands in mute trust, dripping, comic,
obscenely forlorn. This was not the point.
She meant to send me screaming like any child,
home—but home, if ever I had one
is on another continent, inching away.
The man draws back from the insipid scene,
unpleasant female disappointment gathering
in his room, ruining the evening, filling his shoes,
making the air too close. The offending garden hose
settles far under the ivy, and it is intolerable
that I should keep standing here expectantly,
taking it, asking for more, still too much
in love. It was that, then, that Christy wanted
to wash from my face. In the long minute
of my blindness, the summer afternoon went
cruelly on in my ear. A horsefly. The dog
somewhere itching itself. Smack
of the rubber ball against a boy's toe

down in the field. Small shush of ivy
where the hose falls. Drips on the stone.
It's only water, dummy, she says, disgusted.
I look straight into her eyes and she sees
she hasn't gotten rid of it, that appalling
ardor. Too much of something sticky, serious,
and she hates me for it.

Poem Against Ideas

I read in a book that in the Kishinev pogrom
Forty-seven Jews had been killed
But elsewhere I had read
That forty-*eight* Jews had been murdered
By fire, by stoning, by rifle, knife, and strangling.

And I wondered if the author had accidentally left out
My great-uncle Ephraim Belkin, perhaps because
He was passing through, a boy, about ten years old
I was told by my aunt, and somebody had thrown
A rock at his head as he stood in a bread line.

They were starving, a family of eleven. They had fled
Odessa, and though I don't remember my geography
They must have been headed west and south
By foot towards Egypt, which was next to the Promised Land.

In Egypt, there's a family story about a camel and a bride.
And years later, in America, one sister
Would become a Communist, let her hair
Grow long, join the Polar Bear Club at Far Rockaway.
She would smoke those foul-smelling Turkish cigarettes.

One afternoon, a cornice from the roof would fall down
And crush the head of her only daughter, four years old.

Similarly, a woman wrote a book
Called *One by One by One*, referring to the deaths
Of Jews in the Holocaust, meaning to remind us

That this is the only way to think about
The deaths of so many. The book begins with stories

Of a particular group of survivors revisiting
Their hometown in Germany fifty years after the war,

Calling on old neighbors, Herr Schmidt and Frau Hamberger,
The graveyard with its misplaced, upended stones,
The Jewish school now a cultural center.
Some of them even "felt more German," a paradox
I can barely understand.

They were quite moving, these stories, quirky,
As individual stories usually are,
But the rest of the book, which I didn't finish,
Is an intellectual history and less personal.

I told my son (who had asked) that an intellectual
Is a person who thinks a lot, and then
Thinks about what he thought about, and so on,

Until all experience, all emotions, all relationships,
All stories, can be reduced to single words:

Morality, Myth, Paradox, Guilt, and so on.
Then what good is an idea? he asked. It was an idea

About the International Jewish Banking Conspiracy
That got Hitler moving
Toward the Final Solution, and certain ideas

Are right now moving the various
Local militia to take action against blacks, browns,
Asians, Jews, and homosexuals. It was an idea

That got Marx going, and Einstein, and look
What happened there. Even Democracy, that grand
Ongoing experiment, was another bad idea
That gained currency because some good men
Took it in their heads to write a document
We could argue about for a millennium.

I remember once getting punched in the mouth
In seventh grade and I will never forget it.

And I once had an idea about the essential differences
Between men and women, between my wife
And me, between my wife and all women,
But I've since forgotten it. Today a woman told me

My use of the term "son of a bitch"
Was demeaning to women. Behind her, in the bushes,
Was a good idea all tangled up.

There are many petty people in the world.
Just look around you. Their ideas
May be right-sounding as the Ten Commandments
God gave to Moses on the mountain,
As seductive as the Risen Christ,
As rational as Fascism, as elegant as e=mc².

But I'd rather be punched in the mouth
Because I'd tried my hardest to take that boy's
Girlfriend away from him. I succeeded,
And landed in the hedges, while she stood by,

Trembling, not knowing what to say or do. I suppose
She felt ambivalent, but that, too,
Is a story shrunk to a word.

I had a great-uncle named Ephraim
Who undertook a long walk from Odessa to Egypt.
He was just a boy. I can't imagine much about him

Except he was the same age my son is now. He was probably
Silly, like my son, he probably liked sweets,
He probably thought girls were put here by mistake
And probably his feet were sore.

He was a good Jew, and he probably thought
God would rescue him and his whole family
From the mess his little world was in.
He probably thought Government was a bad idea

Because it was the government that was murdering
His people. Someone, probably a man
With a bad idea planted in his brain,
Bent over in the rain—I know it was raining—
And picked up a rock and threw it.

What marked the boy as a Jew?
Maybe he had a nose like mine, maybe
He wore a funny hat and had those curly

Little side locks that seem to sprout
From each ear like tassels from corn. The stone
Struck his temple. The boy fell down,

My great-uncle Ephraim, on the wet pavement.
Maybe he was dead before he hit the ground.

The Talmud tells us that the Biblical injunction
We call "an eye for an eye, a tooth for a tooth"
Is not to be practiced by Jews. The Talmud tells us

If we save one life we save a thousand lives,
And if we take one life
We take a thousand lives, an idea I can grasp.

I have a few friends who think, as they say,
Conceptually. They don't tell stories.

They sit around a room and argue. Each
Has an idea, which gets tossed around
Like a hot potato from person to person.

When they talk like that
My attention wanders, and I feel dumb.

But if one of them leaned across the table
Right now and slugged me for disagreeing with him,
Which I hope he won't, and he knows who he is,
I'd remember that forever. Right here, in the mouth,

So that my upper lip smashed against my eyetooth,
And I'd continue loving him.

A boy named Quegariello, who was in love,
Did just that. He's a story in my mind, a face
Suffused with blood, a quick sucker punch,

And then the stiff green hedges
Holding up my body.

He was righteous, so I didn't hit him back.

No idea could displace him, and all my poems
Are dedicated to him, and to my great-uncle
Ephraim, who's only a name and a scrap of story
Told me by my aunt, a boy my boy's age

Who died in the rain in a bread line in Kishinev.
As I recall, the year was 1903.

My friend is still talking in the parlor
Under an overhanging lamp that illuminates us all. The key words
Are *binomial* and *paradox*. He wants us all to give up
Thinking one way and start thinking another.

And while he is talking I confess I want
To stroke the wonderfully bony ankle and high arch
Of the woman sitting next to me. She is wearing
A gold ring on one toe, which is linked
To a gold ring on another toe. As she fidgets
The metal catches and reflects the light.

from *Orpheus and Eurydice*

If your gaze takes in
the world
a person's a puny thing.

If a person is all
you see,
the rest falls away
and she becomes the world.

But there's another world
into which a person
can disappear.

Then what remains?
Only your word for her:
Eurydice.

*

She paused at the stone
gates and saw
a story like hers
carved there:

the child, Persephone,
fleeing the dark god,
stumbles.
        A crack
appears
beneath her feet.
Her head's thrown back,
its sunburst of curls

a golden chrysanthemum
snapped from its stalk.

A mortal's a blossom
the earth opens for.

*

When I was alive—only glimpses,
moments of bliss but
always the body resisting,
refusing to let go.

          There
I was the fish too eager
to enter the nets; here,
I'm a river.

          There, a bird
in search of its nest;
here, a wind that needs no rest.

When I died, all he heard
was a small, ambiguous cry.
How could he know how free I felt
as I unwound the long bandage
of my skin and stepped out?

*

He stood before the throne
and we stared, astonished,
at his breath pluming
in the cold air.

And then he strummed
his lyre and sang
the things we knew
and had forgot—
the earth in all its seasons
but especially spring
whose kiss melts
the icicle's bone
and makes the dead bush
bloom again.

He sang the splendid wings
sex lends.

He sang the years passing
like sparks
flung in the dark:
anvil, tongs, and hammer
toiling at pleasure's forge.

Last of all it was loss
he sang, how like a vine
it climbs the wall,
sends roots and tendrils
inward, bringing
to the heart
of the hardest stone
the deep bursting emptiness of song.

*

When they said I must leave hell
and I put on flesh again,
it felt like a soiled dress.

And as I followed him
up the steep path
I kept staring at his feet,
callused, bleeding. How
could I once have held
and kissed them?
                    My sandal
came undone. I paused
for breath because
the air hurt my lungs.

A hundred delays offered
their help, their hope,
but still the opening
grew until at last I saw
his body silhouetted
against the entrance glare:
dark pupil
of an eye that stared.

*

The light was like a wall
and I was afraid.
I turned to her as I had before:

to save myself.

She was something between
the abyss and me,
something my eyes could cling to.

*

Far below, plowed fields vibrated
in the spring heat like black harps.

But all that was behind him now:
the lakes and swamps, the low places,
the lilacs with their heart-shaped
leaves shading the clustered huts.

He turned to the cliffs and pathless
slopes above the tree line
where each wind-swept boulder gave forth
its single, inconsolable note.

Who knows? Maybe it would be simpler.
When she was alive, her body
confused him; he couldn't think
clearly when she was close. Smells
of her skin made him dizzy.

Now, where she had been: only
a gaping hole in the air,
an emptiness he could fill with song.

Air Guitar

The women in my family were full of still water;
they churned out piecework as quietly as glands.
Plopped in America with only the wrong words
hobbling their tongues, they liked one thing
about the sweatshop, the glove factory,
and it was this: you didn't have to say much.
All you had to do was stitch the leather fingers
until you came up with a hand; the rest
they kept tucked to their ribs like a secret book.
Why was not said, though it doesn't seem natural
the way the women ripped the pages out
and chewed them silently and swallowed—where
is the *ur*-mother holding court beside her soup pot,
where is Scheherazade and the rest of those Persians
who wove their yodeled tragedies in rugs?
Once I tutored a Cambodian girl; each week
I rolled the language like a newspaper and used it
to club her on the head. In return she spoke
a mangled English that made all her stories sad,
about how she'd been chased through the jungle
by ruthless henchmen of Pol Pot; for months
she and her sisters mothers grandmothers aunts
lived in the crowns of trees and ate what grew there
and did not touch down. When she told the story,
her beautiful and elaborately painted face
loosened at each corner of her eyes and mouth
to remind me of a galosh too big for its shoe.
It was rubbery, her face, like these words
that sometimes haunt me with their absence,
when I wake up gargling the ghost of one
stuck like a wild hair far back in my mouth.
This morning it took me till noon to fish out
cathexis, and even then I did not know

what this meant until I looked it up.
As it was not until I met her sister
that I learned what the girl was telling me
was not the story she was telling: there were
no women in trees, no myrmidons of Comrade Pot,
their father was, is, had always been,
a greengrocer in Cleveland. Cathexis:
fixing emotional energy on some object
or idea—say the jungle, or the guy
getting rubbery with a guitar that isn't there.
Yet see how he can't keep from naming
the gut that spills above his belt *Lucille*—
as music starts to pour from his belly
and the one hiked-up corner of his lip. This
is part of a legend we tell ourselves about the tribe,
that men are stuffed and full to bursting
with their quiet, that this is why they've had to go
into the wilderness, searching for visions
that would deliver up their names. While women
stayed in the villages, with language at their center
like a totem log tipped lengthwise to the ground.
And they chipped at it and picked at it,
making a hole big enough to climb in, a dugout
in which they all paddled off to hunt up
other villages, the other members of the tribe.
And when the men returned they found no one home,
just cold fire pits that would not speak—an old
old forsakenness they bring to the bar stools
while the jukebox music washes over each of them
like a tricolored lightwheel on a silver tree.
Though someone might argue that none of whatever
I've just said is true: it was men who made boats
while the women sat clumped in private guilds,
weaving their baskets tight enough to trap
the molecules of water. You can see
that the trail from here to the glove factory
would not be terribly long or hard to read,
and how it might eventually lead to the railroad flat
where, alone at night for many years, my grandmother

works deep into her privacy with a common nail
that she scratches across the backs of copper sheets.
She is making either the hands clasped in prayer
or the three-quarter profile of Jesus.
As far as I know there is nothing
the radio can play now that will make her sing.

Trees

I.

In late October, daylight stood with one leg in the dark.
A boy swung himself through his unzipped jacket
to work his feet up. Then monkey-handed he headed
for a part of the branch he was heavier than
and bobbed there like a hunk of suet.
But with girls it was different: you came to a place
where the weight of your fear equaled
the pull of going up, and that was where you stayed.
Your crotch was the anchor you sunk
hard on a limb, and it was enough
to stay hidden in a bonnet of dead leaves
until your mother called your name:
once, twice, her vowelings broke into two notes
that came to you as from whole continents away

II.

and I never craved any more perilous instincts,
though sometimes their absence struck:
the plaster of Paris like a missing white fur muff
& my mother never fearful of me falling.
The way I saw her that day my brother shinnied
up our one tall-enough-to-kill-you tree.
The yard sloped from the window above the kitchen sink,
so she could see only where the top of the trunk
tapered, leafless, to a spine that ran
the long axis of his body. I remember
how glamorously—absently, breathlessly—
her hand touched the divot in her neck
as, like a compass needle gauged against the mullion,
he tilted, righted, then slowly tipped the other way.

Pomegranate

How charitable to call it fruit, when almost nothing
inside it can be eaten. Just the gelatin
that thinly rinds the unpalatable seed.
The rest of it all pith, all bitter,
hardly a meal, even for a thin girl. But enough,

at least in the myth, to be what ties Persephone
half the year to hell. From thenceforward her name
makes the corn stalks wither: that's why
the Greeks called her *Kore,*
just Kore, meaning *the girl* or *the maid,* the one

who because she was hungry stood no chance against even
the meager pomegranate—though it's never clear
this future isn't the one she wants,
her other choice being daylight, sure,
but also living with her mother. In some versions

she willingly eats the plush red seeds, signing on
with the underground gods and their motorbikes
and their dark shades. Oh . . . all right—
no motorbikes. And *eat*'s not right either.
But what, then, "sucks"? "Strains the seeds against her teeth"?

Of course it would have made more sense for Hades to tempt her
with something full of juice: a grapefruit, say,
or a peach. But maybe these
would be too close to her mother's food.
And only a girl like Eve could be so blank a slate

to ruin herself with a meal as salutary as the apple.
Give her instead the kind of nourishment
that takes its own hydraulics to extract,
like the pomegranate, or the spiny
asteroid of the Chinese chestnut. Or the oyster,

from which, between the riffled shell and shucking knife,
there is no exciting unscathed: a *delicacy,* we say,
whenever the hand hangs out its little
flag of broken skin.
But doesn't the blood that salts the mouth

somehow make the meat taste sweeter? As when she turns
toward us in the moonlight with the red pulp
mottling her teeth: don't our innards
—even if to spite us—start to sing?
I know that's what mine did on those nights

when our girl got called out of the junipers
where the rest of us hid her—all it took was his
deep voice, and she stepped out.
Then came sounds that, instead of meaning
carried all of punctuation's weight: the exclamation

when she had her air knocked out, and the question
that was her sudden, inswept breath.
And the parentheses when time went on forever,
when there was no sound because he'd got her by the throat.
He seemed to like our watching, his imperiousness

saying books about how much we didn't know: the jelly
sluiced inside the mouth or the seeds rasped
back and forth across the palate,
until it came time for her to hide behind her own hand
when she had to tongue them out. Sometimes

it would end when the boyfriend strolled her off,
steering as if she were the boat and her skinny arm
were its tiller. But just as often
he'd have somewhere to get to, or lose interest
as if so much activity had pushed him to the brink of sleep,

and that's how she came back to us kneeling
in our moonlit patch of stunted trees
whose evergreenery wove our hair and pressed

its crewelwork in our haunches. In the half-dark
it would be hard to make out what he'd done: lip pearled,

her chin gleaming like the hemisphere of a tarnished spoon.
But didn't the leaves seem brighter then,
if it can be said that junipers have leaves?
As our hard panting rattled through
...but no. Stop here. No of course it can't be said.

Birthday

While you suffered I measured
flour for a birthday cake, the bleached
grinding of wheat flowing from a tin scoop
like water, like cold

air I split walking in winter woods,
snow a long white apron flung against the fissured
maples, the smooth trunks of birches.
While you wept I sang, the candles

flared to flush my daughter's face
with greed and joy. A neighbor scraped
his shovel on asphalt, whistling.
He drank deeply from a steaming cup

as you gasped your fugitive sleep. Constellations
blinked at their own bloody stories,
I reached for the broom, the dustpan,
I filled my mouth with sweetness of leftover

ice cream and cake. While you suffered
to live, I lived, it seemed, without effort
or thought. Ribbons and ripped, lustrous
paper emptied of gifts, their shiny reason for being,

I thrust into plastic garbage bags, and marched
that row of headless torsos toward the curb.

Wind

in spring revises bright calligraphies of grass.
Small revisions. Not like winter's chop-
logic. For you who seek in nature resurrections:

each green shoot corkscrews a rotten leaf,
and though our DNA's the same, my twin's
not me. Wind's a death wish rumor hissed

from green to yellow head all summer. I wish
I'd gotten my grandmother's optimism
instead of these pinhole glasses. Look

at trees the hurricane limbed and quartered,
fields scythed bare, the bush blasted; picture
saying, "Don't cry, children, at the wind's long division."

CLENN REED

Catatonia: In a Classroom
for the Slow-to-Learn

I say Jason, look at this book,
but feel like I'm in a dream he's having,
a ship at anchor off the island he is
that dispenses words like boats to shore.
He knows better than to talk.
So, I ask, Jason, do you like to read?
and lift the cover, letting a few
pages flip between us. His small fingers
jitter uncontrollably on the desk.
Caught here, with heckles of children
filling a blurred world behind me,
I'm looking for the key that can unlock
this mouth squirreled into a mute nest.
Where is the cure that is close at hand?
A bright sky of winter moves across
the rectangular panes—sharp light.
What am I here, on an edge
where senses never get sorted out,
too large for the chair I'm sitting in
before this putty-faced boy. Eyes—
brown leaves blown into white cups.
Why would a stranger place himself
where nobody was before and speak?
I say Jason, and name this place,
then turn and head back out to sea.

Oh, Luminous

Yesterday, another dog collapsed, this one
endlessly carrying slippers and bones.

If I don't leave here now, I'll die here,
the ascent to town less than one hour

and my car headed Away, but stalled,
surrounding temperature so extreme

my skin can't distinguish
winter, summer.

In just one hour:
carrots for sight, beets for blood, oh town

where all things good. This house,
where all things bad, barren

skeleton, shelter of leaking rooms,
whose property is this property?

The owner is lost. The house has lost
the owner, the owner has lost the house.

Where there are no chairs
there are plates and silver

scattered across the lawn—sunless,
seedless, wormless lawn—

even the dead and the ones
underneath the dead

crawl away, away, deeper down,
do I still have time?

Oh luminous town.

Browntail

Its gauze tent
Is big as a heart or hand,
Filthy with dots like black sand.
These are its seeds, eggs, which in gooey,
Furred translucency have already sucked in
Twigs and leaves as good as dead,
And will turn into striped,
Puffy, segmented worms,
Whiskered and spotted zinc,
Umber and crimson.

The tent's tissue of unclarity
Is important to the caterpillar's
Success and metamorphosis
Into browntail freedom and flight,
Just as the birthworm's hairs
Are insistently nebulous,
Its excrement invisible
Like the lies you tell someone
To break loose. When caterpillars
Molt, or eat out

Their exterior ovaries,
Those bodiless mothers of gray hair,
Poison is carried awhile
By a dry wind, and this boils
The skin into a rash,
Just as lies, or secretiveness
Generally, is corrosive
To mental balance, all for apotheosis
As a moth, or something
Which claims it is
Unintentionally vicious.

The Little Lie

It was born white. It lay in bed
Between its father and mother
Kicking its tiny feet, so pretty
You wanted to suck them and all their piggies.

The mother kept looking nervously at the father,
Hoping the little lie made him happier.
"I'm telling you the truth," she said.
"It's you I love. The other was a mistake

And it's over." The father was sick
To his stomach. He tried to be wise.
He muttered, "Well, let everyone have another,
You a Byron, me a ballerina."

The mother had to rise from bed
And change the diaper on the little lie,
An infantile truth which laughed
And cried and smelled of mild excrement.

She had to slip off her shirt
Because the little lie needed to suck
And she needed that doomed orphan
To nourish, nothing if not a mom,

Yet hating for a minute all
Her instincts and her little lie.
Out in the world she swore it didn't exist,
That there was nothing between her

And her partner but an occult malaise,
Though maybe a ballerina. The white lie
Was growing up. It became a pink
And purple bundle, a little mulberry

Bitter to try, from a tree whose leaves
Have differently numbered lobes, each
A different version of the green truth.
Worms eat these and make silk,

Shiny and smooth, an ideal avatar of a lie.
No such luck with our little vagabond,
Our Alice or Atlas in Motherland. It grew
Like a tumor and paralyzed everything,

Twisting faces into snails and owls
Until our King and Queen of Prevarication
Ran from each other, paradise a forest
Of petrified trees dropping stone leaves,

A shock to lots of people, especially
Byron left holding his quill-pen hatchet
In the woodpile. He didn't understand awhile
Or see the lie had become a ton of tar,

Poisoning the sweet river of once
Upon a time. It was too big to explain
And in the midst of this blight it was easy
For him to believe he was vile, insane,

A failure, or to blame, until he saw the lie's
Mother out strolling with a new porker
On a leash, a young boar with a sore tail.
Now he understood the whole saga, and if he could

He would have told her, You should have lied
To your husband, saved the truth for your lover.
"Did you tell him about me?" he implored her.
"Just go away," she whispered, starting to cry.

The Dying Gull

In Portland, every once in a while, one encounters
A dying gull, eyes milky as clams,
Lying on a patch of grass or safe gutter,
Shivering with death fever, black back
And white breast dotted over
With stationary yet excited flies
Drunk on salt and the heaving propinquity
Of deathly fresh fowl flesh, and here it is,
The vicious essence, the dissimilar illusion-fusion
Of similarity, the stupid, awkward, squawking flounderer
Encountered inevitably like mental wreckage
Or magical trash: the metaphor.
Jesus Christ! The immense black and white bird, wildly
Trembling and covered with trembling
Gluttonous flies, looks like, awk, a newspaper,
And the flies, ugh, fuck, are words
Sucking delirious bitterness
From a disaster so much larger,
A fucking Mount Everest of hunger and sex,
Love mindless and fierce,
Sharp-eyed, pitiless, pure and impure,
Devastating, fast, which could soar higher
Than a housefly can dream, though sometimes it rests,
A white star very high and immobile in blue sky,
Sustained by what's effortless and invisible,
This disgusting bird, this piece of street shit
A symbol, not a dying gull but Alaric the Hun
Who sacked Rome, or Vercingetorix,
The name Romans gave forever to the one
Captured and killed, a lost Gaul
And early king of love and death.

The Coat

Not night now, not the night's
one chilling vocable
of sharp air, not the cross
parental babble of it
burning your infant ear,
not anything you say
in answer, no good, not fair,
the fiercest syllables
that turn, as soon as spoken,
into steam that lifts away,

no, none of these is the
beloved in the story.
There's no beloved, none,
except the coat you wear,
the heavy coat you've clung
so long, so hard to that
the only warmth you sense
now is the warmth that seeks
an arctic bitterness
to hoard itself against.

Here you are easiest
where only phantom shapes
across the honeyed vagueness
of the window pass—
easiest where no lock
is turned, no door is opened,
no one at all to find
in your greeting that the coat
that kept you warm outside
has brought the cold in with it.

What

After I flung you down
at last onto the bed
because it was two a.m.
and you'd been crying for hours,
it seemed, and would not stop,
all my comforting
defeated, spent; because
you were too frantic by then
to say what it was you wanted,
sobbing too much to say it,
though you kept on trying
to say it till you were frantic
now because I didn't
understand; in the stunned moment
after I flung you down,
before you wailed again,
in your amazed look

I saw how having done
to you just that much had
already brought me that
much closer to doing more;
I saw how memory
in me is a collapsing
universe sucked back
in toward its black
original adhesion,
while in you it is
a universe too suddenly
expanded where my never
before seen or suspected
fury whirls away
forever now as
something possible
from what you won't recall.

Ruins

The first one was in Michigan and I loved him
   like I was digging in a foreign land and he was
      the ruin I came to discover. Michigan is as cold

as people imagine and when I remember him now
   he is leaned against one of those gaudy American
      cars, big as boats, and all but his face is lost

in layers. This was a campus full of kids in knickers
   and baby blue sweaters who, when they laughed, shielded
      their mouths with mittened hands. I longed to uncover

flesh the same way I longed to uncover earth in a place
   where winter long outstayed its welcome. I wanted
      my beauty, whatever it was, held up to my blind eye

and described; I thought loving was the same as
   sifting down through ash to find Pompeii. In Michigan
      there were layers of snow and layers of clothing

and with that first boy it was as if I kept undressing
   until I was naked but I found a way, that young, to take
      off more. Down in the dirt of each other every clue we

uncovered was not enough. The snow did not stop falling
   and now, a decade later, there is the shape of him outlined
      again and again until he is larger but less detailed:
         a relic from the ancient landscape explaining me.

Sway

A noose of moonlight—

I think I see what my father saw
That night when he went out
To the leaning barn—

He followed the light,

Scared up some rope in the tack room
To toss over the beam.

The wind rending itself
through barbed fences.

I found him
The next morning,

Kneeling on a hay bale, his head
In his hands,
Under the dangling rope
He'd left unknotted.

Asterisks of ice on the glass.
Frozen stars to look past.

He was chilled and wretched.
The night had made a penitent of him.
Under the thrum of winter wind, his sobs.

The bay mare seemed embarrassed.
The rafters creaked like a boat.
Steam rising
From the yellow palace of hay bales.

    The wind blows and turns
        another page.

Oddly elating
To see him that way.
For the first time in years

It was easy to reach for him.
I led him back to the house,

    the rope left there
      swaying.

RALPH SNEEDEN

Off Little Misery Island

The bass we catch is too big with years,
its dark stripes notched and wavering
like a cut trunk's rings.
We drag it over the gunnel, stand back, and no one
will touch it, at first. The children cry
and want it gone. And when we do let it go,
it is not out of kindness, but loathing.
We are seeing what usually isn't seen,
the completenesses, the ends, the fish
trailing a red scarf of vomit and blood
back to where we pulled it from.

The white tide is nothing but time
crowding the reef's rusted warning spindle,
sinking more deeply the reef itself,
and the bell in the buoy has not flinched
at its own trite plagiarism. So why are we most happy
when our lives are most visibly not in our hands?
Even when we can name the sea ducks,
or start the engine before the swells
fling the drifting boat against the rocks?
We knew what we'd find here;
we could see it from shore.
But that hasn't stopped us from circling it twice,
rounding every point, looking
for the single unrecognizable shape,
and the old shape of our lives
broken for a moment if not forever.
We coax it with lures—plastic fish
hurled into the wash again and again.
We sniff the air and sigh.

After thousands of miles of open water
the fish and the waves that carry them
must rise against the island's sudden contour.
From all that blue-black they must rise,
shocked, to a sanctuary of coves
and the testament of motion in sunlit shallows,
the strange sun on their cold backs.
But where is *our* world of new green foam,
the oxygen of effervescent sluices,
the brushing life of kelp and assault of barnacles?
The engine revs in a fit of blue smoke
and drags us backward off the rocks.
Water slaps the stern, fills the transom
and drains. We're out of trouble again,
drinking beer, talking of money, rinsing
in a fresh bucket the bloody pliers, the bent hooks.
And our children, trussed in their orange preservers,
are playing in the cutty as if they were home.

Rapunzel's Exile

I was told to lie down in the cart, and I did. My braided hair mixed with straw under me to catch the blood I seeped. Then she covered me with heavy furs and brush. The night was stark and cold, the stars close and multiplying like cells as we creaked along under them a long time. We crossed several creeks, water hissing up through shelves of ice. She pulled the whole time. She was a strong woman.

When I'd first felt the blood darken my skirt in the garden, I knew she'd cursed me for my new game, tossing stones over the wall, and someone—who?—tossing them back. All that day, she paced while I lay in her bed, waiting to die. All that night we traveled.

At dawn we were deep in a forest, so tangled we had to ditch the cart and pick by foot through roots and brambles. Ravines pitched and rose. We waded thigh-deep in leaves and water. I watched her tough haunches, the rope around her waist that tethered my neck. The sky grew heavy with pent snow, and still we walked in woods so old and dark at noon the owls cried.

The one who'd held my face, called it her "sun," had turned to me her wordless back. Behind her, I had no choice but follow, twelve years old, bent and sopping wet with shame and terror. Even when we came, finally, to the cleared place where the tower rose dully in weak moonlight, and I gasped "Godmother!," she would not turn to look at me. Her knife flashed quick to cut the rope, then pointed through the low door. I cried and said "No, no"—I pleaded and grasped for her—but the bright blade held me back. On my knees inside, I groped the stairs. The cellar draft above me fell upon my face, and I knew that this place had been made ready for me all the years that she had loved me. And I guessed that this was love, too—not the seesaw play of stones lopped over a garden wall, but my lonely climb upward, and the thick scrape of mortar over shoved and piled stones, behind.

The Company We Keep

1.

The one she loves she hates. And too
late, she says, for the thing love's become
to let her loose from its grip.

They take it to the hills. Green tent
in blue mountains. They'd bought themselves
fishing licenses, and the conversation began

on trout—cutthroat and Dolly V's—names
bruised and asthmatically deep
inside the second then the third pint

of flat gin. And maybe she'd said brown trout
when she'd meant to say brook.
Which is what got him started,

sent his boot across her hip. Though some—
and just now she can't remember which
blotches of purple and which red welts—

came from her own damn fault,
her own tripping, falling, running
in the general direction of the lake.

2.

The loved thing is so punched in
it's beyond them. A deputy tried
to get pictures: pop and flash at her eyes,
her mouth, the wrung flesh of her forearm.
And what she flashed back—a wince,
a shrug, an abandoned stare. Please
won't someone hunt for her glasses. She can't

drive home without them, though I
had the keys, for Christ's sake, in my hand.

Lake in the hills. It always eludes us.
Its great slick dark. The weather comes
out of it. And then memory's
weather. Were all her answers
to the sheriff's questions *No*? Maybe
a few were *Maybe*. Or *I suppose*. *I don't
know*. The words she wouldn't say
had already fallen underwater, syllables
of stones on the bottom's roiling muck.

3.
Four measly tent stakes pull loose.
Hunched, huddled figure in the hills.
Didn't the fire out there blaze up?
Didn't any of the nearby campers,
anglers, fishwives awaken? Or the lake
rouse itself to flash back at the moonlight?

How much negation till thunder
sets its own charge? Makes up a rain
and releases it? In the tent's huge
gaping puddle: the sleeping bags still tied
in two tight fists. She can't see
her glasses among the broken bottles,

wants to hang nothing, no, nothing,
out to dry. Did you have them on
when you ran—and listen, the thing
to say now is not *I don't know*, since
in a minute we'll find them, since they're
just waiting to be seen, to be lifted.

4.
There must have been smoke
if there was rain on that campfire.

Smoke disappearing into what
other campers turned over in warm bags

to whisper once and roll their eyes at
in the dark. Don't let us look their way

or stare. It's a private matter, no matter
the noise inside, the echoes. Don't let us trespass.

Later she could be heard to pull herself
from the lake. To shake out

her bones of melodrama, her shirt
of cliché. Though the lake might fill

and empty itself a couple more times
this millennium, it's half a block of ice

between us in a few months. The cold
that comes out of it goes back in.

Unsettles its stones, inches them
over. They burrow down.

Liza

In the ambulance a child
is turning blue around the edges.
The sweep of time has lifted up her life
and we are a blur of hands trying
to refasten her to it. Two fingers
press a rhythm on her birdcage
chest. The muscle clenched inside
has a hole too wide. Time sweeps by
like wind. We sweep wind into her mouth
and her lips pink up. This allows us
to pretend she is alive. On the highway's
shoulder, doors flash open
to the Crit Team, to the clear bell
of a mother's calling. Our hands do
what they are told. We watch a man drill
a needle through to a small leg's marrow,
hear the chant from our mouths. We are inside
a tiny cell of time, far from the dull hallway
of hours and disbelief that will follow:
a toddler's groin—red, blue, yellow—
splayed open on a table in an airless room,
our hands thundering blanks in our laps
our tongues so much paper in our mouths.

Now that the Fields

Now that the fields belong to the crows
and the dark rolls in on a cart with supper,
we thicken the skin of the house, tuck a caterpillar
of hay, a reverse moat, around the foundation.

Half the crickets in Conway died last night
under cold rocks—or do they all go at once, once
chain saws are oiled and this new air reeks of apples?
Now that the last chrysalis has refused to open and our ears

are full of frantic roadwork, emergencies are blooming
like chrysanthemums—four in one weekend: first a heart
forgets the rhythm, then a woman leaps a ditch and hears
a loud crack in one of her body's branches; one man falls

off his roof, another sits up and says: *This is just too hard,*
now that the leaves are blushing to see their true selves
and the flies droning their *I told you so* song.
One blazing maple has taken over the town.

from *German Chronicle*

You can't abandon me
now when I'm dead and need tenderness.
    —*Zbigniew Herbert*

1. *Cut Photograph: 1941*

My mother cared most about beauty. Its absence
hurt her like sickness, like loss of life.
So she cut the photograph where I ride on my father's shoulders
at that place on his chest below the heart
where the belly begins, leaving my body intact
and his tanned grin and shoulders, his arms
stretched out above his head, holding my hands in his hands.
A band of sky and sea behind us—bereft of the wet sand
where we'd been walking—we floated now, relieved
of beach and history with its brutal endings
into a sky where our laughter mingled like breath and air.
For years within the plastic window of my wallet
I carried this proof that beauty lives
like something clipped out of a tangled story and freed,
a world of its own, complete with its own plot:
the tiny rider lifting a man out of the sea
where he is half-submerged. She's pulling him firmly,
her legs slung around his neck: at any moment now
he will emerge dripping down to his ankles,
and they'll float higher into orbit
far in the distance of a cloudless day.

II. Cigarette Case: 1942

When I think of them now, those men
drafted to work for a war they didn't believe in,
I see their gray suits arriving at our house after dark,
hands buried in their pockets. Once the door to my father's room
closed, with the flick of a hand, they opened
those sleek silver cases filled with the slim wrapped shapes,
miniature corpses lined up in a row, lit them
all over the room like small funeral pyres, saying some things
aloud and others in whispers—and I, in my father's lap,
crying into his big white handkerchief about my first
pulled tooth, watched as if I already knew
that men can be extracted and leave a space, not only gaping
but blank and dismissive: a lid clicked shut for good—
They knew their turn would come, being not only tools
but targets. They waited and watched the smoke unfurl
across their faces, still young and eager—
Even the spy in their midst was only a man who wanted to live.

III. Eels: 1943

On the Sundays when they emptied the wicker traps
the men would enter the kitchen. Their rubber boots
tracked across the tiles and left them streaked and smeary.
Some brought buckets of salt, some the heavy tubs
of muscled mass, thick as a man's arm, but pliable
as rope and slimy: too slippery for bare hands.
My father with his friends would frost his palms
with salt before he'd lift each dangling beast
and rub down its length of taut and blackish skin.
They scrubbed and rinsed them. They mopped the floor.
But even when they'd driven off to the smokehouse
a sickening smell stayed and trapped our breath.
From the bottom of one tub the cut-off heads would glint
like cold steel buttons on military leather.

iv. My Father's Tailor: 1943

His hands at home in yards of fabric,
woolens, flannel, and fine cotton, they were so nimble
he could fix anything. His vests were famous
for their fit around the trunks of men who liked to eat well.
He knew how to shape fabric as if it were clay,
as if he could fashion the man himself. And he could tell
the latest gossip in the city of Riga,
while holding five pins in the left corner of his mouth.
The last time he came to the apartment
a guard stayed by the door with a gun,
and while he fixed the stove in our kitchen
I watched my mother stuff cigarettes and bread
    into his baggy pockets.
Her hands were trembling. No words were said.
And after he was gone, she cried
over the little wreaths of bluish flame made by the gas.

v. 5,000 Head of Cattle: 1944

In some history recorded by Baltic refugees
my father is acknowledged for rescuing
5,000 head of cattle from being overrun by the Eastern front.
Whom else he might have helped or counseled—or
whom he failed—is not recorded, nor what he said or thought.
But there are five thousand cows that made it, thanks to him,
in the last minute onto a freight train heading west.
There are moments when I think of them
and their descendants, grazing contentedly somewhere near
what was Danzig once or Prussia. I see them
lift their heads to pause while masticating,
not caring whether they're Polish or German,
and look east with their big dreamy eyes—
then bow their heads down to the grass.

VIII.   Berlin: 1940/1945

I remember nothing of that city but a dead mouse
we buried together, how my mother scooped out a hole
in my grandfather's garden and I placed the small corpse
inside, wrapped in its shroud of maple leaf.
How I filled in the earth until it made a mound
and marked it with a small oval of stones.
Later when we found out about my father,
how he had died in that city, I remembered
that mouse and how my mother had wiped the earth from the ring
on her finger so carefully. Then I saw that soil
on the ring of his hand. And he and the mouse
became inseparable, so when I thought of him walking through
      the streets
in those last days, there was always a mouse on the sidewalk
scampering ahead like a shadow before him.

Lunacy

The ocean all day turning its pages, as if the swelling would come,
finally, to an end; as if the ending this time
would be a different story.

It's that the gulls cried or laughed when I passed them.
And the gritty itch of sand in every corner, every crevice,
    every fold.
The air so moist with wild rose scent and krill gone bad
you could tongue brine from the breeze
if there were a breeze.

You think none of this is of consequence?
Even now, as the moon writhes from the grassy dune?
Even as it falls through the dark, like an egg?

Green House

When I decided to ask Recita Holguin to marry me, I visited my confessor, The Bishop, in his place of banishment. He is not a bishop now, but he was once.

"Red!" he said. "Red!" And he hugged me close, his cheek and ear pressed hard against my chest. He stepped back, and raised up on his toes, and held his arms over my shoulders to bless me: "Fountain of Heaven. Mother of God. Ark of Peace." This old blessing of strange and disturbing power brought tears to us both. His bony chest contracted against me. My nose ran. I had no handkerchief and had to use my hand. I snicked the stickiness from one side of my nose, then the other, onto the La Florida Deluxe Motel parking lot.

"God bless you," he said as if I had sneezed. His one-room apartment had a hide-a-bed sofa, long, wide, but with thin cushions. He said, "It is the place to sit."

I said, "Nice," rested my butt and hands on the dull green and vermilion mysteries in the fabric.

The band of freckles across his dark nose and cheeks made his face a galaxy of amazement, made his large eyes seem larger, and his wide forehead wider. No end to the horizons of his joy. I had admired these freckles when we met for the first time as children in 1915; I had seen them for eighty-one years of friendship. When he sat down near me, he said, "I have planned! I have imagined your visit, Red. You are a dream!"

He rested his hands inside mine. Yes, I held them. Holding them gave me such pleasure I should be ashamed to confess it. But I am less afraid than I once was of allowing that there is a kind of touching friends do that should be called lovemaking.

How dear The Bishop's hands were to me! And how different. They, too, were now covered with freckles. I said, "What are these?"

"Nasturtiums," he said, thinking I had asked about the overlapping vermilion and green faces in his sofa. Perennially, flowers blossomed in his thoughts.

I asked again: *"These?"* His fingers were freckled, and his palms. "They're everywhere!"

His wrists and arms were freckled. His neck. He bowed his head to show me his freckled scalp. He said, "God is Lord of Tattooists, no?"

I strained not to imagine the number of freckles. But I am a counter, I don't know why. All my life I have felt the need. I counted rocks in the rock walls my father built for a living; the number of people who received communion at Sunday Mass; the hats on the heads in Albertson's supermarket; the trees in the Christmas tree lots. I counted money in my dreams before I ever stole it, counted it as I stole it (put back anything over the planned amount), counted it after I stole it. Money, trees, hats, holy people, rocks. Whatever was beautiful to me I wanted to know the amount of its beauty. The Bishop's freckles. Numberless.

"I have a fire over me," The Bishop said. They did look like tiny rising or collapsing flames. "What dark angels hover over you, Red?"

"My problems are nothing," I said. "My sins are crumbs."

"Impossible!" he said. "Your sins have always been loaves! I have feasted on your sins, Red! Have you stolen nothing lately?"

I wanted to please him. How could I not want that? I said, "I have kept secrets. From Recita."

"You have. You have? Of course you have!" He tugged at my hands to lift me from the sofa. "Don't start your confession yet. We'll eat first. Eggs. Wine. Cottage cheese. Everything is already prepared."

He sliced hard-boiled eggs with the egg slicer I had given him. He served full glasses of wine, one of the twelve bottles I had lifted for him from the cellar of my friend Eusebio. The cottage cheese was small curd. We sprinkled red chili powder over the egg slices (ten for me, twelve for him) and into the cheese.

I said, "I will be direct. I'm going to ask Recita to marry me."

"Wonderful," he said.

"Wonderful," I said. "It is. Wonderful. But I worry." The golden yoke on my tongue crumbled. I didn't know what to say next.

"Tell what you can, Red."

"After so many years. There are questions."

"On earth as in heaven, Red." He coughed. "What is the big question—*la pregunta grande?*"

"Impotency," I said. "Will I be impotent?"

"*Dios!*" He coughed hard. He wiped bits of shiny egg from his lips. "I think—I think we should finish our meal," he said.

"I don't know. I might be unready. Alone twenty-three years."

The chili powder, too much chili powder, made him gasp. He said, "You are old, my friend. But she is also." He sprinkled more powder on his egg slice, both sides. "The dust settles. It can be kicked up again." His lips were red as a harlot's.

"Sins are involved," I said. "Impure thoughts. Things I have not told her."

"Oh. Oh!" What food before him could satisfy him like this news? He said, "The coffee is already made. Fresh-ground. Smell it?" He wiped his hands with his napkin, but not his mouth. "So. We will go to the confessional sofa. You will tell me."

I told him about *La Memoria.*

You have heard of the tradition of setting the table for a dead loved one? People will do this in order to pretend. They will invite The Memory back. They will put the chair and setting where La Memoria sits. They will serve the soup and bread that are La Memoria's favorites. How many ice cubes does La Memoria like in the glass? What brand of creamed corn gave so much simple pleasure? This is how the ritual of the meal with the dead goes. For a while after the person first dies we set a place for and serve a meal to La Memoria. We invite others among the living to come. Then, we do this on the family birthdays, the name-saint day, the anniversary of marriage, the holidays, the anniversary of death. We invite others among the dead to come. The ritual is crowded with memories. The table is laden with good food. It gets expensive. Eventually, we invite La Memoria less often to the table. We celebrate alone. Once a year maybe.

We pretend. We imagine the departed one, La Memoria, is clever at the table, clever and kind, and a generous listener and always interested and utterly infatuated and in love with us and transformed by our love, the ways that, truly, the departed one was. Except better. We pretend everything was better.

Or we imagine the departed one swilling food and drinking like a sow, grunting and cruelly ignoring our cleverness, our kindness and generosity, our perfect love. La Memoria makes us do the dishes, clean the table, sweep the floors. La Memoria leaves us to go watch the television. Good riddance to this memory. "Praise God," we say until the next meal for the dead.

When my wife, Cecilia, died in 1972, I honored her. La Memoria. Alone in our bedroom, I made our bed, small, queen-size, caved-in bed, as she liked it. I washed the lace flounce, a falling rain pattern of lace, and I ironed it, and said, "Cecilia. How much?" I sprayed as much starch as she liked, and I ironed out every wrinkle. I put on the beaten bed pad she had always said was good enough, and I heard my dead wife, La Memoria, say that it was, it was "Good enough, dear Red."

With my hands and with the insides of my arms, I made the white sheets smooth. I put on Cecilia's quilt, the prized quilt. Her mother had bought it for her in Tijuana from someone who said it was an American Civil War quilt traded across the border and traded back, and worth fortunes. Across her quilt flew lariats of morning glory vines, and inside the lariats flew stars the same pale blue color as the flowers. When everything was made right, I closed the curtains of our room.

Well. You can imagine. A man alone. I pretended. And each time I pretended, La Memoria became a more remarkable lover, and La Memoria's lover, Red Greet, became a lover's dream.

I lay longer with La Memoria. I lay every afternoon, in the late afternoons, with La Memoria. Already, I was in love with Recita Holguin—in celibate but passionate love. I should have separated from my dead wife. Death should have helped me. But La Memoria and I would not give up this time together, which was like no time we had ever known in the living years.

One day, I stripped off the quilt. I piled all our old wraps and cloaks and coats and jackets on top of the bed. We seemed to be hosting a party, La Memoria and I. So many people had come, the dead and living, and I imagined them as gracious guests, excited by each other's company, sharing the dip and heaven and earth's gossip, pouring each other wine from bottles that never emptied, linking arms and hands and spilling everywhere, singing badly and angelically, burying old miseries and raising up old joys.

La Memoria and I had crawled naked under the coverings our

guests had shed in our bedroom. I had caressed her cool, bare head, that is how we began. We did not rest, not one part of our bodies rested. Even if I wished her to, La Memoria would not rest. We heard the banging of our guests at the bedroom door, and we could not stop, not pause. We heard the joking pleas for us to stop making love long enough to let them take what they needed and leave, and we would not.

Through the door, one guest said, "Cecilia, you should be ashamed of yourself. You are dead!"

La Memoria groaned, "How can I be sure?"

Another guest said, "Red! This is sad. This is not good."

"How can I be sure?" I said.

Our guests said goodbye from behind the door, and we said goodbye back. "Goodbye," we said to them. "Goodbye! Blessings! Goodbye!" and said it to each other, and we closed the spaces between us. Tightly. And La Memoria and I remembered she was dead, but the sadness sharpened our pleasure. In my bliss, I flung off the wraps and jackets, coats and cloaks. The last of our guests left. ("It is not sad," the guest whispered through the door. "It is beautiful." Her voice was Sister Josefa's. Ex-Carmelite.)

The front door closed with a sound like a last breath. I flung off more coverings. The bed was bare. I was alone. I moved my hands and the insides of my arms over the bed and could barely believe La Memoria had gone.

What more do I need to confess?

I still make the bed so many ways. Year after year. I hardly recognize the bed. And who is this La Memoria who visits? A thousand different Cecilias, and none of them really Cecilia. Who is this man who almost every afternoon for twenty-three years has been pretending? How will I ask Recita, dear Recita, a living woman, to lie with me? I will disappoint her. I will disappoint me.

"Complicated," The Bishop said. "Weird. And complicated. And familiar." He leaned toward me on the confessional sofa. His freckles were tiny tilmas. "I am celibate. I know this story. If this is a confession, I do not know absolution that will fit."

"Huh?" I said.

He said, "I have old beer in my refrigerator. Bring it."

"No absolution?" I said. I went to the refrigerator.

Dos Equis. Four of them. I put them on the counter and wrestled with the tops. "They're not screwtops," I said. "Do you have an opener?"

"Bring them, Red."

He unscrewed them, of course. He is an angel, The Bishop. He wiped the moist bottom of the bottle across the fabric of the sofa. He swigged. "You need a plan," he said.

"Right!" I said. "That's what I need."

The Bishop had no plan. "You must pray for a plan," he said.

"Damn!" I said. "You have to do better than that."

He swished beer in his mouth. The freckles over his skin were filled with dark red roses no larger than motes. "It is what I do," he said. "I pray to the saints and holy martyrs for a plan."

I asked, "Which ones do you pray to?"

"The women. Saint Joan. Teresa of Avila. Saint Bridget, Saint Monica."

"The real lookers," I said.

He hummed. His hum meant yes.

"And? And you have a plan?"

"I have no plan," he said.

"Sixty years! Sixty years of praying, and you have no plan!" I stood up. "This is not encouraging," I said.

What could he say? He said nothing. Finally, he asked me to sit back down. "I love you, Red," he said. "You know this?"

"I know," I said.

"You love me?"

"I love you."

"Red! That is a miracle, is it not? A miracle!"

We had some flan. The flan and the beer did not go good together, but it inspired him. The nutmeg on the flan upset his stomach, and the indigestion inspired him. "Here is my advice," he said. "Do not pray alone. When you are with Recita and La Memoria, when the three of you are together, pray then."

In Christ Is King Church, at the evening service, I whispered, "Marry me," to Recita Holguin. We were standing close, too close, singing. I made sure she heard. Into her good ear I whispered, "Marry me." This was during the processional song so that she would have the liturgy, Eucharist, and final blessing to consider.

When we left the church, wind freed wisps of Recita's black, red, and silver hair around her dark face. She lifted her head and neck to let wind expose her however it wished. The blue-brown slackness under her eyes was dear to me. And the sharp brightness at her cheeks where the bones grew dull beneath the skin. Her jaw and chin looked small when she gritted her teeth, closed her mouth in a tight smile that showed fear but no shame.

My nose watered. I had to wipe it and my eyes, too. I am a broken, leaking donkey. She saw this, and lent me a Kleenex from her purse, white alligator-skin vinyl. She handed me the whole purse so I could take another. Never had she done this, though my nose always watered in the cold and watered when I ate and watered when I laughed good, and so I had often asked her for Kleenexes.

She *had* decided to marry me.

I knew for sure because she let me hold her hand on the steps of the church. At the bottom steps she closed her long, wrinkled fingers over mine and pressed our bony fingers, five flinty petals holding up another five, to her breast. She held that flower of old bones to her breast, and bowed her head and smelled the flower. Or it seemed like she smelled it, the way she drew in her breath, so far inside.

In my other hand I held her purse, small, almost empty. Through the vinyl skin I felt coins, two lipsticks, no, three, and a balled-up scarf and a fork and knife, a spoon. Soup spoon.

This was March 31, 1995, the feast of Eucharist and the Holy Orders. A frost sometimes comes in late March to our valley, a murdering frost. It is carried in the winds that have been waiting in the Sierra de la Soledad, waiting until they can come down to claim all the green, hopeful souls of plum and peach and apple trees.

"What do you plan for us?" Recita asked.

"*Plan?*" I said. I wondered if she had made her own visit to The Bishop's motel room. "I am *eighty-six*. You are *eighty-five*."

"You have no plan?" She, of course, did. Instantly, I saw she did, that during the Mass she had made A Plan.

Our hands fell apart. We walked beside each other. No words. Had she said yes to my marriage proposal? Now I was not sure. Would she tell me her plan? Was part of her plan to keep The Plan secret? Already, maybe we were following Her Plan.

An Old Woman with a Plan—nothing can save you from this. If Christ in the desert had met An Old Woman with a Plan and Two Lipsticks and a Soup Spoon instead of meeting only Satan, His suffering, death, and resurrection, all of it, would have begun that very moment—no apostles, no Judas, no high priests, no soldiers, no Barrabas, no Pilate, no heaven-bound thief on His right side, no hellbound thief on His left. And no words. None. On the corner of Mr. Telles's front yard, we passed a shivering old Santa Rosa plum tree, all its fruit doomed. I thought of La Memoria. How strange I must have looked: Recita on one arm, La Memoria on the other.

Finally, I asked, "*You* have a plan?" For the first time, I realized we were not walking to her apartment on Espina and Boutz, where I would usually be allowed one kiss, one embrace, a long one sometimes, but only one. I asked, "Where are we going?" We were not holding hands, but she was leading, I was following. "Where?" I asked.

She did not answer. We walked, Recita and I. And La Memoria. Recita's old legs were tough as the roots of sarsaparilla, and lovely all the way up. I could imagine. I did imagine. Too much I imagined. Inviting legs, but no words. I am a dishonest man, everyone knows this about me. But I am a little honest whenever I tell a story, and I do not put words where there are no words.

We came to The Bishop's house, which had once been my friend Francisco Velasco's house when he was still bishop. She said, "We will go into his garden. He has a greeeen house." She did not say "greenhouse," she said, "greeeen house," a very sly way she said this, a sixteen-year-old girl's smile on her face. We opened the gate at the back of The Bishop's garden, Recita pushing it open, La Memoria pushing it closed behind us, do you see? Her Plan.

It was true. The small house was greeeen. I had sometimes been the caretaker for it, but, I admit, I had ignored it. The door was a brighter yellow-green, the doorknob was emerald-green glass. Its good coldness made my hand ache, my palm burn. I said, "Doesn't open."

"No?" She opened it without a sound. This made her giggle. "Like I dreamed," she said. She had a dime-size coffee-spill birthmark on her thick, wide nose, right in the center. It had fingerprint whorls in it. I liked this mark, an uneven oval, which she said was twin to such a mark on her mother and all her mother's ancestors.

Moonlight splashed silver upon the windows that had been painted green. On the wooden floor everywhere were shriveled, sharp-smelling bulbs we scooted our feet through. "Irises," she said. The warped tables along the walls were bare, and their speckled Formica had been washed clean, so clean the black-green light on them was like one current of river flowing over another darker current.

"Tell me," she whispered. She was behind me, close enough I could feel her long dress sweep the back of my ankles. Her nose brushed against my ear, and she kissed the tender place behind it and then before it, and whispered, "Tell me," and she kissed the place beneath my ear, old, wrinkled, smelly, hairy ear. Ear of a donkey. I was supposed to tell her. Tell her what? Tell her My Plan, which I didn't have?

"Are you there?" I asked. You can see, I was asking La Memoria, who was once Cecilia herself, if she was still there with us. I didn't feel her at my side.

Recita said, "She is gone."

"She is, isn't she?" I said.

When I dropped Recita's purse on the floor, the things inside it clinked. She turned me around to face her, and in the turning, she slipped off her shoes. Pale yellow, to match her straw-gold dress. Long sleeves, gold trim at the neck and wrists and hem. Tiny, gold cloth buttons down the front. She was as tall as me without her shoes.

The purse slumped, and it clinked. Alone, untouched, it made a racket. Recita pushed away the purse with her bare feet. She took my hands, both at the same time, and tugged at them until they understood where they should go. My fingers slid into my back pants pockets where she sent them. She kissed a burning path across my jaw, nudged my chin with her chin. She tucked in my thumbs, too.

Her cheek pressed against mine. With her own hands she touched her face, her jaw and chin, her fingers blessing her own eyebrows and eyelids. She closed her eyes to touch her ears, old but worn smooth by time or by the caressing of her own fingers over time. "Red. Tell me. You have a plan?"

I swear, the bulbs strewn over the floor gathered around my ankles, gathered and grew fingers. I kicked them away. They crept back. At the same moment my hands tried escaping, her arms captured my waist; her hands flew into my back pockets. She said to me, said to my hands, "Stay inside." Her fingers between my fingers, she pushed my hands flat against my hips. She wanted my hands to go deeper into my pockets, and so she forced them down, gentle but sure, which brought my pants low on my hips. "Stay there," she said, and her fingertips showed my fingertips the curve of my own ass, inviting me to touch. Touch myself.

"Recita," I said. "My dear."

She said, "You are shy."

I said, "This place is muggy."

"Ohhh, Red," she whispered, "we are in a greeeen house." Her hands withdrew, her moist palms dampening my wrists. I watched her hands move behind her. How they moved was mysterious, reaching down behind her. Her lips tried to kiss my eyes closed, but I watched her hands. You would not?

She turned her back to me and bent her knees and waist in order to lift the golden hem of her straw-colored dress, the whole hem. And now I saw how the moonlit green light of the green house made her golden dress the green-gold of cotton blossoms. The smooth material still in her hands, she drew her fingers up against the skin of her ankles and legs, and, slowly, her thighs.

Oh, my dear.

Old woman's underwear. You will not see this underwear in magazines. No designer names, no printed words, no lace or floral wonders, but puckered elastic, plain, faded pink cloth, enough to cover a chair.

I have my theories. When this underwear goes on, it does not take itself too seriously. When this underwear comes off (Recita's thumbs hooking the waistband, her hands almost completely inside, pushing this underwear down over her knees and ankles), when this underwear comes off (one dance step, and she has kicked it away, and it lands around the purse, the silent purse), when this underwear comes off, it is part of A Plan.

Facing me again, she dropped the hem all at once. She did not take off the dress, under which she now had nothing but her legs, lovelier than they had ever been in my imagination. She touched but did not unbutton the cloth buttons at her breast and neck. How nice they must have felt, the material rougher than the material of her dress. I saw her pleasure. Under her eyes and at her cheeks was lovely greenness gilded by the deep brown of her skin. I became aware of my fingertips enjoying my own flesh.

"Where is your purse?" I asked. I looked around for it. Why did I look for it? Concerned for her purse!

She asked, "You are worried?"

"Where has it gone?"

"Not far," she said. "She never goes far." She made a little clap of her hands. "Heeeere, purse. Heeeere, purse."

"Lost," I said. My nose trickled.

"Wipe your nose," she said, tender, funny, loving three words, good as any I have ever heard. She leaned her body against me, she reached behind me to free my hands.

I wiped, sniffed, and blew my nose right in front of her, and this seemed not at all strange. She took the rag from me and balled it up and put it back in my pocket for me. What do the young know of this kind of love?

I touched the buttons of her dress, the cloth still heated from her touch. She unbuckled my belt. Buckled it one notch tighter.

We kissed. Our eyes were open. Recita's hair was black, red, and silver, more red than black or silver, and I looked close. I leaned back from her and looked close at the falling waves on the top, the retreating flatter waves on the sides, the unbrushed tumble in back.

We kissed. I touched her woman's beard, barely there, but there enough to illuminate the moonsilver on the skin of her neck and jaw. And around her mouth. Silver and seedling green. I tried to pray. This would be the time I should pray. Where was La Memoria? Where had La Memoria gone?

We kissed. Recita's ears were low on her head. Smooth, small ears, low and far back on her head. I prayed: What now, God? When I touched her ears, I swear this, I felt them move back under my fingertips. They *moved.* What plan, God? I need a plan.

We kissed. I had a crazy notion I could move her ears, and if I moved them far enough, they would be small wings at the back of her neck. She would fly a little ahead of me with them. Like a golden bee, she would hover over me. I pushed her ears back with my thumbs. She cupped my ears with her hands, my donkey ears.

How our ears delighted us! We laughed together. We kissed. In the greeeen house.

Skeleton

I grew up in Garden City, a small Pennsylvania community where my brother, Adrian, and I were the only Jews in our elementary school. I got along better with the kids than Adrian, played sports and made friends more easily, but still I had my troubles.

One day I went into Mrs. Nick's—short for Nicodemus—a corner grocery store and fountain down the street from us. I sat at the counter with Warren Banks, my best friend. We didn't sit next to each other. You always had a seat between you, even when you went to the movies. It hinted of homosexuality to sit next to each other, to wish to be that close to another boy, and also maybe there was just the thing of wanting to spread out, establish your territory. I don't know, but I do remember that day in Mrs. Nick's store when Warren and I sat there spinning the stool between us, its silver sides whistling as we slapped the green vinyl top to make it go faster.

"Cut it out," said Mrs. Nick. We stopped. "What do you want?" she asked Warren.

"Root beer float," Warren said. Mrs. Nick nodded at him, looked at me. She had her hair up in blue curlers. She lived in the back with her husband, who worked at the shipyards in nearby Chester. My father was a doctor in the town.

"What about you, moneybags?"

I heard laughter from down the counter, where the teenagers hung out.

"Black and white," I said inaudibly.

"What?"

"Milkshake. Black and white." I was burning up with shame. Warren looked straight ahead. The three teenagers at the other end snickered. They were just out of high school and worked the night shift in Chester at Scott Paper.

Mrs. Nick went over to the fountain and mixed up ice cream and root beer and filled it with soda water. She brought the frosted ribbed glass over to Warren and set it down in front of him. Then she disappeared into the back of the store.

I sat there with my head down. I could hear Warren sucking gently on his straw. We came here every day after school to have drinks at the counter. Why had she said that? "Moneybags."

Five minutes passed. Mrs. Nick didn't come out. I slid off the stool and glanced at Warren. He was trying to go slow on his drink but was already down to the dregs. I went over to the magazine rack and looked at the cover of the new Superman comic. Jimmy Olsen had superpowers. His freckled face and red hair were still there, but his arms and shoulders rippled with muscles. Superman, meanwhile, had changed places with him and looked puny and frightened. Lois Lane was in the background glancing desirably at Jimmy. It was all turned around and all temporary, of course. I knew Superman would be restored to his powers, Jimmy would return to being a cub reporter, and Lois would get straight her hopeless crush on the Man of Steel.

I reached in my pants pocket for a quarter left over from lunch. It was 1959, and Superman comics had just gone up from ten to twelve cents. When I'd first started collecting them, they were only five cents each.

Warren came over and stood next to me at the cash register. He was from the project, where many of the kids whom I went to school with lived. The project consisted of squat, brown stucco buildings built during the Second World War. They had tiny yards tied together by a maze of chain-link fences. A metal pole webbed with clothesline stood in the corner of each yard, taking the place of a shade tree. The driveways were concrete runners with weeds growing between them. Fights broke out regularly, dogs choked on their chains, and mothers screamed openly at their kids. I wasn't allowed to go in there, except to Warren's house, which was on the edge closest to our home.

"Hey, Mrs. Nick," said Corky Innes, shooting a thumb my way, "you got a customer." Corky "Kong" Innes lived with his brother, Richie, down the street from us. They called him "Kong" because of his car, a souped-up, black Dodge so shiny "you can see your pimples in it," Corky would say. With a 426 Hemi, dual quads, a Detroit locker, and hooker headers, the car was rumored to need a parachute to stop. Under its dash, the Kongmobile had a record player installed that played forty-fives. Warren and I would sit in it at Mrs. Nick's, listen to "Sea of Love," "Mr. Blue," and "Kansas City," stick our elbows out the windows, and pretend to peel out.

Mrs. Nick stayed at the other end of the counter washing a glass by hand.

"Hey, Mrs. Nick," said Corky, and I wished he would shut up. "You got a paying customer here."

"That's all right," I said quietly.

"I can buy it for you," said Warren.

I shook my head. I just wanted to get out of here. My face had turned red, and I was afraid if I stayed around I'd start crying.

But Corky, whose father owned a tavern in Chester, and who I was beginning to see was a true lunkhead when it came to social matters that I instinctively understood, wouldn't drop the subject. He grabbed the quarter from my hand and swaggered it over to Mrs. Nick. "Here you go," he said, and slapped the coin onto the counter. The quarter wobbled in front of her, then stopped dead with a dull tink. Mrs. Nick let it lay there, as I knew she would. Corky, dimwit, confidant to his gonads, palmed the quarter, tossed it in his mouth, and swallowed it down with an audible gulp. It was one of his tricks. Years later he would develop cancer of the larynx, an irony that was lost on us all now. We weren't thinking about cancer, nor what would become of us, including Mrs. Nick, whose store would close up in five years after she had a fatal heart attack, her store becoming a beauty parlor, then a funeral home, and there would be no sign of that day when I was refused service, and Corky ate my quarter and then pretended to barf it up and hand it back to me, a true idiot, who had forgotten why he was even holding it.

I walked out of the store, Warren following. We didn't talk about what happened on the way home. But we did pass the Olans' house. Broken bottles and trash were in their front yard, and freshly painted since the last time they'd erased it was GO HOME NIGGERS on the side of their white clapboard house with blue shutters. Two weeks ago they'd moved into the home on Rynard Road, the only black family in Garden City, including the all-white project. Their house had been stoned, their car's windshield smashed, their two children taunted when they'd tried to attend the local elementary school.

"Hi, Officer Dennis," Warren said, as we walked past the Olans' house. He was patrolling back and forth on the sidewalk in front. His uniform said "Garden City Township Police."

"Howdy," he said. "You boys just getting home from school?"

"We went to Mrs. Nick's," said Warren.

"Where's my hoagie, then?" said Officer Dennis. He was Gloria Dennis's father. Gloria was two grades ahead of us, in fifth, and "developed."

"We ate it," said Warren.

"You ate it, did you?" Officer Dennis joked. "Well, that's not going to help me now is it?"

I wanted to keep walking, but Warren had stopped and was staring at the Olans' home. You couldn't see any movement inside. They kept their curtains drawn even in daytime. Their father, I'd heard, was escorted in and out of the house to work at his accounting office. Groceries were brought to them through the back door. Officer Dennis said, "So what's new at school?" Officer Dennis seemed to want company. "Your father doing all right now, David?" he asked me.

I nodded. After the Olans had moved in, their baby needed a doctor. My father had gone over, and on the way into the house, a brick had hit him in the back. It had knocked him down, but he'd gotten up and gone inside anyway.

That was two weeks ago, and I knew that my father going there, his speaking out against the attacks, his telling reporters that he was ashamed of the community, all this had to do with why Mrs. Nick had called me moneybags and not served me.

"Well, you tell him hello for me," Officer Dennis said, and I nodded again. He was being so kind to me that I wanted to drag him back to Mrs. Nick's and have him make her sell me a milkshake and my comic book.

I saw the curtains part and a little girl peek out the window; then they were closed again, quickly. The house still had the name Stewart on the wood plaque that hung from the porch. The papers had said that the Stewarts, who had moved to Kennett Square, had been threatened for selling the house to Negroes. My father pored over the newspaper every day, shook his head, and mumbled angrily. "Like hostages, they're kept inside like hostages," he said one night at dinner. My mother sat in silence, not disagreeing, but not sharing his fury. She had never wanted to move into this neighborhood anyway.

At my house, Warren and I scuffed our sneakers against the flagstone steps.

"Want to come in?" I said to Warren. He shook his head no; he had to go home and help with dinner. His dad worked the grave-yard shift at Sun Ship, and his mom worked late at Crozer hospital in the cafeteria. His sister and he fixed dinner for themselves at night. I looked up at the bedrooms of our house. My brother would be in his, my mother in hers. I didn't want to go in.

"Maybe I could go home with you," I said.

"Yeah," said Warren, "ask."

But I knew my mother wouldn't let me. She'd be too afraid for me to be alone at Warren's in the project at night, and I didn't want to make her any more anxious than she was already. Or unhappy. She'd been "sad," she told me, which meant she spent a lot of time alone in her room.

We lived across the street from a park, in the biggest, most conspicuously affluent home in Garden City, a three-story fieldstone Colonial with white shutters, a tall peaked roof, and a large picture window that looked out on the park. My father had wanted to live here, a working-class section outside of Chester, a pocket among the more prosperous communities of Swarthmore, Rose Valley, and Wallingford, because he'd found a piece of property across the street from the park and fallen in love with the location and the unpretentious neighborhood. But there were no Jews besides us, no one my mother socialized with, and my brother was regularly beaten up at school. I had done better, making friends, "passing," and fitting in, except now for Mrs. Nick.

I punched Warren in the arm, and he punched me back, and then I went inside. No sounds were in the house, just the ticking of the grandfather clock in the foyer. The living room, which we never used, enjoyed the last of the winter light coming into it through the picture window. My mother collected glass bottles displayed along the wide ledge under the window. My favorite was a translucent blue bottle about four feet high with a gently fluted opening and spired top. I couldn't explain it exactly, but the bottle looked desirable to me, I suppose I mean sexual, and I had sensations of excitement whenever I gazed at it. It was graceful and slender, an ice-blue color that shimmered in the morning light. The other bottles rose in height from either side toward the blue one in the middle, like the pipes of an organ. I went over and touched its tip, a frozen tear on top.

I heard a toilet flush upstairs, my parents' bathroom.

My brother, who was two years older than me, lay on his bed reading. His teacher, Mrs. Fitzsimmons, had sent a note home recommending that he not read so much. Adrian was spending his time at recess reading rather than playing kickball or baseball or getting fresh air. Mrs. Fitzsimmons believed he should involve himself more in physical activity and the company of his classmates.

"Hi," I said, standing in his doorway, not wanting to go all the way into his room. He didn't like to build model airplanes and aircraft carriers. He didn't have baseball pennants on his walls as I did, or pictures of wild animals. Adrian had movie posters: Charlie Chaplin in *Modern Times,* Marlene Dietrich in *Blue Angel,* Humphrey Bogart and Walter Huston in *The Treasure of the Sierra Madre.* It was the other thing he did besides read, watch movies and pretend to make them. He spent a lot of time looking at me with his thumb up to his right eye. "Tracking shot," he'd say as I came out of the bathroom. Or he'd cup his hands to his face: "Close-up." It was annoying. I'd lie in bed at night and wish Warren was my brother, or somebody like him. Adrian was heavyset—the term I'd been told to use by my father—and kids at school called him swivel hips, because of the way he walked. He had one friend, Perry, who lived across town and, like Adrian, had "introverted" interests, the other term I'd learned to describe Adrian's unpopularity. I held my breath during every recess that Adrian wouldn't get picked on and beat up (no doubt why he stayed inside and read). Unlike me, he didn't fight back, or even try to, nor did he have a protector like Warren. Adrian just lay there and covered his face with his arms and let them wallop him. He didn't cry or make a fuss afterward, and for that reason maybe nobody really tried to hurt him. It was just to humiliate him, pound on the fat boy, like a stop along an obstacle course. They'd thump him a while and then go back to what they were doing, playing softball or using the swings or pitching pennies, and Adrian would stand up, brush himself off, and go find a book somewhere.

"Where's Mom?" I said.

"In her room," said Adrian. "You just get home?"

"Yes." I thought of telling him about Mrs. Nick, but I knew there was nothing he'd say to help. What could you say when you were a whipping boy for the whole class?

"Look at this," he said, and pulled a long wooden box out from under his bed.

He opened the latches. It was a skeleton.

"Where'd you get that?" I said, impressed.

"Dad loaned it to me. It's a teaching skeleton."

"What do you mean?"

"They use it in medical school. *This is a child,*" he said, conspiratorially.

"A child?"

"About six years old."

I reached out and touched the small skull.

"I'm going to make a film with it," said Adrian. He was squatting down as was I next to the skeleton, and I could see the rolls of fat under his T-shirt. His forehead had broken out in perspiration, his fair cheeks reddened. I wondered what he'd been doing in here before I came in, and then I realized it was just excitement, excitement about an idea. Nobody I knew at school got excited about ideas. Just Adrian.

"What kind of movie?" I asked.

"A horror film," said Adrian. "I'm writing the script," and he nodded at the Royal typewriter on his desk. He'd gotten it for his last birthday. *"Buried Coccyx,"* said Adrian.

"What?"

"That's the title."

"What's it mean?"

Adrian shifted his hips with irritation. He was sitting on the bed, holding the skeleton in his lap. "It's a mystery, stupid. The victims lose their coccyx."

"Their what?"

"Their tailbones. The murderer cuts them off. He collects them like arrowheads."

I looked at the small skeleton. It was frail and delicate. "He does this to children?"

Adrian hesitated. "Well, I haven't decided that part yet. I can make the skeleton look bigger on camera."

"Do you have a camera?"

"Dad's going to help me rent one. A sixteen millimeter."

Adrian tilted his head back and hooded his eyes. "I vill be zee greatest director of ze century! I'll find a part for you," he added.

"All right," I said, and got up to go.

"Where you going?"

"To see Mom."

Adrian shook his head. "She's resting." Resting. It could mean anything, but it probably meant she was "sad."

"I'll check on her anyway," I said.

"Fade out," called Adrian as I exited through his doorway.

I went down the hall to my mother's room. She was sitting by the window staring out. She was still in her nightgown, at four-thirty in the afternoon. "David," she said, as if surprised to see me. I had the feeling she'd been sitting here for hours.

"Hi," I said, not going into her room too far, either. It smelled of sleep and unwashed sheets. My parents' bed was still rumpled, the room unstraightened, clothes on the floor. Several bottles of pills that my father prescribed for her were on the nightstand. A round tray with a coffee cup and a plate with an uneaten roll caught the last of the afternoon light at the small table for two.

"Do you want your lunch?" she asked.

"Lunch?"

My mother stared at me, as if trying to remember. She closed her eyes and swallowed. "I mean, dinner. *Dinner*, David."

"Are you all right?" I asked.

"I'm fine," she said. "You go play now. I'll be down in a minute to fix dinner." She turned away, and I felt my chest tighten, my eyes start to water. I thought of the child skeleton in the box under Adrian's bed.

An hour later my father returned from his office, and the house came to life. He'd been tied up with patients all day. He made us grilled cheese sandwiches and milkshakes. Mother joined us. She'd gotten dressed, a blue sweater and a tan skirt, and she sat at the table with her cheek resting on one hand, smiling pleasantly. Everything would be all right. Everything was fine. We were a family. Dad was home.

Adrian ate one helping of chocolate cream pie for dessert, and when he asked for another, my mother gently turned him down. She picked up our plates and began to wash the dishes at the sink. Except for her having been upstairs all day, she was fine. Maybe she was just resting, after all. Tired. And I started to feel better. I didn't even mind after dinner when Adrian stood in our old Radio Flyer wagon and asked me to pull him along the wall of the dining room while he shouted, "Dolly shot! Quiet on the set!"

Not long after I went to bed, I heard raised voices in my parents' bedroom. I could make out my father saying something about keeping the house clean, and my mother answering she hated it here and she missed her sisters in New York and why had she ever agreed to move, and then my mother crying and my father saying, "Oh, for God's sake," and leaving the bedroom. I got up to use the bathroom and saw that Adrian's light was still on. He was typing. I thought about going in, but either he had been listening or he hadn't been listening. Either way, like Warren and I with Mrs. Nick, we wouldn't talk about what was right in front of us.

Downstairs the phone rang, and I heard my father answer it and say, "Yes," then a long pause. "How high is it?" he asked, and then he said, "Okay, I'll be right over." He came upstairs and saw me standing in the hallway. "Why are you still up, David?"

"I—"

"Go to bed. Right now." I glanced at Adrian's door, as if to excuse my behavior by my brother's, but my father didn't care. They never bothered Adrian. He stayed up all night, read and wrote and went to school and got straight A's and that was Adrian. But me, I was going to be normal, sleep regular hours, have decent friends, make average grades, not be a budding, precious genius. Live a boy's life. I hurried back into my room.

I couldn't sleep, especially when I heard my parents raising their voices again. It was like a storm that never went away entirely, the thunder becoming distant enough that you forgot about it, but not for long. "Take your pill," my father said, "just take it," and I heard the bathroom water running and then silence. I imagined my mother's mouth opening submissively, my father placing the pill on her tongue and tipping her water glass up to her lips. Her swallowing mechanically. I don't know for sure if that's what happened or if she even took a pill that night, but I know sitting alone on my bed I felt her complete helplessness.

My father came out from their bedroom. He closed their door and stepped quietly down the stairs. The hall closet opened, then the front door. I heard him leave.

I ran to the window. He'd parked the Buick on the street. We only had one car. Some families, some of the kids I knew from Hebrew school, the wealthier doctors, had two cars, but nobody in Garden City had a second car.

The headlights flickered on and off as he tried to start the car. Mother had been complaining about the battery for weeks now. I saw him get out and angrily slam the door and start walking down the street.

There was something instinctive, if crazy, about what I did next. I pulled on my clothes and ran after him. I followed him down Chestnut Parkway onto Locust Lane. I knew by this time where he was going. He stepped so purposefully, with long determined strides, that it couldn't be a regular house call. I ran across the winter lawns trying to keep up. Once, he stopped and looked around when he heard me, but I had already ducked down behind the McClearys' wheelbarrow that always stayed in their cluttered front yard. When he turned from Hastings onto Rynard Road, I saw the Olans' house.

I was surprised to see no policeman patrolling out front, but then I'd never been here this late.

Still, though, there were floodlights on the lawn, and the house was lit up like a stage. My father went up the front walk, the same walk where a brick two weeks earlier had knocked him to the ground. A policeman opened the front door, and my father disappeared inside.

What to do? I could go home. Wearing just a flannel shirt, I was starting to freeze. But I hadn't come all this way only to fade back into my own home. Well, I didn't want to escape. My nature was too curious to let me turn away. My mother's "sadness" terrified me, that I might catch it, or some form of it, which perhaps Adrian, sitting at his typewriter, had already contracted. I wanted to follow my father into his world.

I was standing in the yard adjacent to the Olans', the Wileys'. Mrs. Wiley worked at the school as a dietitian, and her husband was in maintenance. My father had read us Mrs. Wiley's comment to *The Philadelphia Evening Bulletin:* "Nothing yet has convinced us they won't make good neighbors." It was less forceful than my father's comment that the neighborhood was holding this family hostage, and perhaps the reason he'd gotten a brick in the back, and why Mrs. Nick wouldn't serve me. In some way, I'd wished he hadn't spoken out. I'd worked so hard to be like the other kids in my school. My hair, curly like my father's, I kept short now. I wore lavender hi-boy shirts and stuck a greasy black comb in my back pocket. I had rat-stabber shoes from Flagg Brothers, and I said "That's boss" as often as I could work it into a sentence. Meanwhile, the kids with whom I went to Hebrew school and who lived across the township line looked and dressed like the young lawyers most of them would eventually become. They wore Arrow shirts and khaki slacks, navy turtlenecks and corduroy sport coats with green suede patches on the elbows. Their hair, wavy and dark and Semitic like mine, was parted down the left side in a clean white scalp line. At Hebrew school I studied about everybody from Theodor Herzl to Hank Greenberg, and when I went back to Garden City Elementary in the morning, these people and my heritage didn't—and never had— existed.

I was fascinated by the Olans, because they'd tried to break into the new neighborhood, as we had, and because they were having an even harder time than we did. When I stood on a milk crate under their back window, I had only wanted a glimpse of ourselves in the extreme. Their kitchen, tidy, clean, had the same Formica breakfast table as ours, a light blue oval with a large toaster on it. Right below my nose, under the window, was a wash sink filled with soaking clothes. I was amazed, given everything that was happening to them, that the Olans could carry on with life inside. Suddenly my shoulders were grabbed from behind, and I was yanked backwards. Two seconds later I was flat on my back on the cold grass with a flashlight shining in my eyes.

I could see through the glare that it was a policeman, and that he was from Garden City. "What are you doing here?" He was young, or young compared to Officer Dennis, who would have understood why I was here and to whom I could have explained my curiosity.

"I'm just looking," I said.

"You're just looking for trouble," he said. "Now get out of here."

But at that moment the back door opened, and Officer Dennis, who was indeed inside and had come out to see what all the commotion was about, saw me and said, "David?"

"Yes, sir," I said.

"Bring him inside, Tim," he told the officer.

And I wound up at the Olans' kitchen table. Mrs. Olan had just made a pot of coffee. She was a tall, thin woman with glistening black hair and long, lanky arms that seemed to be in every place at one time. She brought me milk and cookies and put her hand warmly on the back of my head, and I missed my own mother doing that. My mother hadn't touched me or held me much in the last year, and it seemed she was always wringing her hands or looking at me too anxiously for me to want her to touch me.

Mrs. Olan, though, had been crying. Her eyes were red, and against her dark skin they looked fiery. Mr. Olan came into the kitchen with his head down, saw me, and blinked hard. "He's Dr. Pete's boy," explained Mrs. Olan. Mr. Olan nodded at me, and I said, "Hello, sir," as I'd been trained to do. Officer Dennis leaned back against the kitchen counter, sipping the coffee Mrs. Olan had made. Everyone was quiet in the kitchen, and when Mrs. Olan sat down at the blue Formica table, Mr. Olan came over and patted her shoulder, and she took his hand and pressed her face against his palm. "She sleeping now," Mr. Olan said. Officer Dennis looked down at his coffee cup. Something was wrong, terribly wrong, I realized, beyond the neighbors hating these people. Something at the center of their lives that mattered more and was less comprehensible than any forces outside their home.

I put down the chocolate chip cookie. They were homemade and tasted delicious, but I thought it was insensitive to be gobbling cookies and gulping milk right now.

I heard footsteps down the stairs, and my father came into the kitchen with his black doctor's bag. His face was pale and the shadows deep around his eyes. He had sharp, handsome features and dark curls, and people had said he reminded them of Tony Curtis, but he looked worn down, sunken and dented like my old basketball in the garage. When he saw me, it startled him, but only momentarily. So thick was his distress that even my inexplicable presence here couldn't jar him from his heaviness. He turned to the Olans. "The ambulance will be here soon," he told them, and Mrs. Olan put her hands up to her face.

My father and I walked home. I carried his black doctor's bag. I felt immensely important to be at his side. He didn't ask me what I was doing at the Olans' house. If anything, he seemed glad for the company on the long walk home, much longer than it had taken either of us to get here. He said that he wished the baby hadn't been allergic to penicillin, and that he should have made the decision earlier to put the child in the hospital, but he didn't want to split up the family. "Under the circumstances, David," he told me, although it was as if he were talking to himself.

Two hours later I heard sirens going by our house, then more sirens. I heard my father run downstairs, followed by my mother. My father woke up our next-door neighbor, Mr. Phillips, for a ride to the Olans'. The fire that had been set would destroy the Olans' garage and most of their kitchen. The only good thing— and it wasn't good, as it turned out—was that the Olans hadn't been at home. They'd gone with their baby to the hospital, bringing along the two younger children asleep in their pajamas.

But the Olans' baby had passed away during the night: I couldn't bring myself to say "died" for a long while, because it was just the same as with my mother's "sadness," a soft phrase that let everybody, including me, off the hook. They had lost their baby and they'd lost their house in the same night. Smoke damage would make the place uninhabitable, and they'd soon leave, surrender and move to Darby. The neighborhood, which would not become integrated for twenty-one years, would never quite recover from it, as I would never recover from that day Mrs. Nick didn't serve me, and I allowed myself to slink away. The next year was 1960, and Warren and his family would move away, my mother would be hospitalized for depression, Adrian would break his shoulder trying to take an aerial shot of the park from our garage roof with his rented sixteen-millimeter camera, and I would decide I was going to be a doctor, a good doctor like my father, part of the great chain of cause and effect.

Why We're Here

In the room in Mexico where they finally reunited, Bird knelt by the bed, Kin lay on it as he'd done for weeks, and JJ settled into the canvas butterfly chair at its foot. Bird often knelt by Kin's bed these days, as if praying—which she also often did these days, though not on her knees. She had written JJ at last because Kin had grown weak so quickly here. Propping another pillow behind Kin's head now, Bird noticed he'd muted the new plum-dark lesion on his chin with base and powder. JJ seemed to be studying that very spot. He unhooked from his ears the sunglasses he'd worn for his car trip from Phoenix. His eyes were as Bird remembered—blue and green and gray. All three at once.

Awkward after eight years apart from them, JJ shifted in the chair. He fiddled with his sunglasses. Bird blushed, wishing she could set him at ease. But Kin, she knew, would waste no time on small talk.

"After me," Kin asked JJ, "were there any other men?"

JJ's bony face remained blank. His voice came out flatly matter-of-fact. "No," he said. "None after my summer with you, you and Bird..."

"Well, *I've* had a few." Kin managed a grin. Half closing his eyes, he described the lovers Bird knew to be his favorites. The fellow Pan Am steward he worked with for a year; the man he met on a beach in Greece; the young man in Brazil; the older man he seduced in his mom's native Taiwan. Except for the steward, none had spoken much English. "But then, that's what I craved." Kin raised one delicate eyebrow. "Touching without talking."

JJ nodded. Bird watched his hands fondle the sunglasses.

"Of course," Kin went on more slowly, "I've always gotten plenty of talk with Bird. Plenty of soul food, all these years we've been traveling. And sometimes now I worry that she didn't—" Kin slid his black eyes to her, a cough rumbling in his throat. His lusterless hair swayed.

"Get anything else," she finished for him. She touched his shoulder, steadied him as his cough died down. "Then again," she added in a rush, "I worry that I didn't *want* you to have much more than sex with those men." Kin gave a slight nod, looking drained by his coughs. "And me," Bird continued softly. "God. You know better than anyone, Sister Kin, that except for our summer with JJ, I haven't wanted anything *but* talking…"

Nervously, she ran her hand over her scalp, her hair bleached white by the desert sun and chopped short—like a monk's, Kin used to say. He'd dropped that description these past weeks, once she'd begun seeing Estella Hinojosa.

"And now-ow?" Kin asked in his old Sister Kin voice. "Want to tell JJ how things've heated up for you, down here?" The voice was more hoarse than its original version. But Bird smiled, knowing it must remind JJ, too, of Kin's old apartment, the fondue that had smelled of Sterno, the lingering talks in which Kin drew out his two shy guests, the long nights on Kin's small futon. Sister Kin lowered his voice coaxingly. "Tell us, come on. What all *did* happen with you and Estella last night?"

Bird looked down. She lifted Kin's ice bag off a battered paperback on Buddhism. Books in English were hard to come by here. She handed him a chip of ice. As she drew a shuddery breath to speak, Kin cracked the ice between his teeth, then told JJ, "Estella is Bird's new sweetie. Estella Hinojosa."

Bird felt her flush deepen. Her leather jacket was ridiculously hot, but she didn't want to take it off. She glanced up at JJ, freshly amazed by his presence. His eyes fixed wholly on her now, as if he'd been waiting for a chance to stare. And Bird sensed that something more than talk might yet happen among the three of them.

Staying on her knees, Bird told JJ how one June evening she'd walked with the kids down the hill to a small racetrack outside of town. She'd wanted to see the imported greyhounds run. To try her luck at betting, raise some pesos.

"And I did. Won my first-ever bet. Which was great since we'd been living on the last of Kin's Pan Am money. So I was grinning, feeling good, wishing Kin could've come. Then at the cash-in booth, a guy tried to pick me up. Bragged that he spoke English, that he worked at the track, that he had to 'take care of' this white-speckled greyhound that'd snapped its leg in the race I'd won. I said, What do you mean, take care of? He said, The opposite of what it usually means. I was so high on winning that I followed him under the stands to these cages. This stink of raw meat and dogshit and dog. One greyhound was lying outside a cage. So thin, his organs showed through his skin. I swear: round shapes of his liver and intestines. Like meat through butcher paper. The guy told me, That dog won't even make it into your tacos."

As if he hadn't heard all this before, Kin winced. Bird pulled herself up, brushing off her jeans. Weighted by her jacket, she paced beside the bed.

"You were getting scared—?" Kin prompted from his pillow.

"Scared to be alone with this guy—he *smelled* like dog meat—when I spotted *another* guy stepping from behind the cages, holding another starved-looking dog. I backed away, *real* scared till the other guy stepped into light. And it wasn't a guy but a tall, wide—a *big* woman. Estella."

Bird stopped at the doorway, her back to JJ as she remembered Estella holding out the limp, whimpering dog. Slowly, Bird slipped off her leather jacket and draped it over her arm. Her skin tingled with relief. She breathed in, feeling her breasts strain her tank top. Exhaling, she met JJ's eyes.

"Right from the start, Estella was staring at me like—" Bird grinned at JJ, showing her teeth with all their gaps. "You, right now."

Kin choked, laughing. And JJ—looking startled, as if he hadn't known he was staring—joined in with his low, dry laugh. Bird widened her grin. Their laughter mixed as naturally now as eight years before. All of them barely in their twenties then.

"Anyhow." She paced more slowly, wondering where she was leading. "I wound up helping Estella Hinojosa load the dog into her old Bonneville convertible. She'd bought the dog, see. And she gave me a cigarette. Like this." Bird shook one from a pack lying on the radio. Lighting it, she sucked a mouthful of smoke. As gently as Estella had done in the hot, starry dark of the parking lot, Bird knelt on the bed and slipped the cigarette between Kin's lips. They'd been smoking together since high school.

"*Muchas gracias,*" he murmured. These days, though he barely inhaled, he savored his cigarettes.

"Then she asked if I was hungry." Bird resettled the jacket on her arm, watching JJ watch Kin. "I rode with the dog's head in my lap. Her house was off by itself—lotsa roses climbing the walls and a yard full of dogs." Bird breathed Kin's smoke, remembering the rich smells of Estella's kitchen. "She fed the dog first, then me. Hauled out a pot to make *sopa*. She had—has—big hands and a long horsey face. A ponytail—black hair but not like Kin's. Coarser, like a real horse's tail. Like—" Bird glanced at JJ. He was still watching Kin smoke. "Yours." She stood, surprised and ashamed by a little flare of jealousy inside her.

"So anyhow, I ate. The kitchen was steamy, and we both smelled of dog. Estella asked, real polite, in Spanish, if I wanted a bath."

Kin cleared his throat loudly. Bird looked down. "And I asked myself: Do I want a bath?" She drew a breath of smoke, feeling JJ's eyes shift to her. "I did. So she ran me a bath in her old-fashioned boat tub, and I—don't know why; I just knew it was what she wanted—I said, in Spanish, You wanna watch?" Bird met JJ's gaze. She wanted him to understand what had happened to her this summer, how it was the first time since the summer she'd loved him and Kin.

"That's how it started, our routine. Couple of nights a week. We'd meet at the track and bet. Then we'd pick up any dogs worth saving. I'd help feed the dogs and we'd eat and if I felt like it, I'd take a bath. She'd lean on the sink, smoking and watching. Then"—Bird turned from JJ—"she'd pay me. For feeding the dogs, she said. But it was for the bath. I *wanted* to bathe for her, so it seemed..." She silently asked Kin to find a word. The Spanish she'd been learning escaped her now.

"Cool," he muttered through his smoke.

Bird nodded. "Round July," she hurried on, watching JJ half smile at Kin, "I managed to tell her I wanted to, needed to, learn to drive."

"You still aren't driving?" JJ blinked and turned to her.

"You *do* remember," Bird said straight to him, "why I never learned?"

JJ nodded slowly. Only he and Kin knew what Stepdad #2 had done to her when he was supposed to be teaching her to drive the family Vega. Two of his fingers thrust up inside her. Bird slung her jacket over her bare shoulder. As she paced again by the bed, she described how Estella let her bump the Bonneville up and down her dusty side street. How sometimes Estella's thigh would brush her own, or how Estella's hand would rest on her knee. Estella would slip her a few more pesos on those nights. Kin nodded, releasing slight streams of smoke.

And, Bird went on, Estella helped out when Kin got so sick. She paid for Kin's hospital stay. She paid, last week, for the *dentista* who pulled Bird's bad teeth.

"But last night"—Bird faced Kin—"I wasn't trying to pay her back."

"Real-ly?" Sister Kin asked, almost with his old New York edge. Had *he* been feeling little flares of jealousy over Estella?

"Really." Bird looked from Kin and his elegantly suspended, barely smoked cigarette to JJ. She wanted them both to understand that it hadn't been for money.

"So," Kin murmured, pointing to her with his cigarette as he used to do during their fondue suppers. Their conductor. "What all *happened* last night?"

Bird fingered her onyx ring. Kin's gift. "Estella," she told JJ, "knew Kin was my husband. That's all she knew. Last night, I told her that Kin and I would have to leave Mexico soon. Move to Texas, find a hospital."

JJ looked at the floor and folded his arms. Impulsively, Bird stepped toward him, trailing her jacket. "So Estella and I, we went on this long last ride. She let me drive—a celebration, I was driving fast and easy." Bird draped her jacket onto JJ's lap. His knees supported it like tent poles. He stiffened but—still—kept his face deadpan, eyes downcast. "For protection," Bird said. She smoothed the leather over his rigid knees. "Case anyone decides to sit on you." His eyes flicked up to her, a forbidding gray-green.

Bird plucked JJ's sunglasses from his pocket, unfolded them, and slipped them on him. "Case we do anything now you don't want to see."

JJ reached up as if to take them off but merely adjusted the curved stems around his ears. His pock-scarred face was flushed, as was hers. Half-scared and half-exhilarated by what she was doing, Bird backed away.

"So you drove," Kin said, easing her into the story again. He ground out his cigarette in a seashell.

"I drove all the way to Nogales," Bird went on. "With the roof down."

Estella's horse hair had streamed in wind; Estella had yelled, *"Ai ya,"* as they rolled into Nogales, rolled along streets thronged by tourists, by burros painted with zebra stripes, by bouquets of paper flowers huge as bunches of balloons, by streetcarts of lemons and peeled cukes and sweets with beautiful names. The layered pastry they'd shared was called a *buñuelo.*

Bird hugged herself, remembering the leather and silver-polish smell of the shop where she'd tried on jacket after jacket. "As a going-away present, Estella bought me just what I wanted." Bird stepped back to JJ. "Plus coconut oil to protect the leather."

She bent and touched the jacket on JJ's lap. Daring herself, she rested her hand on JJ's shoulder as she straightened. Through the cotton, she felt his skin, its surface cool. "Anyhow," she went on, her voice shaking slightly, "when we got back, I parked her Bonneville behind the dog fence." JJ's body was stiffening under her touch. "No one around but the dogs..." Tentatively, Bird pressed his shoulder. "We sat there awhile under these big bright stars, me in my jacket—even in the heat, I wanted it on. And I could've just driven myself home, said goodbye in her car. But I said to myself: What do I want to do?"

Keeping hold of JJ's shoulder, she asked herself again that same question. Then bent closer to him. She felt Kin observing them through his lingering smoke. "So I slid out from under the steering wheel, and I climbed into her lap."

Unsteadily, Bird started to ease herself onto JJ's lap. He gripped her bare arm hard. "No, Bird." Half-relieved, she pulled away.

"Want me to show *you?*" she asked Kin. He gave a slow-motion nod and eased himself into a sitting position, propping his pillows upright behind him. His legs stretched in a V over the red-striped sheets.

Abruptly, Bird lifted the jacket from JJ's lap and held it up like a bullfighter's cape. Kneeling on the bed, she spread it over Kin's white-clad thighs and crotch.

"I sat in her lap," Bird repeated softly, to Kin. "In my jacket." She eased down in front of Kin as if they were on a bobsled. Careful not to rest her full weight on him, she settled between his outstretched legs. Leather squeaked beneath her. "She helped me unbutton. Her body was all...round. Watermelon breasts and a big belly, and at first, Sister Kin, I felt kinda overwhelmed." Bird settled more heavily against him. "But gradually I *sank* into all that flesh. All brown and firm, not soft. Before I knew what was happening, I was—my first time, y'know—sucking her breasts." Bird leaned fully on Kin as she'd done during a few long afternoons here, once letting him reach around and feel her breasts as if they were his own.

"Then we were kissing, hard, too." Bird slowed her words, remembering Estella's wide tongue filling her mouth, filling the gaps between her teeth. "I took hold of her hand." Bird groped at her side for Kin's hand. Light, compared to Estella's. Drawing it around her body, she rested Kin's warm bony hand in her lap. "I eased her hand under my skirt..."

"*Bueno, bueno,*" Kin said, his smoky breath in her hair. Bird shut her eyes, unable to describe how delicately Estella's strong fingers had separated her vaginal lips. Like flesh petals. How Estella's fingertips held traces of the *buñuelo* they'd shared, its oil and flour and powdered sugar.

"Just a touch," Bird whispered only to Kin, her eyes shut. "But she knew—" Bird pressed her hand over Kin's in her lap. "Just where."

She blinked open her eyes. In the growing window sun, she made out JJ's sunglasses, his locked jaw. His lips were tightly sealed. But his face had reddened.

"My first time ever with a woman," she said to JJ. "And the first time in years, first time since you, I've en*joyed* anything like that."

Lit by the sun, JJ's hair shimmered with reddish browns. Steadily behind his glasses, he studied Bird and half-hidden Kin.

"I've let men kiss and touch me. All my Would-Be Lovers. But never—" Bird was the one to lower her eyes. "Never like you, Jimmy Joe."

"*Nunca.*" Kin propped his chin on Bird's bare shoulder. JJ leaned forward, his forearms resting on his knees again, his hands re-clasped. His expression seemed even more closed, sunglasses still in place.

"So." Bird stretched her legs. She leveled her voice, stating a fact. "We can't help it. We keep...thinking about you, Jimmy Joe."

"And you?" Kin asked, his jaw moving against Bird's shoulder.

He was speaking to JJ now, confidentially. Man to man. "You think about us, much?"

JJ swallowed. "Till I got Bird's letter, I didn't. Much. Didn't let myself. I'd gotten good at, I don't know. Control. In some good ways, I think." He swallowed again. "But once I started, I couldn't stop. Thinking of you two."

Bird nodded, feeling her hair brush Kin's. "We never could get very far alone, Sister Kin and me." She kept leaning back. In the dim silken Comm. Ave. apartment, she used to lean on Kin, spreading her thighs for JJ.

Slowly now, she let her knees loll open. Even with her jeans on, the gesture made her feel bold. She breathed the faint rotted-fish smell under Kin's perfume. And she held her breath with longing, though not the old longing. Not for Kin stroking her while JJ entered her. No, she was distracted now, worried about leaning on Kin too hard. Her heart knotted up as JJ stared, its ache stronger than the slight moist ache between her legs.

Ceremonially slow, JJ pulled off his sunglasses. He folded them. He gave Kin and Bird his heavy-lidded stare. "Bird, I can't." He shook his head, his face more darkly reddened. "My wife back in Phoenix. You know. I can't do that now, to you. Can't do it."

Bird cupped her knees. "Yeah, I know," she said. Behind her, Kin exhaled as if he'd known, all along. She eased forward to relieve his tense, frail body.

Kin cleared his throat to speak. He'd always been the calm one, the one who relaxed Bird and JJ their first times together. "Jimmy Joe, Jimmy Joe," Kin said. "We aren't trying to ... force anything." A cough erupted inside him, but Bird felt him swallow it back, hard. "Not with every-thing—all of us—so changed. Especially me. *I* know we can't do like we used to ... ."

"But still." Bird drew her knees closed. Kin's hand slipped out of her lap. She stood up by the bed as Kin let loose his rumbling cough. Then she stepped over to JJ, who sank low in the butterfly chair. Unmistakably, his bony face was heated like hers. His lips had taken on their old color. "Still, Jimmy Joe." Bird struggled to keep her own voice calm. "I feel like there ... might be something we could do. Not you and me. That's not it now, you know?" She waited a beat, and he raised his eyes. He nodded as if sensing this might've been the point of her story about Estella. "But what I said in my letter," Bird went on, remembering that letter herself. "You read it. You knew coming down here I wanted to try...something—"

"For Kin," JJ said and looked past her at Kin on the bed. Impassively, Kin met JJ's stare. His black eyes formed the only slashes of color in his face. He didn't blink.

"In her letter," JJ told Kin, studying him, "she said...lately you felt. In bursts. All your senses overcharged?"

Kin gave a slow matter-of-fact nod. "Comes and goes in waves," he said. "Like my fear." He switched to a mock-teacherly tone, another persona that dated back to the old days. "It's an ex-peri-ence, boys and girls. And you know I'm a glutton for experience." He dropped the voice. "The best part is how sometimes some things—just smoking or playing guitar chords or smelling mint—feel all at once overwhelming...like seeing you two together." He squinted at them as if they gave off light. His jaw made the chewing motion that Bird knew meant he couldn't speak. He dipped a hand into his ice bag. Shutting his eyes abruptly, he ran a piece of ice over his face. It washed off the powder that hid his lesion, revealing a purple deeper than a mere bruise.

"What *I* fucking need is a cold shower." Kin reverted now to his Southern Belle voice. "'S all too much ex-citement for my del-i-cate condition." He wiped his face with one slow sweeping motion, then lowered his hand.

JJ bent more sharply forward. "You still have...I mean you always have that—" He gestured to Kin's limp, slender hand. "Grace."

Kin still didn't blink. Bird drew a breath, half-hopeful and half-afraid she was going to see him cry. Even when he'd first found out he'd tested positive, he hadn't cried. But his bright gaze stayed steady.

She whispered, "If we could even just lie down together. Just now, once more." Her whisper seemed to her disembodied, a voice from the room's shadows. "You don't have to do anything, Jimmy Joe. Except lie there, maybe, between us." His eyes flicked up. "It'd be safe, I swear. There's nothing dangerous in, you know, sweat."

JJ blinked, his face opening but his jaw still clenched. Bird raised one hand to him as if to shake his hand. The knot in her chest tightened. She found herself longing for the twenty-year-old Jimmy Joe. Shy like her, yet bold, too.

"See," she said to him, suddenly inspired, "my jacket, that leather. It'll protect us." JJ studied her outstretched hand as if unsure what it was. Bird bent down to his ear. She whispered, "You're the only one who could join us."

JJ raised his eyes to her face. "I know." He said this flatly. As if it were the one thing in his life he was certain about.

Slowly, maybe experimentally, he took her hand. She didn't tug. He pulled himself up. She let go of his hand, remembering Jimmy Joe gazing at Kin that first night, no longer asking why she'd insisted Kin come along, young Jimmy Joe's eyes burning with a kind of fascination. She'd seen a flicker of it when he'd watched Kin smoke minutes before. Now, his gaze seemed lit by something stronger. His eyes shone with a liquid that looked thicker than tears.

"Don't," Kin said to JJ from the bed. "Don't do anything you don't want to do, love."

What Sister Kin always told them, Bird thought, turning. She felt sure JJ was remembering that, too. The single rule of their old game.

"I won't," JJ answered, low-voiced like a groom taking his vow.

As she had never done years before, Bird led JJ. Together, they stepped away from the butterfly chair and edged between the bed and stucco wall. JJ stopped behind Bird. She froze, wondering what next. JJ moved first. He sat on the mattress to pull off his black sneakers. Then he stood again. Kin on the bed eased his body sideways.

JJ lowered himself onto his knees, the mattress sinking under his weight, springs squeaking. Bird touched his shoulder. And he touched Kin's shoulder. One light touch, one nod. Hello, they seemed to be saying at last.

Bird breathed JJ's sweat, the welcome smell of healthy flesh. "If we can all just . . . lie down here . . ." Her voice faltered. "In . . . a row?"

Deliberately, JJ rolled onto his side. Bird touched his rib cage, more padded with flesh than before. But his hipbones still jutted out, his limbs and haunches still lean. A foot of space stretched between JJ's long curved back and Kin, who sat propped against his pillow as if weighted in place by the jacket on his lap.

Bird heard the buzzing flies and the sun outside, its hum as it beat down harder. Time was running short, the limited time they could spend together again. But didn't she already feel a charge in the air among their bodies? Tentatively, Kin shifted his weight, trying to hold the jacket on his lap.

"Let me." Bird edged around the bed, sensing what Kin might want.

She rested her hand on Kin's shirt, his rib cage. Padded by the thinnest skin. Her fingers pressed between his ribs as she helped him roll on his side, the jacket sliding off his lap. Bird took its empty arms. "Wait now."

She held up the unlined jacket. Then remembered Estella's test last night: how droplets of water had sunk into the leather. Leather is skin, and all skin is porous. She lowered the jacket, wondering what could wholly protect them. She hadn't thought of buying condoms, wasn't even sure Kin would be able to get erect. She blinked over at Kin's ice bag, then stepped quickly around the bed. She lifted the bag, dumped its remaining ice into the trash basket. "Kin calls this the Buddhist brand." She smoothed the airtight plastic to warm it, reading its label. " 'Clear Pure Ice.' "

"Oh, right," Kin said to JJ, his ragged voice sounding somehow reassured. "This Buddhist book I read for fun. Tells how to reach the State of Not-Self. A clear state, they say. Clear, pure."

"Right." Bird draped the plastic bag over Kin's crotch. She lifted the jacket again and tied its creaking leather arms around Kin's waist. The jacket over the plastic covered Kin's crotch and thighs like an apron. A smithy apron, she thought.

"Perfect," she said, stepping back to view her work. The unlined leather was thin enough to let Kin feel the body in front of him. Which was what Kin wanted, Bird felt sure. To feel JJ close to him now. To feel her close, too.

JJ propped himself on one elbow, twisting around to face them. "I had to work my leather in here somehow," Bird said. Kin smiled, curled on his side, his legs bent under the jacket. JJ rested his head again on the bed's second pillow, his back to Kin. His long body poised.

Bird kicked off her sandals. She had read Kin's Buddhist book, too. It compared its series of meditations to the process of refining gold from ore. How the first stages were bound to be—in the book's curious word—gross. Straightening, she touched the knot of Kin's jacket apron, making sure it would hold. The early stages were gross, the end result pure. Bird lifted her hand from the leather.

"The State of Not-Self," Kin repeated, musing over the words. "Such a bad translation." He coughed, but softly. As Bird padded barefoot around the bed, Kin's voice took on his familiar, gently mocking tone. "I only know one way to reach any such state, Jimmy Joe. Remember? We used to call it going, not coming. All your desires, even your body itself. Just . . . gone."

Bird stopped in front of JJ. She was wedged between the bed and wall.

"I remember," JJ whispered, almost too quietly to be heard.

"Course it only lasts a moment or so," Kin went on, sounding almost sleepy.

"But what doesn't?" Bird asked, her voice softened, too.

"*Nada,*" Kin answered. "Like the book tells us. It all depends on what you mean by a 'moment.'"

JJ eased closer to Kin to make room for Bird. She hesitated, half wanting to strip off her jeans. But she climbed onto the bed fully clothed. "Like the summer we were together," she whispered, curling herself at the edge, her back to JJ. The three of them lay in a row. "Only a few months, but it's lasted and lasted. Inside Kin and me, anyhow."

"And me," JJ added, his breath hot in her hair.

"We always remembered," she dared to go on. "How the three of us, together, always had this . . ."

"Grace," JJ said.

In answer, Bird moved back close enough so that JJ's zippered crotch brushed her ass. Then she heard and felt Kin inch closer to JJ from his side, the mattress springs squealing and the jacket creaking. Under it all, the plastic crackled. Kin was pressing his crotch through the leather against JJ's ass.

Bird began to rock a little, listening to the crackle. So many layers of protection needed now to do what used to be simple. Natural. She rocked harder, feeling Kin rock, too. The mattress springs sounded strange, new. Always before, they had lain together on a springless futon. Bird breathed leather and smoke and sweat, all stronger than the sickly perfumed smell of Kin's body. Not fish, Bird thought now, inhaling. But oysters, rotted oysters. Behind her, JJ's body stiffened. Could he detect that smell? Or was he thinking of the wife Bird had never seen? His Alice.

"C'mon," Bird murmured, trying not to sound anxious. She rolled around onto her other side. Then she giggled into JJ's solemn, intently expectant face, much older than Jimmy Joe's. A computer programmer's face now. Yet the same bones showed, and the same nerves were strung inside his pockmarked skin. His same lips sealed as if he were holding his breath. This has to work for Kin, Bird thought. She wanted JJ to understand by her own serious stare. It has to work.

Chastely, she kissed JJ on his flat bristled cheek. "Swans," she said, half shutting her eyes. JJ made no answer but tilted back his head slightly, just enough. She rubbed her neck against his neck, feeling his Adam's apple fill the hollow of her throat.

JJ moaned. A sound deep in his throat like the purr in a cat. She pressed her throat harder against his and opened her eyes to meet, sideways over JJ's broad shoulder, Kin's upraised eyes.

"Swans," she whispered down to Kin. Kin shut his eyes prayerfully hard. He bowed his head. Bird watched him ease forward a last few creaking inches and rest his forehead between JJ's large, beautifully tensed shoulder blades.

JJ gave a low gasp, as if remembering something long forgotten. Then he exhaled, a softly drawn-out vowel of pleasure.

Sighing, too, her throat thoroughly warmed, Bird pulled back her head. "Remember our first time, all together?" She knew JJ did; she wanted him to acknowledge it. "In Kin's apartment, way off-campus?" She ran her hand over JJ's chest, feeling through his shirt his stiffened nipples. He breathed hard again. But he held still. "How Kin showed us both what to do?" Slowly, so he could stop her if he wanted, she reached down to his waist.

"I promise," she whispered as she unsnapped his pants. He tensed his bent legs, but held his body still for her. "We'll stay safe, Jimmy Joe." She inched his zipper down as carefully as Kin had undone her bra that first night, his fingertips barely brushing her skin. She could feel Kin hold his breath at the zipper's last notches. "Just hands," she whispered shakily.

JJ's eyes stayed shut. His breathing came steadily now, as if he were concentrating. He shifted his weight so Bird could tug on his pants and his cotton briefs, pulling them halfway down. She heard Kin's own slow zipper. JJ held his body expectantly still.

"Remember the night I first touched you?" she whispered to JJ, but loud enough for Kin to hear. "Really touched you?" Balancing on one elbow, she reached behind JJ and clasped Kin's hand. "Remember," she continued in whisper, easing Kin's arm over JJ's side, "how scared I was? But Sister Kin guided me, my hands?"

She rested Kin's palm on JJ's abdomen. His shirttails half hid his mass of brown pubic hair, his velvety purplish balls, his shadowed cock—a dusky reddish-pink, thick at its base. She felt the extra warmth that had made her think, years before, that it was— the word had frightened her then—*alive.*

"The only cock I've ever touched," she whispered to JJ.

He opened his eyes. "God, Bird," he whispered back. "Why?"

She shrugged one bare shoulder. "There wasn't ever anyone else we both, Kin and I . . ."

JJ nodded.

She began to hum. Kin's leather and plastic apron creaked and crackled as he pressed closer to JJ. She eased his hand down, her own curved thumb brushing JJ's cock, its warmth and grainy texture deeply familiar. Kin gave the throaty moan Bird hadn't heard for eight years. Only with JJ had they been able to share this, too. Under her hand, Kin's hand held JJ's cock. With his own lower-pitched moan, JJ began rocking to Bird's low hum.

And she embraced JJ, her breasts pressing against his chest. He shut his eyes again. Kin had begun to pump JJ's cock. Still humming, her hum vibrating in her outstretched throat, Bird kissed JJ. His mouth warmed hers, but he kept his lips closed.

As she pulled back, she remembered how, when Estella's tongue had filled her mouth, filled all its holes, she'd felt she knew the answer. Why we were here. She took hold of JJ's solid shoulders, feeling Kin's knuckles brush her crotch, imagining Kin's voice. To fill each other's holes, love.

Kin moaned again. Bird's fingers sank into JJ's firm flesh. All skin, Bird thought. Full of pores, holes. Kin's hand was pumping up and down between her and JJ, warming them both. Could Kin reach that moment he wanted? Bird braced her own body.

Moments of purified awareness; that was how Kin's book defined Buddhism. A stream of such moments leading to a Perfect Emptiness. She held her breath. Through vibrations in JJ's body, she felt Kin's hips moving. He was breathing hard, like a runner who knows just where he's going. JJ, too, was breathing hard, his eyes shut tighter, the skin about them rayed with new creases. Kin's hand pumped steadily along with his hips. Bird had stopped humming, but she was still hearing her hum. She shut her eyes, the three of them sharing a smoke-tinged silence. A chapel full of candles, everybody praying.

Please, she was saying inside, gripping JJ's arms. The muscle under the meat. She squeezed, holding JJ steady as Kin pressed him harder from behind. Bird's heartbeat speeded with Kin's rough breaths and the singing springs, the shuddery mattress. *Please, please.* The words beat with thumps of her pulse. *Please let Kin come.*

Leather creaked, suddenly louder than the springs. "Go," Kin breathed hoarsely from the other side of JJ.

JJ sucked in a harsh-sounding breath. Bird gasped, too, tasting JJ's sweat, losing hold of JJ's arms as his big hips jolted forward. His hipbones swallowed hers. His chest flattened her breasts, her nipples prickling. Between her legs, Kin's hand slipped away, replaced by the bare swollen warmth of JJ's cock, its wetness seeping through her denim.

"Oh—" JJ gasped. Suddenly he'd wrapped his arms around Bird, his hands cupping her ass. As JJ held and rocked her, as heat spread inside her own skin, Bird gripped Kin's hands, his arm wedged now under JJ's rocking side. His palm coated with JJ's semen, warm and milky between them.

With strength she didn't think he had, strength he hadn't had minutes before, Kin pulled Bird toward him through JJ. Their arms bent; their bodies strained. Her onyx ring dug into their interlocked fingers. Bird felt Kin grind against JJ's haunches, the leather and plastic crackling together. Blacksmith fire, she thought: hot enough to meld solid metal, to separate from gross ore purest gold.

JJ's Adam's apple bobbed; Bird opened her mouth and closed her lips around his throat, his bristly sweaty skin. Sucking so hard her teeth ached, she tightened her hold on Kin's miraculously strong, bony hands. He squeezed her hands back, gasping with a sharp inhale like silk torn.

Through JJ, Bird felt Kin's body convulse, her lips fastened to JJ's throat. Her body remembered what she'd felt last night, what she'd felt years before with JJ and Kin, what she felt Kin feel now: veins filled with air, flesh buoyant. Not coming but going, taking off.

Those Poor Devils

In 1969, except for the yearly wardrobe changes of the young officers' wives, Randolph Air Force Base had barely acknowledged the decade. The young officers discussed shoeshines, the laundry that put the sharpest crease in their everyday khakis, which colonel gave the best TDY. Friday afternoons the wives met them at the Officers Club. The best wives ordered pink drinks and said little. Others drank beer or bourbon and seven, swiveled on their bar stools, and looked toward the door.

None of the young officers talked about the war on base. They had made their choices: Air Force ROTC or Officer Candidate School, emphasis ground duty, stateside. Some felt smug and safely patriotic about their decision. Some regretted it, felt that anything, even a tour of duty in Nam, would be better than reporting every day to the Education and Training Division, three years of Orwellian routine, a complex of duties so particular and minute that only a few realized there was nothing to do. All the young officers performed assiduously, earning their promotions, striving for the recognition of Colonel Teale and Colonel Dunne.

Here is a second lieutenant from Grand Island, Nebraska, a town that was neither grand nor on or near an island. If he had a metaphorical turn of mind, he might draw some parallels. He has a master's degree in elementary education and a wife, but has run out of military deferments and has made his choice. He says it's the right thing. No one asks if he believes it.

He bought his wife the Air Force Officers' Wives Handbook, and half hoped she wouldn't get a job when they moved south so late in the summer, but the Eli Whitney High School needed a teacher to take over its accelerated program and her credentials were good. He went with her to the job interview, but no one asked her age so he couldn't accuse her of lying. The first weeks of the term she'd come home late, crying, and he said she was too young and ought to get the vice principal to monitor her classes. After a few months, he didn't hear any more about the twenty-year-old senior and part-time bull rider who came to her class drunk or the student ROTC hall guard who demanded her hall pass, but she still came home late, every night.

He asked his parents for the down payment for a house just off-base. His next-door neighbor was a staff sergeant who encouraged the young second looey and his wife to poison the clover that swept the front lawn and to set in pale squares of greenhouse grass. "Those poor devils who lived here before," the sergeant kept saying, "they didn't know shit about grass, poor devils."

Colonel Teale and Colonel Dunne liked to tease the new second lieutenant's wife because she looked cute when she argued with them about *Easy Rider* or the naked teenagers in *Romeo and Juliet*. At school, one of her students gave a report on Kent State and another was called down to the office because in a class discussion he said Communism as an ideal made sense. The second lieutenant's wife was called down to the office, too, but it was for skirt length. The vice principal requested that she wear a longer skirt to Parents' Night. She asked if a pants suit would be all right, but he started tapping the black book she'd heard about in the Communist incident so she said yes, of course. Later, she would describe this as an ignominious epiphany: for want of a below-the-knee dress, a good little girl was lost.

Some of the young officers had almost completed their three years. They had parties where people wandered around with glow-in-the-dark flowers and symbols painted on their faces. Even enlisted men came to these parties. One of them drove a white van with a big yellow peace sign emblazoned on the side. The young second lieutenant wasn't so comfortable at these gatherings, although he painted FUCK on his forehead with lime-green Day-Glo and thought it was pretty funny because he forgot about it when he went on a beer run.

He knew he shouldn't have left his wife alone. She was sitting in a corner with a guy everyone called Dopey who'd received a dishonorable discharge for mental incompetence. It was time to get his wife out of there so he pulled on her hand. Even though he always teased her about her weight, there wasn't very much to her, never had been, and he was surprised to feel the strength of her resistance, surprised to hear the power in her scream. After that, everything moved in slow motion, the way cinematographers were starting to film riots, protests, police brutality. He felt her go limp beneath him, as if she'd been trained. He saw people rush to her, heard the man with the yellow peace sign say she could stay in his van. Someone slipped her what looked like a business card.

The young second lieutenant made love to his wife that night. He said everything had evened out. She had hurt him, and he had hurt her.

When the second lieutenant's wife moved out, he wrote a letter to her parents, blaming liberal friends and how they put ideas in an innocent girl's head. Her mother saved that letter twenty years before showing it to her daughter. "You should have it," she said. "I didn't want you to throw it away. I think you can use it."

A Profile by Don Lee

In many ways, Robert Boswell fits the mythology of the contemporary man in the American West. Known as Boz, he's a lanky, laconic six-footer with a closely cropped beard. Typically garbed in jeans and rumpled shirts with rolled-up sleeves, he drives a pickup truck and listens to Bruce Springsteen. He lives in an adobe house near the Rio Grande in Las Cruces, New Mexico, less than fifty miles from the Mexican border. His voice is a baritone, coming from way deep, and he's a slow talker—slower still with strangers. He claims the desert as his landscape of preference, insisting that the sky really is larger out there, and too much time away from the West makes him claustrophobic.

But the stereotypes end there. The acclaimed author of three novels and two collections of short stories, Boswell is no cowboy, and certainly no redneck. The lonesome highway may be the chosen path for some of Boswell's characters, but not him. He's a devoted family man, married to the writer Antonya Nelson since their graduate-school days at the University of Arizona in Tucson, and their two young children, daughter Jade and son Noah, are the center of their lives; Boswell even helps out one day a week at Jade's school, running a writers' workshop for the fourth graders, going over what the kids call their "sloppy copy." Moreover, Boswell, a card-carrying member of the ACLU, is an activist and supporter for a number of liberal organizations, including the Southern Poverty Law Center, Planned Parenthood, NOW, and Share Our Strength.

He was born in Sikeston, Missouri, in 1953 and spent his childhood on a tobacco farm in Wickliffe, Kentucky, a literary landmark of sorts. The town is where the Mississippi and Ohio rivers meet, a dramatic turning point in *The Adventures of Huckleberry Finn,* a book that Boswell says changed his life, forever instilling in him the desire to become a writer. When he was in sixth grade, his family moved to Yuma, Arizona. There, his father, formerly an elementary school principal, taught high school government, and

PHOTO: MARION ETTLINGER

his mother worked mostly as a realtor. Alongside two brothers and a sister, Boswell grew up to be a "shy extrovert," a member of student government and the basketball team, but also a brooder, frequently depressed and insecure. A child of the sixties, he was preoccupied with the draft and Vietnam and was heavily involved in recreational drugs. "If you go the long way," he says, "Yuma is fifteen miles from the border, and there were a lot of drugs available cheap, a lot of people running across the border, and I found that an interesting pastime."

Chemically distracted, it took Boswell five and a half years to finish his undergraduate studies at the University of Arizona in Tucson. "I finally made a conscious decision to quit doing drugs. I thought I'd never get through college otherwise, and I knew I wanted to accomplish something. But it took me years, really, to quit." Another protractive factor was his indecision about his major. He started in government, thinking he might become a lawyer, as his father had always wanted to be, then switched to psychology, to English, and then to creative writing. He had so many credits in psychology, he graduated with a double major.

Still not ready to commit to writing fully, he continued at the University of Arizona for a master's degree in rehabilitation counseling. "I was looking for a way to have a life that wasn't an obscenity, and this seemed like a possibility, doing important work," he says. In 1979, he was hired as a counselor just outside of San Diego and guided immigrants, schizophrenics, and the poor into job training programs. The experience radicalized his politics, and would later deeply inform his writing. Pointedly, he remembers seeing single mothers who were trying to attend college while supporting their kids with part-time jobs, then having the Reagan administration change the eligibility rules, forcing the women to quit working in order to keep their welfare benefits. "The government had plenty of programs," Boswell says, "but at the same time the programs were compromised, so there seemed to be a genuine effort to keep people from getting the benefits they were entitled to. A very strange and frustrating experience, Kafkaesque in some ways."

His job began to consume him, and after two years, he decided to return to the University of Arizona to pursue his abiding love, entering the M.F.A. program in creative writing. His class had quite a few incipient stars, including David Foster Wallace and Richard Russo, but Boswell wasn't among them. Concentrating on poetry at first, he admits he was near the bottom of the talent pool. During one conference, his teacher, Steve Orlen, told Boswell, "It seems to me you're always trying to tell a story," then added, "It seems to me that there's not much music in your poetry." Laughing, Boswell says, "It was a euphemistic way of telling me that I was writing one clunker after another, and the light bulb came on over my head that I should be writing fiction."

He might have had a natural instinct for storytelling, but he knew next to nothing about the craft, and he invested himself in learning it. The summer after his first year in the M.F.A. program, he maniacally wrote for sixteen to eighteen hours a day, then would go to a dive called The Country Club Lounge, drinking and dancing to a rock 'n' roll band, Los Lasers, until closing time. "I wrote one bad thing after another, but after that my work got better. I think it had to do with finally understanding something writers were often saying—when you're writing fiction, what you pursue is truth. I managed to get ruthless, and hack away at the things that were dishonest in my stories." It's an attitude, a work ethic, that has held true to this day. "To write good fiction, typically I have to push it beyond any point I could have anticipated, and then be willing to give up on the story as *my* story, and work back into it on its own terms." Thus, he will sometimes sacrifice favorite scenes or entire novel chapters as he is churning out draft after draft. "I have to write about thirty drafts of a book, or a story, or a letter, to get something I'm happy with," he says.

His efforts that long-ago summer quickly paid off. Larry McMurtry, while visiting the University of Arizona campus, read a story of Boswell's and then met with him. "He said we didn't need to talk about the story itself, we just needed to talk about having a life as a writer." The short story, "The Right Thing," became Boswell's first publication, appearing in *The Antioch Review* in 1983. Around the same time, he met Antonya Nelson in a workshop. He was in his last year of the three-year program, and she was in her first. "Tony and I first started going out in November, and we were engaged in January, got married in July. It was really quite a whirlwind affair."

His literary career moved rapidly as well. Submitting many of the stories from his thesis, he won the Iowa School of Letters Award for Short Fiction in 1985, and his collection, *Dancing in the Movies,* was published by the University of Iowa Press the subsequent year. His agent, to whom he was introduced by McMurtry, sold his first novel, *Crooked Hearts,* about an eccentric Arizona family, to Knopf, and it came out to phenomenal reviews in 1987. *Geography of Desire,* a novel about a Californian in Central America, was released in 1989, followed by his breakthrough novel, *Mystery Ride,* which became a bestseller in 1993. A second story collection, *Living to Be a Hundred,* was released in 1994.

Most of Boswell's work explores the themes of family, fidelity, morality, and the nature of love, and by and large, his characters are intelligent, ordinary, middle-class folk trying to live decently, with "integrity" (an obsessive principle in Boswell's lexicon), but of course failing for one reason or another. A hallmark of Boswell's fiction is the extraordinary empathy he generates for each character, even those who have beliefs antithetical to his— the pro-life, born-again Christians in *Mystery Ride,* for instance. In that novel, Boswell weaves together twenty years with brilliant technical skill, portraying an idealistic couple, Stephen and Angela Landis—who meet in the sixties and have a daughter, Dulcie—

through their marriage and divorce, through their separate lives in Iowa and California. The original title for the book was *Fidelity*. "Although this couple has been divorced for twelve years," Boswell explains, "in the most important ways, they're still faithful, they're still true to the things they believe in, the things that had brought them together."

In the haunting final scene of the first chapter, Stephen and Angela set a mound of trash afire. They've just bought their first piece of property, a farm in Iowa, but they've discovered that the cellar of the house is filled with years of accumulated garbage— coffee grounds, liquefied vegetables, piles of rotting filth. They haul everything outside to burn:

> The fire rose high over the dark field, high over the rancid mound. Above the blue and yellow center, flames twisted red and orange. Shards of pure green appeared and vanished. The fire did not crackle but howled, a wall of sound, heat, and color. . . .
>
> Their love was young enough and powerful enough for each to think it: we have taken something putrid and made it into something beautiful.
>
> Years later, a decade after Angela left him, Stephen would remember the great flame burning behind the house, how it had seemed to push against their faces like a wind, how the raw heat had finally made them turn away.
>
> The memory of those days would come back to Angela as well, rising up before her whenever she felt doubt or longing, looming over every disappointment—the inexhaustible mystery of love found and lost.

Boswell's new novel, *American Owned Love*, which will be published in April, takes place on the Rio Grande and examines the area's unique border culture. The title came to him looking at roadside marquees for motels, many of which proclaim they are American-owned. "It's their little racist way of letting you know that there won't be a Pakistani running the place," Boswell says. The marquees often include spiritual messages as well, and one said, without any punctuation: "American Owned Christ Gives Eternal Life Couples $20."

Life is hectic for Boswell these days. After two years at Northwestern University, he began teaching at New Mexico State University in 1989, splitting teaching duties with his wife. Along with

Antonya Nelson, he also teaches at Warren Wilson College, and he is dedicated to the students in both writing programs, viewing them as an extended family. He writes when he can, tapping away on a laptop computer while watching his children, sometimes sneaking away to the guest house, which was once used to dry chili peppers. Owing to his schedule, and also to a blown anterior cruciate ligament in his left knee, he can no longer really indulge his passion for basketball, which he had played at least twice a week.

Yet Boswell wouldn't change his life in any way. He knows he is lucky. He is universally well-liked and respected. He has a family he loves, a teaching position that excites him, good friends, an enviable writing career with the same publisher, Knopf, and the same editor, Ashbel Green, since 1986, and each summer, he is able to relax at a second home in Telluride, Colorado. He might launch into a diatribe about the sociopolitical injustices in this country, but he would never suggest he himself is wanting for anything. To do so, he believes, would be an outrage. "My life has already exceeded my expectations by a long shot."

A Profile by Tony Hoagland

When asked about her poetic influences, Ellen Bryant Voigt's answer is somewhat surprising, but delivered with typical certitude. "Bach and, later, Brahms." It was the pure forms of music from which she started; poetry was, as she tells it, a sort of accident, something she happened on to late in her undergraduate career at Converse College, where she was initially a music major.

Born in 1943, she grew up on a farm in south-central Virginia, in a culture she describes as now completely vanished. She played the piano everywhere as a girl—at church, in school, and for her father's barbershop quartet. Her Southern Baptist family was large, extended, and close-knit; all of her cousins lived near enough to come to Sunday dinner, and summertime meant no fewer than three family reunions. Despite her evident participation in that world, Voigt says she found being so surrounded by family "extremely claustrophobic." The great thing about music, she says, was that "it was an accepted form of solitude," and perhaps it is in that detail we can see the life of poetry predicted. "As long as music was coming from that piano, nobody bothered you."

She attended the all-women's Converse College in South Carolina because it included a music conservatory. It was there she fell under the spell of literature, gradually taking more poetry and fewer music classes. Her professors, disciples of New Criticism, presented poetry as an art form transcending context, released from the "merely" personal. At the time, that suited Voigt.

That urge towards the purity of music, language for its own sake, is audible in all of her poetic work. Voigt, even in this epoch of the meditative narrative, unashamedly owns herself as a lyric poet, and any of her readers knows the value she places on tautness and compression. Her particular specialty is the phrase which indelibly combines austerity of mind and sonic richness. But as Yeats said, out of the quarrels with ourselves, we make poetry. And that dialectic, between the sheer spirituality available in music and the more circumstantially bound facts of life, between the beauti-

PHOTO: THOMAS VICTOR

ful phrase and the bloody body, runs throughout her work. Eventually, she says, "I needed a poetry that could accommodate the soul in the messy world of PTA meetings and sick children." Her first book, *Claiming Kin,* is filled with the dense imagery of rural life, snakes and cornfields, decapitated hens and flowering vines, the fertile fallen world. And in one of her many poems about music, "At the Piano," Voigt describes a girl practicing, "driving triplets against the duple meter": "She knows nothing, but Bach knows everything. / Outside, in the vast, disordered world, / the calves have been taken from their mothers; / both groups bawled and hooted all night long—" Those two chords of experience— transcendent pleasure and earthly suffering—are what Voigt has constantly sought to incorporate into *her* music.

The journey away from the world of her family took her far afield, and also provided her a ringside seat at several singular chapters of American culture. One such experience was being a member of the Iowa Writer's Workshop. She recalls being one of only three women in a class of sixty, the whole group meeting in a Quonset hut on the University of Iowa campus. She remembers having just one poem workshopped that year, though her classmate Stephen Dobyns claims she may have had as many as three.

After a teaching stint at Iowa Wesleyan College, her next stop was the revolutionary Goddard College, then in the full fever of the Aquarian Age. The opening day festivities at that campus in 1969 included sliding, nude, down a mud slope created by the college fire truck.

It is hard to imagine, as she tells these stories with fondness and bemusement, that Voigt has ever *not* had an unusually clear sense of who she is, and both feet solidly planted on the ground. In her home base of Cabot, Vermont, a town which she says remarkably resembles the town of her Virginia childhood, she has raised a family, stayed married, and, in a moment which has had great significance for American poetry, founded the Goddard M.F.A. creative writing program: six-month tutorial semesters in poetry and fiction, initiated by a two-week residency.

That program, of course, became the model for other "low-residence" writing programs at Bennington and Vermont College, and was eventually reincarnated, in 1981, at Warren Wilson College in North Carolina. The point, as Voigt explains it, was not "community," a term she is still suspicious of, but *access* for talented writers, particularly women, who had little opportunity to attend conventional graduate schools or were not served well by them.

Despite Voigt's suspicions of institutional communities—it is notable that she is not a tenured member of any conventional college or university—she seems to have created one. The list of early Goddard M.F.A. faculty is a roster of young powerhouses, including Robert Hass, Michael Ryan, Tobias Wolff, Louise Glück, and Richard Ford. And both faculty and students speak of the program with nothing less than reverence and a sense of their own good fortune.

Of Voigt herself, the two adjectives most commonly employed by others are apparent contradictions: "fierce" and "motherly." Just mention Voigt's name to graduates, and their eyes get filmy; she is famous not only for knowing every student's name, but for possessing an apparently encyclopedic memory of their work, being able to discuss it at a moment's notice. This summer, at the program's twentieth-anniversary celebration in Swannanoa, North Carolina, colleague Heather McHugh dubbed her "the alloy of silk and steel."

Where the steel comes into play is in her tireless ability to administer, guide, and preside over the complex workings of the program as chair of its academic board, and to help make the highly intense residencies flow with purpose and balance. And in workshops, her rigorous standards for poetry are a daunting, incisive reminder of how much craft and knowledge are required before the word "art" can be uttered. At Warren Wilson residencies, publication is not a dirty word, exactly—just an irrelevant one, belonging to the "outside" world.

In the outside world, Voigt has published five books of her own poems, won NEAs and Guggenheims, and taught, it seems, at every writers' conference in the country. Her most recent collection, *Kyrie*, was nominated for the National Book Critics Circle Award, and her second, *The Forces of Plenty*, has just been reissued from Carnegie-Mellon.

Art and life, community and privacy, immense practicality and the growth of the soul—to meet Voigt is to recognize that you are meeting a person of remarkable integration, and to be heartened by the possibility. As this issue of *Ploughshares* was going to press, she was en route to a house in southern France for several weeks (a gift from Warren Wilson alumni), to do nothing but read, write, and walk around. It seemed only fair that she should have her turn at the experience she has fostered for so many—that moment when the writer turns his or her back on the world and begins to play, like the girl in the poem "At the Piano": "she pushes off in her wooden boat—/ she knows nothing, she thinks / no one could be happier than this."

Tony Hoagland currently teaches at New Mexico State University and at Warren Wilson College. His second collection of poems, Donkey Gospel, *will be published by Graywolf Press in 1997.*

PERFECT HELL *Poems by H. L. Hix. Gibbs Smith, $9.95 paper. Reviewed by Dana Gioia.*

H. L. Hix's *Perfect Hell* is the most original, accomplished, and intriguing debut volume I have seen in several years. I am so impressed by this dark and disturbing book by a little known poet that I could easily offer up a dozen more plaudits, but these three terms of commendation seem especially appropriate. *Perfect Hell* speaks in a wonderfully *original* voice—an unexpected but alluring combination of almost surreal procedures set to formal music. Not uncommonly Hix's poems consist only of sentence fragments or catalogues of mysterious unconnected images. A few of his titles will illustrate his queer and quirky sensibility: "So Many Rats, So Many Florins," "As with the Skull, So with the Nose," "The Spindle Turns on the Knees of Necessity." But Hix's poems are utterly *accomplished*. Unlike most experimental poems, his succeed as forceful, expressive, and memorable lyrics. Their poetic frisson makes us realize how many allowances we normally give experimental works of art. So grateful for some meaningful novelty, we forgive avant-garde literature many failings if it does something new well. Finally, Hix is consummately *intriguing* in his unrestrained exploration of the poetic possibilities of our eclectic *fin de siècle*.

Perfect Hell joyfully combines stylistic elements we seldom see joined. To Hix, rhyme and meter do not seem incompatible with fragmented syntax, surreal dream logic, or Keesian collage. In less capable hands (or without a perfectly pitched ear), this postmodern eclecticism might prove disastrous, but, *mirabile dictu,* Hix brings it off. The poems not only cohere; they emanate energy. Hix's nonpartisan omnivorous aesthetic is particularly intriguing because it hints at the potential of American poetry beyond the current Poetry Wars. Why not combine the seldom-realized associational excitement of Language Poetry with the musical rigor and narrative savvy of New Formalism and then add the dark violence and sexuality of early Surrealism? One might create, as Hix has, sonnets that sound like inspired collaborations between Richard Wilbur, Nathanael West, and André Breton, as in the macabre opening of "No Less Than Twenty-six Distinct Necronyms": "*Father dead,* we will call her, or *Niece dead. / Cousin in car crash.* So many names fit. / *Sister cut wrists, Brother shot in the head. / Grandfather wandered off, Great uncle hit / By train while drunk…*" Partial quotation does not adequately convey the intricate musical effect of Hix's poems, but this brief passage provides at least a sense of his deliberately disturbing subject matter.

How will a poet who has debuted so remarkably develop? This is an impossible question to answer, but I worry. Hix's voice is so extreme and idiosyncratic that if he wrote with less consummate musicality or probed less deeply into his secret and uneasy material, the poems might seem merely odd. But *Perfect Hell* stands beyond such criticism. Sadly, however, I must end on a cautionary note. Although Hix's poems are superb, the typography of *Perfect Hell* is dumbfoundingly dreadful. But Hix shouldn't fret. Poems this good will be reset and reprinted many times.

Dana Gioia is the author of Can Poetry Matter? Essays on Poetry and American Culture *(Graywolf).*

CHEATERS AND OTHER STORIES *Stories by Dean Albarelli. St. Martin's, $20.95 cloth. Reviewed by Joan Wickersham.*

Dean Albarelli's *Cheaters and Other Stories* is a collection about moral responsibility, as considered by people who have, for the most part, disappointed themselves. "What he needed was the energy and idealism of his younger self, back when he was so damn sure he'd be a flawless husband and father," one character thinks ruefully. Another flirts with the possibility of an affair that would betray his longtime girlfriend, even though he can already predict his own disillusionment: "Then again, wasn't this only the novelty of someone new? A novelty that will no doubt wear off in time, given the chance. And what would he be left with then?"

What distinguishes these from other tales of emotional fatigue is their crisp, often comic specificity: these are stories about weariness written with tremendous energy. A character drifting toward adultery with an older woman picks up her feet and notices she has very long toes. He fits his fingers between them. "I'm holding hands with your feet, Margaret." The silly irreverence of this, and the complexity—it's partly affectionate, partly cruel, and partly just weird—juxtapose memorably with the weight of the character's guilt and confusion.

Albarelli's energy in this first collection is also apparent in the admirable range of the stories. In one, he writes in the guise of a twenty-nine-year-old female book designer, who is ambivalent about her own Jewishness and alternately irritated by, ashamed of, and deeply tied to her Orthodox twin brother. In another, the storyteller is a father, acutely aware of how flawed he looks in the eyes of his beloved, mercilessly secure sixteen-year-old son. And there's a story written from the viewpoint of a disillusioned, drugged-out journalist whose adventures spin along in a bizarre series of causes and effects with the unreal, inevitable quality of a dream.

This variety is more than mere virtuosity; Albarelli is a patient writer who fully explores the consequences of each of his choices, never hastening a story to a conclusion. In most of these pieces, it is not the language that is embellished, it is the world of the story itself; every revealed detail implies many more that the writer has chosen not to include, and the fact that he knows so much more than he tells gives each story a satisfying heft.

In the stunning, understated "Honeymoon," for example, Albarelli tells the entire story of Shane, an IRA terrorist, from idealistic commitment to ruthless skill to disillusioned horror, without actually narrating any of the formative events. In fact, the drama of the IRA is downplayed; Shane compares his loss of purpose with his feelings about the university track team: "Somehow it has always been that way with me; just when I become quite serious about something, or committed to it, or proficient at it, I lose interest in the thing." The story's only violent image is one that haunts Shane's dreams: that of a young woman killed by a bomb, whose half-naked body he has seen lying beside a bathtub in a supposedly "safe house." This image is implicitly recalled on his wedding night, when his bride, a virgin, is frightened and baffled by her own pain: " 'Shane, we're after doing something wrong; I'm bleeding.' " And we are left gazing into the unbridgeable gulf between her utter innocence, and his utter lack of it.

Joan Wickersham's fiction has appeared in Ploughshares, The Hudson Review, Story, *and* Best American Short Stories. *Her first novel,* The Paper Anniversary, *was recently issued in paperback by Washington Square Press.*

GLASS, IRONY, AND GOD *Poems by Anne Carson. New Directions, $14.00 paper. Reviewed by Liam Rector.*

Poet and editor James Laughlin, publisher of New Directions, is still acquiring poetry that is importantly new, poetry that still sets and extends new directions. Again taking up the battle cry of his essential mentor, Ezra Pound, Laughlin has most recently made literature new by publishing Canadian poet Anne Carson's *Glass, Irony, and God,* one of the most important events so far in the poetry of the 1990's.

Carson's verse is Modernism at its old-fashioned, newfangled best: a use of montage that is slicing, dramatic, antic, learned, wise, wicked, and surprising; a use of fractured narrative which tells the story while also telling the consciousness and sensibility; and a use of elliptical, simultaneous musics rendered in precise, memorable phrasings. It's as if other poets of the time have largely been fiddling around with lyric and narrative, expressionist and constructivist modes, while Carson sweeps by with the entire kit and caboodle. And she throws in a closing essay, "The Gender of Sound," for good measure.

With titles such as "The Glass Essay," "The Truth About God," "TV Men," and "The Fall of Rome: A Traveller's Guide," Carson sets out the audacious breadth, themes, and obsessions of her book, meanings and musics captured and propelled by an equally audacious sense and use of forms. With *Glass, Irony, and God,* one senses the personal vision and hand at work in, say, the finest auteur film, and one is also amidst a vast impersonality that lights up and orchestrates historical figures such as the Brontë sisters, Artaud, Socrates, Sappho, and others. These figures are not arcanely referenced for the footnoters among us, but brought alive again in the very actions of the poem.

Carson's work is suggestively, luridly, and simultaneously all closure and horizon. Her village-explaining voices are akin to the tone Robert Pinsky struck in *An Explanation of America,* and her fastening of the voice to the page suggests the unmannered manner at work in the poems of Frank Bidart. In a useful introduction to the book, Guy Davenport notes that Carson "writes in a kind of mathematics of the emotions," and I'd add that she does this in a terrain where classicism and romanticism hold equal tension, equipoise.

Her tale of a woman separating from a man called Law (which

should be a special delight for those conspiracy buffs hot on the trail of patriarchy) is among the most complex and poignant in contemporary literature: "Yes, I said, as I began to remove my clothes. / / Everything gets crazy. When nude / I turned my back because he likes the back. / He moved onto me. / / Everything I know about love and its necessities / I learned in that one moment / when I found myself / / thrusting my little burning red backside like a baboon / at a man who no longer cherished me. / There was no area of my mind / / Not appalled by this action, no part of my body / that could have done otherwise. / But to talk of mind and body begs the question. / / Soul is the place, / stretched like a surface of millstone grit between body and mind, / where such necessity grinds itself out."

Carson's sense of romance is experienced and imaginative, rather than deluded and feckless. She goes for the inner adult and finds her (and him), as in "Perhaps the hardest thing about losing a lover is / to watch the year repeat its days. / It is as if I could dip my hand down / / into time and scoop up / blue and green lozenges of April heat / a year ago in another country."

If you have been wondering, sorrowing, or worrying about the fate of reading in an electronic age, the electric intelligence and artistry here may be your book back, your book forward.

Liam Rector's collections of poetry are The Sorrow of Architecture *and* American Prodigal. *He edited* The Day I Was Older: On the Poetry of Donald Hall, *and he directs the graduate Writing Seminars at Bennington College.*

OUT WEST *A novel by Fred G. Leebron. Doubleday, $21.95 cloth. Reviewed by Don Lee.*

There is nothing timid about Fred G. Leebron's first novel, *Out West*. He takes two basically decent, highly educated, young social do-gooders and quickly steeps them into the squalid heart of two murders, and then asks us, his readers, to side with the couple. That we mostly do is evidence of Leebron's remarkable talents as a writer.

Of course, Benjamin West and Amber Keenan, both around thirty, are not exactly irreproachable to begin with. Benjamin worked for ten years at an institute for handicapped children, but he never fulfilled his promising academic career, never even mailed out his applications for Ph.D. programs. Instead, he got caught with two ounces of marijuana and a seventeen-year-old girl. After a six-month prison term, he drives cross-country from Pennsylvania to San Francisco, looking for a fresh start. Not much is waiting for him there. A dead-end, minimum-wage job as a desk clerk at a seedy residential hotel in the Tenderloin. But he views this new station, as he sits in the hotel lobby behind a grillwork of bars, as proper penance: "It was, indisputably, a kind of cell. He liked it."

Likewise, Amber, a VISTA worker who is staying in the hotel, is trapped in contrition. Three months before, she had tried to kill her rich, indolent boyfriend, Dean, whom she had lived with in Los Angeles for three years. A poet teaching part-time at a college, he slept with a fellow teacher, then cruelly flaunted the affair in Amber's face. Amber, numb, temporarily demented, opened up the oven vents in his apartment, hoping Dean would ignite the gas when he lit a cigarette. Yet his new lover, not Dean, was killed, and Amber is now unable to sleep: "she had drawn a line between herself and a place—the place of innocence and simplicity, or at least the place of indifferent interaction with humanity—and while it was overwrought and self-pitying to think of it like this, it was true. She had killed someone. . . . She was guilty."

A day after his arrival, Benjamin and Amber have sex, and while he is immediately taken by her, she has misgivings. She is ready to break it off, when Dean arrives and attacks her in her hotel room. Benjamin intercedes and in self-defense kills him. With their past deeds, they can hardly go to the police, and they are now, however reluctantly, bound to each other. What follows is a road nightmare, ripe with dark humor, as they drive first around San Francisco and then to L.A., trying to dump Dean's decomposing body and cover their tracks. Leebron's prose is lucid and evocative throughout the novel, and he seamlessly shifts between Benjamin and Amber's points of view. He is especially adept at describing the particulars of these California cities, the misery of the Tenderloin, the surreal beauty of the highway landscapes, the prefab constructs of convenience stores, gas stations, and fast-food restaurants that substitute as architecture. Granted, this novel is not for everyone. The scenes can become gruesome, fetid, and at times, there are lapses in credibility, gaps in background and explication. Yet *Out West* progresses with tremendous momentum, rushing through a harrowing week in these characters' lives, and with great skill, Leebron creates a rarity: an original, provocative, literary page-turner.

Books Recommended by
Our Advisory Editors

Madeline DeFrees recommends *Beethoven and the Birds,* poems by Judith Skillman: "Forty-five poems from the author whose first collection, *Worship of the Visible Spectrum,* won the King County Arts Commission's Book Award in 1988. The poems celebrate the author's return to playing the violin after a lapse of nine years. Images drawn from music and ornithology dominate in these finely crafted poems. The book is beautifully produced with a cover painting of wisteria in sumi on rice paper. If sumi is the common medium of painter and writer, these poems are the common medium of violinist and poet." (Blue Begonia)

George Garrett recommends *Hockey Sur Glacé,* stories by Peter LaSalle: "It may sound crazy, but seven stories and four poems, all involving ice hockey, really work. Why? Because LaSalle is a wonderful writer and knows more about hockey than anyone." (Breakaway)

Marilyn Hacker recommends *Harping On,* poems by Carolyn Kizer: "Carolyn Kizer's magisterial new book is a world citizen's witty and lyrical meditations on many of the major events of this century, from the intimate perspective of someone who was there. As she re/members herself in sentences and stanzas—the seventeen-year-old observing Einstein; the twenty-year-old hearing of Roosevelt's death on her way to a Chinese lesson in Manhattan; the mature woman, recalling her youth, tempted to spit on Franco's tomb—readers find a poetry which resolves dichotomies: personal/political; form/content; memory/immediacy. Polyglot, a gifted translator, Kizer often has as subtext the untrustworthiness of mediated language—but her own readers are in fiable, skilled hands." (Copper Canyon)

Maxine Kumin recommends *Forged Correspondences,* poems by Philip Brady: "Wildly inventive, these 'forgeries' roam from Heraclitus to the Queen of Sheba, from Newark to Africa. Highly serious and richly comic, a great trip." (New Myths)

Don Lee recommends *Zip Six,* a first novel by Jack Gantos: "Dark, energetic, and sometimes surprisingly comic, Gantos's novel charts a young drug smuggler's course through prison." (Bridge Works)

Gary Soto recommends *Calle 10,* a first novel by Danny Romero: "*Calle 10* is a novel of Chicano lowlife in Oakland. The main character is a dude named Zero, his name summarizing what this novel is all about. The writing is gritty. If you like chewing on the salty rocks of hard living, this is for you." (Mercury)

Maura Stanton recommends *Pears, Lake, Sun,* a first book of poems by Sandy Solomon: "Sandy Solomon is the winner of the Agnes Lynch Starrett Poetry Prize. The poems in *Pears, Lake, Sun* are tough-minded and impeccably crafted, full of passionate stillness and disciplined commotion." (Pittsburgh)

Mark Strand recommends *Journey to the Land of the Flies,* essays by Aldo Buzzi: "It is impossible to describe the homey exoticism of this book, its associative richness, its great intelligence manifested so casually, its wit, its imaginative scope, its revelations, its dilemmas, e.g., 'I was reflecting on the menu, undecided between serpent soup, roast monkey, or a simple stuffed dog with roast pepper.'" (Random)

EDITORS' CORNER

*New Books by
Our Advisory Editors*

Rita Dove, *The Darker Face of the Earth,* a play: Dove's adaptation of *Oedipus* to a Southern plantation in 1840 premiered at the Oregon Shakespeare Festival this past summer, and this second edition reflects major changes made to the script as it was brought to the stage. (Story Line)

George Garrett, *The King of Babylon Shall Not Come Against You,* a novel: A reporter goes to a Florida town to reinvestigate a series of shocking crimes that occurred twenty-five years ago during the week that Martin Luther King, Jr., was assassinated. (Harcourt Brace)

Marilyn Hacker, *Edge,* translations of poems by Claire Malroux: Sandra Gilbert comments: "Claire Malroux's piercing and subtly nuanced poems have been sensitively mediated for English readers in Marilyn Hacker's poised translations. Malroux has put such American and British writers as Emily Dickinson and Emily Brontë into French with style and grace; her own work has clearly been shaped not just by the brilliance of these writers ... but by the technical expertise she brings to the task of translation. And in Marilyn Hacker ... she has found a worthy counterpart to convey her words into English." (Wake Forest)

Charles Simic, *Walking the Black Cat,* poems: In his thirteenth collection, a National Book Award finalist, Simic melds folklore and black magic with everyday life. (Harvest)

Tobias Wolff, *The Night in Question,* short stories: The fourteen tales in this book, Wolff's first collection in over a decade, amply confirm his place as one of the best storytellers of our time. (Knopf)

POSTSCRIPTS

ZACHARIS AWARD *Ploughshares* and Emerson College are pleased to present Kevin Young with the sixth annual John C. Zacharis First Book Award for his poetry collection, *Most Way Home,* published by William Morrow. The $1,500 award—which is funded by Emerson College and named after the college's former president— honors the best debut book published by a *Ploughshares* writer, alternating annually between poetry and fiction.

Kevin Young, who has just turned twenty-six, was born in Lincoln, Nebraska. An only child, he moved six times before he was ten as his parents pursued educational and professional opportunities. Young spent middle and high school in Kansas, then went to Harvard University, where he took poetry workshops with Lucie Brock-Broido and Seamus Heaney and won an Academy of American Poets Prize. While in Cambridge, he joined the Dark Room Collective, a group founded by Thomas Sayers Ellis and Sharan Strange to support and promote young black writers, artists, and filmmakers.

After graduating from Harvard, Young spent two years as a Stegner Fellow at Stanford University, working with Denise Levertov, and then received his M.F.A. from Brown University, where Michael S. Harper was a major influence on him. Young's first publication was in *Callaloo,* followed by appearances in magazines and anthologies such as *Poetry, The Kenyon Review, Agni, Ploughshares,* and *On the Verge.*

Most Way Home, his first collection, was selected by Lucille Clifton as a National Poetry Series winner and published by William Morrow last year. Clifton said of Young, "This poet's gift of storytelling and understanding of the music inherent in the oral tradition of language recreates for us an inner history which is compelling and authentic and American." *The Village Voice Literary Supplement* commented, "In Young's alchemy, succulent scraps are gathered from daily life, distilled, and emerge, finally, as portable nuggets of home, carried wherever the poet may travel."

The book reflects a personalized, largely imagined view of African American history in this century, loosely based on stories from Young's Louisiana family. It considers the dialectic of home and displacement, and the myths and fierce nostalgia that join the two. The poems are arranged to create a narrative arc: in the first section, a family loses their land and a grandfather dies; in the second, a traveling sideshow comes to town; in the third, a woman recalls her rural childhood; and in the last, more contemporary and urban landscapes are explored. Young adds, "The book's also about the two most important things: food and hair."

Currently Young is an assistant professor of English and African American studies at the University of Georgia in Athens, and he is finishing a new book of poems, begun five years ago, about the late artist Jean-Michel Basquiat. "This is not biography," Young says, "nor is it hagiography. Rather, I think it's closer to discography, riffing off his work while recording parts of his life. It's a long poem, a jam session in his honor, bringing in many figures from his time and from history, whether they are musicians, graffiti artists, comedians, or, as Basquiat put it, 'Famous Negro Athletes.'" Individual poems from this series have appeared or are forthcoming in *The New Yorker, Grand Street, Gulf Coast, Hambone,* and *Global City Review.* Young is also featured in an installation called *Two Cents,* an exhibit and catalogue of his poems and Basquiat's works on paper. Beginning at the Miami Dade Art Gallery, the installation has been shown in Niagara, Memphis, Tampa, Los Angeles, and, most recently, Austin, Texas.

The Zacharis First Book Award was inaugurated in 1991. The past winners are: Debra Spark for *Coconuts for the Saint;* Tony Hoagland for *Sweet Ruin;* Jessica Treadway for *Absent Without Leave;* Allison Joseph for *What Keeps Us Here;* and David Wong Louie for *The Pangs of Love.* The award is nominated by the advisory editors of *Ploughshares,* with founding editor DeWitt Henry acting as the final judge. There is no formal application process; all writers who have been published in *Ploughshares* are eligible, and should simply direct two copies of their first book to our office.

CONTRIBUTORS' NOTES

DICK ALLEN's *Ode to the Cold War: Poems New and Selected* is forthcoming from Sarabande Books in April 1997. He has received fellowships from the National Endowment for the Arts and the Ingram Merrill Foundation, and his poems have been included in several recent volumes of *Best American Poetry*. He directs the creative writing program at the University of Bridgeport.

CLAUDIA EMERSON ANDREWS's first book of poems, *Pharaoh, Pharaoh,* will be published in the spring of 1997 as part of Louisiana State University's new signature series, Southern Messenger Poets, edited by Dave Smith. Her poems have appeared or are forthcoming in *Poetry, The Southern Review, The Georgia Review, TriQuarterly, Crazyhorse,* and other journals. A recipient of fellowships from the NEA and the Virginia Commission for the Arts, she lives in Chatham, Virginia.

SALLY BALL is a graduate of Warren Wilson College and lives in St. Louis, where she works at Washington University's International Writers Center. Her work has appeared in *Salmagundi, The Southwest Review, The Threepenny Review,* and *Best American Poetry 1995.*

ANDREA BARRETT is the author of four novels and, most recently, a collection of short fiction, *Ship Fever & Other Stories* (Norton, 1996), which was nominated for a National Book Award. Other stories about the Marburg sisters have appeared in *Story* ("Agnes at Night" and "The Mysteries of Ubiquitin") and *New England Review* ("The Marburg Sisters"). She lives in Rochester, New York.

DINAH BERLAND's poems have appeared in *The Antioch Review, The Iowa Review, New Letters, Ploughshares,* and anthologies including *Nice Jewish Girls: Growing Up in America* (Penguin USA, 1996). She received her M.F.A. from Warren Wilson College in 1995 and works as Publications Coordinator at the Getty Conservation Institute in Los Angeles.

STEVEN CRAMER has published two collections of poetry, *The Eye that Desires to Look Upward* (1987) and *The World Book* (1992), and has finished a third collection entitled *Dialogue for the Left and Right Hand,* which will be published by Lumen Editions in 1997. He teaches literature and writing at Bennington College.

CHARD DENIORD is the author of *Asleep in the Fire,* which was published by the University of Alabama in 1990. His poems have appeared recently in *The Southern Review, The Gettysburg Review, Harvard Magazine, Pequod, Ploughshares, Poetry East, The Iowa Review, New England Review,* and *Agni.* He teaches comparative religions, philosophy, and English at the Putney School.

CARL DENNIS lives in Buffalo, where he teaches in the English department of SUNY at Buffalo. The poems in this issue are part of a manuscript entitled *Ranking the Wishes* that Penguin will be publishing in May 1997.

STUART DISCHELL's poems will appear in his new book, *Evenings and Avenues,* which will be published by Penguin.

STEPHEN DOBYNS is the author of nine books of poetry and seventeen novels. His most recent book of poems is *Common Carnage* (Viking), and his latest novel is *Saratoga Fleshpot* (Norton). His book of essays on poetry, *Best Words, Best Order,* was published by St. Martin's Press last summer. He lives in Watertown, Massachusetts.

LYNN EMANUEL is the author of two books of poetry, *Hotel Fiesta* and *The Dig.* She has received two NEA fellowships, the National Poetry Series Award, and two Pushcart Prizes. With David St. John, she was poetry editor for the 1994–95 edition of *The Pushcart Prize.* Currently, she is a professor at the University of Pittsburgh. Her work has appeared in journals such as *Parnassus, Poetry, The Hudson Review,* and *Ploughshares,* and also was included in *Best American Poetry 1995,* edited by Richard Howard.

CAROLINE FINKELSTEIN is the author of *Windows Facing East* (Dragon Gate, 1986) and *Germany* (Carnegie-Mellon, 1995). She recently completed a third collection, *Justice.*

CAROL FROST's new book of poems, *Venus and Don Juan,* is forthcoming from TriQuarterly Books. The recipient of two fellowships from the NEA, she is Writer-in-Residence at Hartwick College.

GREG GRUMMER manufactures and sells kits used to produce handmade paper for his family's business. He has published in many reviews and quarterlies, including *The American Poetry Review, The Plum Review, Ploughshares, Fine Madness,* and *Indiana Review.*

DONALD HALL's latest book of poems, *The Old Life,* came out earlier this year. "Letter with No Address" is directed toward his late wife, Jane Kenyon, who died in April 1995.

PAUL JENKINS's new book, *Radio Tooth,* won Four Way Books' Award Series Prize—judged by Alberto Ríos—and will be published in the spring of 1997. His recent work has appeared or is forthcoming in *The Gettysburg Review, Grand Street,* and *The New Yorker.* He teaches poetry and writing at Hampshire College and is an editor of *The Massachusetts Review.*

ALICE JONES won the 1992 Beatrice Hawley Award from Alice James Books for her book, *The Knot.* Her poems have appeared in *Poetry, Pequod, The Kenyon Review,* and *Best American Poetry 1994.* She received a poetry fellowship from the NEA in 1994.

SUE KWOCK KIM is a student at the Iowa Writers' Workshop. Her poems have been published in *Poetry, The Nation, The Paris Review, The New Republic, Western Humanities Review, Prairie Schooner, Mudfish,* and the online magazine *Salon,* among other places. *Private Property,* a play she co-wrote, was produced at the Edinburgh Festival Fringe.

LAURIE KUTCHINS has had poems published in *Ploughshares, The Georgia Review, The New Yorker, Poetry,* and numerous other periodicals. Her second book, *The Night Path,* is forthcoming from BOA Editions in 1997. She currently lives and teaches in Albuquerque, New Mexico.

THOMAS LUX teaches at Sarah Lawrence College. His *New and Selected Poems* will be published by Houghton Mifflin in early 1997.

CAMPBELL MCGRATH's new book of poems is *Spring Comes to Chicago,* which has just been published by Ecco Press. He teaches at Florida International University and lives in Miami Beach with his family.

CHRISTOPHER "KIT" MCILROY's short story collection, *All My Relations,* won the 1992 Flannery O'Connor Award and was published by University of Georgia Press. He is the program director of ArtsReach, a nonprofit corporation based in Tucson, Arizona, that conducts writing residencies and workshops in Native American communities.

KEVIN MCILVOY is the editor in chief of *Puerto del Sol.* He has published three novels: *A Waltz* (Lynx House), *The Fifth Station* (Algonquin), and *Little Peg* (Atheneum). His most recent work appeared in *Blue Mesa Review, The Chariton Review,* and *TriQuarterly.*

LESLIE ADRIENNE MILLER's new collection of poems, *Yesterday Had a Man in It,* is forthcoming from Carnegie-Mellon University Press in 1997. She is also the author of *Ungodliness, Staying Up for Love,* and *No River.* She has published in a number of magazines and anthologies, including *The American Poetry Review, The Kenyon Review,* and *The Georgia Review.* Currently she is an associate professor of English at the University of St. Thomas in St. Paul, Minnesota.

STEVE ORLEN's most recent book of poetry is *The Bridge of Sighs,* published by Miami University Press in Ohio. A new book will be published by Miami in 1997, and new poems are forthcoming in *The Gettysburg Review* and *The Yale Review.* He teaches in the creative writing program at the University of Arizona in Tucson and in the low-residency M.F.A. program at Warren Wilson College.

GREGORY ORR's most recent collection is *City of Salt* (Pittsburgh, 1995). His first book, *Burning the Empty Nests,* will soon be reissued by Carnegie-Mellon University Press in its Contemporary Classics series. He is co-editor, with Ellen Bryant Voigt, of the essay collection *Poets Teaching Poets: Self and the World* (Michigan, 1996). He is married to the painter Trisha Orr.

TRISHA ORR exhibits at the Katharina Rich Perlow Gallery in New York City (solo show, December 1996). She has received fellowships from the Mid-Atlantic/NEA and the Virginia Commission for the Arts. Portfolios of her work have been published in *The Georgia Review* (Summer 1995) and the upcoming *New American Paintings VIII* (Open Studios Press). She lives in Charlottesville, Virginia.

LUCIA PERILLO's second book of poems, *The Body Mutinies,* was published by Purdue University Press in 1996. Her previous book, *Dangerous Life,* was published by Northeastern University Press in 1989 and received the Poetry Society of America's Norma Farber Award for the best first book of that year.

JOYCE PESEROFF is the author, most recently, of *A Dog in the Lifeboat* (Carnegie-Mellon).

CLENN REED, a native of western New York, graduated from the University of Akron and recently earned an M.F.A. from Sarah Lawrence College. He now lives in New York City and teaches at Sarah Lawrence. His work appeared in recent issues of *Alaska Quarterly Review* and *Faultline*.

MARTHA RHODES is the author of the collections *At the Gate* (Provincetown Arts, 1995) and the forthcoming *Perfect Disappearance*. She is one of the founding editors of Four Way Books and a member of the writing faculty at The New School in New York City, where she resides.

KENNETH ROSEN of Portland, Maine, recently concluded his tenure as Walter E. Russell Chair of Education and Philosophy at the University of Southern Maine with the public talk "A Spy in the House of the Thought Police." New poems have appeared in *The Paris Review, Agni,* and *The Massachusetts Review,* and in the collection *No Snake, No Paradise*.

STEVEN SCHWARTZ is the author of two collections of stories, *To Leningrad in Winter* (1985) and *Lives of the Fathers* (1991), and a novel, *Therapy* (1994). His new novel, *Shred of God,* will be published by William Morrow in 1998. He lives in Fort Collins, Colorado, where he teaches writing at Colorado State University.

ELIZABETH SEARLE's story, "Why We're Here," was adapted from a chapter of her first novel, *A Four-Sided Bed,* which is forthcoming from Graywolf Press in 1997. Other excerpts have appeared in *Agni, The Kenyon Review,* and the anthologies *Lovers* and *American Fiction.* Her story collection, *My Body to You,* won the 1992 Iowa Short Fiction Prize. A former special education teacher, she now teaches in the graduate writing program at Emerson College.

ALAN SHAPIRO's most recent book of poems, *Mixed Company,* was published in the spring of 1996 by the University of Chicago Press. His memoir, *The Last Happy Occasion* (Chicago), appeared in the fall of 1996.

FAITH SHEARIN received her M.F.A. from Sarah Lawrence College in 1993 and recently completed two consecutive years of fellowship at the Fine Arts Work Center in Provincetown. A recipient of awards from the Michigan Young Playwright's Festival, the National Foundation for Advancement in the Arts, the Ann M. Kaufmann Fund, and Bread Loaf, she has published in a number of journals, including *Shankpainter, The Women's Studies Quarterly,* and *The Chicago Review*.

GARY SHORT is the author of two books of poems, *Theory of Twilight* (Ahsahta) and *Flying Over Sonny Liston* (Nevada), which received the 1996 Western States Book Award. His poems have appeared recently in *The Antioch Review* and *Poetry*. He lives in American Flat, Nevada, population nine.

RALPH SNEEDEN has work forthcoming in *The Southern Review, TriQuarterly, New Virginia Review, Portsmouth Review,* and *The Second Set* (Indiana), an anthology of jazz-related poetry. "Off Little Misery Island" is the title poem of his book-length manuscript. He teaches in Exeter, New Hampshire, where he lives with his wife and three children.

LISA RUSS SPAAR's work has appeared in *Poetry, The Virginia Quarterly Review, Crazyhorse, Shenandoah,* and elsewhere. She has published two chapbooks, and her new manuscript, *Rapunzel's Clock,* won a 1996 Virginia Commission for the Arts award. She teaches creative writing at the University of Virginia, where she administers the M.F.A. program.

NANCE VAN WINCKEL's second collection of poems, *The Dirt* (Miami), was published in 1994. New poems appear in *The North American Review, Denver Quarterly,* and *The Paris Review.* She is also the author of two collections of fiction, *Limited Lifetime Warranty* (1994) and the forthcoming *Quake,* both from University of Missouri Press. She teaches in the M.F.A. program at Eastern Washington University.

ELLEN DORÉ WATSON's full-length collection, *We Live in Bodies,* will be published in February by Alice James Books. New poems are forthcoming in *Prairie Schooner* and *The New Yorker.* She also translates Brazilian literature, including the poems of Adélia Prado (*The Alphabet in the Park,* Wesleyan), and serves as the translation editor of *The Massachusetts Review.*

KATHLEENE WEST is the poetry editor of *Puerto del Sol.* She has published seven books of poetry and fiction, of which two are in print: *Water Witching* (Copper Canyon) and *The Farmer's Daughter* (Sandhills). New work is forthcoming in *Alaska Quarterly Review* and *The Muse Strikes Back!* (Story Line).

RENATE WOOD's collection of poems, *Raised Underground,* was published by Carnegie-Mellon University Press in 1991. The recipient of a grant from the Colorado Council on the Arts and of the 1995 Emily Clark Balch Prize from *The Virginia Quarterly Review,* she teaches in the M.F.A. program at Warren Wilson College.

JODY ZORGDRAGER, a recent grant recipient from the Connecticut Commission on the Arts, has poems forthcoming in *The Literary Review* and *The Antioch Review.* Currently she teaches English literature at Quinsigamond Community College in Worcester, Massachusetts.

~

SUBSCRIBERS Feel free to contact us via E-mail with address changes (the post office usually will not forward journals) or any problems with your subscription. Our E-mail address is: pshares@emerson.edu. Also, please note that on occasion we exchange mailing lists with other literary magazines and organizations. If you would like your name excluded from these exchanges, simply send us an E-mail message or a letter stating so.

SUBMISSION POLICIES *Ploughshares* is published three times a year: usually mixed issues of poetry and fiction in the Spring and Winter and a fiction issue in the Fall, with each guest-edited by a different writer. We welcome unsolicited manuscripts from August 1 to March 31 (postmark dates). All submissions sent from April to July are returned unread. In the past, guest editors often announced specific themes for issues, but we have revised our editorial policies and no longer restrict submissions to thematic topics. Submit your work at any time during our reading period; if a manuscript is not timely for one issue, it will be considered for another. Send one prose piece and/or one to three poems at a time (mail genres separately). Poems should be individually typed either single- or double-spaced on one side of the page. Prose should be typed double-spaced on one side and be no longer than twenty-five pages. Although we look primarily for short stories, we occasionally publish personal essays/memoirs. Novel excerpts are acceptable if self-contained. Unsolicited book reviews and criticism are not considered. Please do not send multiple submissions of the same genre, and do not send another manuscript until you hear about the first. Additional submissions will be returned unread. Mail your manuscript in a page-sized manila envelope, your full name and address written on the outside, to the "Fiction Editor," "Poetry Editor," or "Nonfiction Editor." (Unsolicited work sent directly to a guest editor's home or office will be discarded.) All manuscripts and correspondence regarding submissions should be accompanied by a self-addressed, stamped envelope (S.A.S.E.) for a response. Expect three to five months for a decision. Do not query us until five months have passed, and if you do, please write to us, including an S.A.S.E. and indicating the postmark date of submission, instead of calling. Simultaneous submissions are amenable as long as they are indicated as such and we are notified immediately upon acceptance elsewhere. We cannot accommodate revisions, changes of return address, or forgotten S.A.S.E.'s after the fact. We do not reprint previously published work. Translations are welcome if permission has been granted. We cannot be responsible for delay, loss, or damage. Payment is upon publication: $25/printed page, $50 minimum per title, $250 maximum per author, with two copies of the issue and a one-year subscription.

THE NAME *Ploughshares* 1. The sharp edge of a plough that cuts a furrow in the earth. 2 a. A variation of the name of the pub, the Plough and Stars, in Cambridge, Massachusetts, where a journal was founded. 2 b. The pub's name was inspired by the Sean O'Casey play about the Easter Rising of the Irish "citizen army." The army's flag contained a plough, representing the things of the earth, hence practicality; and stars, the ideals by which the plough is steered. 3. A shared, collaborative, community effort that has endured for twenty-five years. 4. A literary journal that has been energized by a desire for harmony, peace, and reform. Once, that spirit motivated civil rights marches, war protests, and student activism. Today, it still inspirits a desire for beating swords into ploughshares, but through the power and the beauty of the written word.

Ploughshares Patrons

This publication would not be possible without the support of
our readers and the generosity of the following individuals
and organizations. As a nonprofit enterprise,
we welcome donations of any amount.

COUNCIL
Denise and Mel Cohen
Eugenia Gladstone Vogel

PATRONS
Anonymous
John K. Dineen
Scott and Annette Turow
Marillyn Zacharis

FRIENDS
Martin Geer
Richard and Maureen Yelovich

ORGANIZATIONS
Emerson College
Lila Wallace–Reader's Digest Fund
Council of Literary Magazines and Presses
Lannan Foundation
Massachusetts Cultural Council

COUNCIL: $3,000 for two lifetime subscriptions, acknowledgement
in the journal for three years, and votes on the Cohen and Zacharis
Awards. PATRON: $1,000 for a lifetime subscription and acknow-
ledgement in the journal for two years. FRIEND: $500 for a life-
time subscription and acknowledgement in the journal
for one year. All donations are tax-deductible.
Please make your check payable to *Ploughshares*,
Emerson College, 100 Beacon St., Boston, MA 02116.

Ploughshares Donors

With great gratitude, we would like to acknowledge the following
readers who generously made donations to *Ploughshares* during
our 1996 fundraising campaign.

Anonymous (3)
Anne Aldrich
John Wayne Andrews
M. C. Bartek
M. Kuno Bernheim
Mary Clearman Blew
Susan DeWitt Bodemer
Pierce Brennan
Robert Brooks
Ashley Brown
Linda Butler
Steve Cantwell
James Carroll and
  Alexandra Marshall
M. Riesa Clark
Stephanie Cohen
Richard Concannon and
  Smoki Bacon
Margaret Davis
Brian Komei Dempster
Elizabeth Detwiler
Mary Lynn H. Dickson
Susan Dodd
Bruce S. Dole
John Donner
Paula Eder
Betty Ellis
Tara Epstein
Dundas I. Flaherty
David Godine
  David R. Godine Publisher
Barry and Lorrie
  Goldensohn
Jane Goldflies
Joanne Goodrich
Mary Gordon
Greg Grummer
Elizabeth C. Guthrie
Donald Hall
Michael D. Harvey

James Haug
James Hazen
Ray Herles
Connie Hershey
  Artifact Press, Ltd.
Richard Holowka
J. Perry Howland
Kristi Humphries
Joseph Hurka
Alma Johnson
Jennifer Karetnick
X. J. Kennedy
Joann Kobin
Joseph Kostolefsky
Mary Ellen Kreher
Maxine Kumin
Kristin Laxalt
Victor and Joyce Lee
Bob Lewis
H. R. Lohr
Joanne Lyman
Anthony Majahad
Kathryn Maris
Cleopatra Mathis
Ruth Newton Mattos
David McAuliffe
  Angles Gallery
E. McCarthy
Michael McCarty
Fiona McCrae
  Graywolf Press
Eileen McGuire
Lisa Mohnsam
Warren L. Molton
Judith H. Montgomery
Radames Morales
Jeanne Morrel-Franklin
Romola C. Morse
Sandell Morse
Wanda L. Nagy

Joseph A. O'Malley
Phoebe Palmer
Elizabeth Paxson
Joyce Peseroff
Georgiana Porton
Richardson Price
Mollie Pryor
Mildred M. Reed
Kenneth Rosen
M. L. Rosenthal
Kelly Rowe
Tammy J. Senk
Marcia Slutsky
Gary Soto
Debra Spark
S. Spring
James Stacey
Maura Stanton
Joan Stern
Clara Stites
Frank Stricker
Lee Strickland
Esther P. Thomas
Joanne Trafton
Eunice E. Valentine
Richard Vincent
John W. Vineyard
Gale Ward
Alison Weber
Norma Weiss
Lynda M. Wierenga
Paul Wilcox
Jehanne B. Williamson
Miryam Ehrlich Williamson
Sarah S. Wilson
Rodney Wittwer
James Wolcott
Nancy Wynstra
Ria Young
Ellen Zahl

INDEX TO VOLUME XXII

Ploughshares · A Journal of New Writing · 1996

Last Name, First Name, Title, Volume.Issue.Page

FICTION

Barrett, Andrea, *The Forest*, 22.4.12

Bausch, Richard, *Two Altercations*, 22.2&3.66

Beattie, Ann, *Buried Treasure*, 22.2&3.9

Bienen, Leslie McKenzie, *The Star of Africa*, 22.2&3.197

Caldwell, Bo, *Fourteen*, 22.2&3.108

Cheuse, Alan, *Midnight Ride*, 22.2&3.82

DuBow, Shane, *About Fifty Band-Aids*, 22.2&3.154

Fay, Julie, *Hannah*, 22.1.66

Finger, Anne, *Comrade Luxemburg and Comrade Gramsci...*, 22.1.74

Gallagher, Tess, *Coming and Going*, 22.2&3.96

Gammon, Catherine, *Issues of Appropriation*, 22.1.83

Gordon, Mary, *City Life*, 22.1.91

Greer, Andrew Sean, *Come Live with Me and Be My Love*, 22.2&3.126

Hagy, Alyson, *Search Bay*, 22.2&3.165

Keene, John R., *My Son, My Heart, My Life*, 22.1.117

McIlroy, Christopher, *Medicine*, 22.4.34

McIlvoy, Kevin, *Green House*, 22.4.173

Phillips, Dale Ray, *At the Edge of the New World*, 22.2&3.46

Sadoff, Ira, *The Tragic Stiletto of Trabzon*, 22.2&3.37

Schwartz, Steven, *Skeleton*, 22.4.184

Searle, Elizabeth, *Why We're Here*, 22.4.197

West, Kathleene, *Those Poor Devils*, 22.4.213

White, Edmund, *The Tea Ceremony*, 22.1.190

NONFICTION

Boswell, Robert, *Introduction to Winter 1996–97*, 22.4.5

Campo, Rafael, *About Marilyn Hacker: A Profile*, 22.1.195

Derricotte, Toi, *Blacks in the U.*, 22.1.46

Ford, Richard, *Introduction to Fall 1996*, 22.2&3.5

Hacker, Marilyn, *Introduction to Spring 1996*, 22.1.5

Hoagland, Tony, *About Ellen Bryant Voigt: A Profile*, 22.4.222

Lee, Don, *About Richard Ford: A Profile*, 22.2&3.226

About Robert Boswell: A Profile, 22.4.216

Louis, Adrian C., *Earth Bone Connected to the Spirit Bone*, 22.1.145

Voigt, Ellen Bryant, *Introduction to Winter 1996–97*, 22.4.10

POETRY

Alexander, Elizabeth, *Harlem Birthday Party*, 22.1.6

Allen, Dick, *Cassandra in Connecticut*, 22.4.73

Alvarez, Julia, *Folding My Clothes*, 22.1.8

Two Years Too Late, 22.1.9

Andrews, Claudia Emerson, *Bait Man*, 22.4.74

Arroyo, Rane, *Breathing Lessons*, 22.1.12

Ball, Sally, *Gymnasium*, 22.4.78

Berland, Dinah, *Angeline*, 22.4.79

Brackenbury, Alison, *In the General*, 22.1.16

At the Playhouse, 22.1.17

Campo, Rafael, *Route 17*, 22.1.18

Cannon, Melissa, *Fairy Tale and Gloss*, 22.1.21

Corn, Alfred, *Musical Sacrifice*, 22.1.23

Cramer, Steven, *A Brief History of the Enclosure Movement*, 22.4.80

Dempster, Brian Komei, *My Questions to Obachan, Her Answers*, 22.1.38

A Conversation with My Mother, Renko..., 22.1.39

deNiord, Chard, *The Invisible Body*, 22.4.81

Dennis, Carl, *Writing at Night*, 22.4.82
Distinctions, 22.4.84

Dent, Tory, *Everybody Loves a Winner*,
22.1.41
Voice as Gym-Body, 22.1.45

Dischell, Stuart, *Evening II*, 22.4.86
End of the Century, 22.4.87
Psalm, 22.4.88

Dobyns, Stephen, *The Cunning One*,
22.4.89
Artist, 22.4.90
Discord, 22.4.91
Icarus's Flight, 22.4.92
Blemished and Unblemished, 22.4.93
Last Wisdom, 22.4.95

Eady, Cornelius, *How I Got Born*, 22.1.51
My Heart, 22.1.52
Who Am I?, 22.1.53
Sightings, 22.1.54

Ellis, Thomas Sayers, *Atomic Bride*, 22.1.56

Emanuel, Lynn, *Self-Portrait as a Small
Town*, 22.4.97
Poem About a Landscape in the Country,
22.4.98
Painting the Town, 22.4.100

Espada, Martín, *Offerings to an Ulcerated
God*, 22.1.60

Fanthorpe, U. A., *On Worms, and Being
Lucky*, 22.1.62
Née, 22.1.64

Finkelstein, Caroline, *My Little Esperanto*,
22.4.101

Frost, Carol, *Bliss*, 22.4.103
Companion Of, 22.4.104
Self, 22.4.106

García, Diana, *Cotton Rows, Cotton
Blankets*, 22.1.90

Gregor, Arthur, *Chiaroscuro*, 22.1.110

Grummer, Greg, *End of the Road*, 22.4.107
This Has Happened Before, 22.4.108

Hall, Donald, *Letter with No Address*,
22.4.109

Hall, Judith, *Fanny Burney;
Or, The Anatomy Theater*, 22.1.113
The Other Girls in Lettuce, 22.1.115

Jenkins, Paul, *Headboard and Footboard*,
22.4.113

Jones, Alice, *Tap*, 22.4.115

Kim, Sue Kwock, *Flight*, 22.4.116

Komunyakaa, Yusef, *Ogoni*, 22.1.139

Kumin, Maxine, *Letters*, 22.1.142

Kutchins, Laurie, *New Moon, End of
October*, 22.4.118

Lux, Thomas, *Pismire Rising*, 22.4.119

Mattawa, Khaled, *Heartsong*, 22.1.157

McGrath, Campbell, *Praia dos Orixas*,
22.4.121

McLeod, Stephen, *Becoming Kansas*,
22.1.159

Merritt, Constance, *Woman of Color*,
22.1.161

Miller, Leslie Adrienne, *A Connect-the-Dots
Picture*, 22.4.124

Orlen, Steve, *Poem Against Ideas*, 22.4.127

Orr, Gregory, from *Orpheus and Eurydice*,
22.4.132

Ostriker, Alicia, *Another Imaginary Voyage*,
22.1.163

Perillo, Lucia, *Air Guitar*, 22.4.139
Trees, 22.4.142
Pomegranate, 22.4.143

Peseroff, Joyce, *Birthday*, 22.4.146
Wind, 22.4.147

Phillips, Carl, *The Blue Castrato*, 22.1.165

Pratt, Minnie Bruce, *The White Star*,
22.1.169

Raz, Hilda, *Breast/Fever*, 22.1.171
Service, 22.1.173

Reed, Clenn, *Catatonia: In a Classroom for
the Slow-to-Learn*, 22.4.148

Rhodes, Martha, *Oh, Luminous*, 22.4.149

Rickel, Boyer, *Ode (To My Desire)*, 22.1.176

Rodríguez, Aleida, *The First Woman*,
22.1.179
Parts of Speech, 22.1.181

Rosen, Kenneth, *Browntail*, 22.4.151
The Little Lie, 22.4.152
The Dying Gull, 22.4.154

Rumens, Carol, *The Mistaken Nymph*,
22.1.183

Schulman, Grace, *Elegy Written in the
Conservatory Garden*, 22.1.184

Seaton, Maureen, *When I Was White*,
22.1.187

Shapiro, Alan, *The Coat*, 22.4.155
What, 22.4.156

Shearin, Faith, *Ruins*, 22.4.157

Shepherd, Reginald, *Blue*, 22.1.189

Short, Gary, *Sway*, 22.4.158

Sneeden, Ralph, *Off Little Misery Island*,
22.4.160

Spaar, Lisa Russ, *Rapunzel's Exile,* 22.4.162

Van Winckel, Nance, *The Company We Keep,* 22.4.163

Watson, Ellen Doré, *Liza,* 22.4.166

Now that the Fields, 22.4.167

Wood, Renate, from *German Chronicle,* 22.4.168

Zorgdrager, Jody, *Lunacy,* 22.4.172

BOOKSHELF

Gioia, Dana, rev. of *Perfect Hell* by H. L. Hix, 22.4.226

Harleman, Ann, rev. of *Lies of the Saints* by Erin McGraw, 22.2&3.239

Hershman, Marcie, rev. of *Elijah Visible* by Thane Rosenbaum, 22.2&3.242

Hix, H. L., rev. of *The Chain* by Tom Sleigh, 22.1.200

Lee, Don, rev. of *Out West* by Fred G. Leebron, 22.4.230

Leebron, Fred, rev. of *You Have the Wrong Man* by Maria Flook, 22.1.201

rev. of *Large Animals in Everyday Life* by Wendy Brenner, 22.2&3.236

Peseroff, Joyce, rev. of *All-American Girl* by Robin Becker, 22.2&3.238

Rector, Liam, rev. of *Glass, Irony, and God* by Anne Carson, 22.4.229

Rivard, David, rev. of *Red Sauce, Whiskey and Snow* by August Kleinzahler, 22.2&3.240

Rosenthal, M. L., rev. of *The Dual Tradition* by Thomas Kinsella, 22.2&3.243

Shoaf, Diann Blakely, rev. of *Atlantis* and *Heaven's Coast* by Mark Doty, 22.1.203

Stanley, Jodee, rev. of *Emerald City* by Jennifer Egan, 22.1.205

Wickersham, Joan, rev. of *Cheaters and Other Stories* by Dean Albarelli, 22.4.227

IN MEMORIAM

M. L. ROSENTHAL

Be an Expatriate Writer
for Two Weeks

Join an international group of selected fiction writers for an intensive working seminar in the tranquillity of a Dutch Renaissance castle. Guided by six distinguished instructors, this seminar is designed to be intimate and productive. The team-taught workshop is an editorial roundtable where writers are advised on strategies for analyzing structure and developing and sustaining character-in-action. Designated writing sessions and individual conferences enable new or revised work and redefined writing objectives. The seminar concentrates on the craft and technique of fiction while also considering the pragmatics of the literary market. The dynamics of the seminar are carefully planned to include both published writers and those in the early stages of promising careers. The seminar is sponsored by Emerson College and inspired by the literary traditions of the journal *Ploughshares*, an Emerson College publication. Four academic credits are offered and all applications received by April 1 are considered for the $1,000 Robie Macauley fellowship.

DIRECTOR: Alexandra Marshall. FACULTY: James Carroll, Pamela Painter, Thomas E. Kennedy, Alexandra Johnson, Askold Melnyczuk.

Eighth Annual
Ploughshares
International
Fiction
Writing
Seminar

Kasteel Well
The Netherlands
August 11-22, 1997
Emerson College
European Center

For a brochure and application to the seminar, mail or fax this form to
David Griffin • Assistant Director of Continuing Education
Emerson College • 100 Beacon Street • Boston, MA 02116 USA
Tel. 617-824-8567 • Fax 617-824-8618 • E-mail: dgriffin@emerson.edu

Name _____

Address_____

_____

wc&f

THE MFA PROGRAM FOR WRITERS
AT WARREN WILSON COLLEGE CELEBRATES
TWENTY YEARS OF TEACHING WRITING

S emesters in our rigorous low-residency program in poetry and fiction begin with a 10-day residency of classes, workshops and lectures on 1,100 acres in the Swannanoa Valley. Join us, and study under the close supervision of outstanding faculty, each of whom works with no more than five students.

Need-based grants, federal loans, and a Holden Minority Scholarship are available.

For more information, call or write Peter Turchi, Director, MFA Program for Writers, PO Box 9000, Warren Wilson College, Asheville NC 28815-9000. (704) 298-3325 x380   FAX (704) 298-1405 http://www.warren-wilson.edu/mfa

Recent graduates worked one-to-one with

Joan Aleshire	Carl Dennis	Margot Livesey	Ira Sadoff
Agha Shahid Ali	Stephen Dobyns	Thomas Lux	Jim Shepard
Debra Allbery	Roland Flint	Michael Martone	Joan Silber
Andrea Barrett	Reginald Gibbons	Campbell McGrath	Dave Smith
Charles Baxter	Ehud Havazelet	Heather McHugh	Irini Spanidou
Pinckney Benedict	Brooks Haxton	Christopher McIlroy	Debra Spark
Marianne Boruch	David Haynes	Kevin McIlvoy	Darcey Steinke
Robert Boswell	Tony Hoagland	James McMichael	Peter Turchi
Karen Brennan	Marie Howe	Pablo Medina	Ellen Bryant Voigt
Robert Cohen	C. J. Hribal	Antonya Nelson	Chuck Wachtel
Michael Collier	Edward P. Jones	Susan Neville	Alan Williamson
	Brigit Pegeen Kelly	Steve Orlen	Eleanor Wilner
	Larry Levis	Janet Peery	Geoffrey Wolff
		Mary Elsie Robertson	Renate Wood
		Richard Russo	

Look for Poets Teaching Poets: Self in the World,
a collection of essays by our poetry faculty,
just published by the University of Michigan Press.

New from Graywolf Press

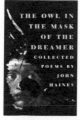

BENNINGTON WRITING SEMINARS

MFA in Writing and Literature
Two-Year Low-Residency Program

A. BLAKE GARDNER

FICTION
NONFICTION
POETRY

For more information contact:
Writing Seminars
Box PL
Bennington College
Bennington, VT 05201
802-442-5401, ext. 160, Fax 802-442-6164

MFA in Writing
at Vermont College

Intensive 11-day residencies on our beautiful central Vermont campus alternate with **six-month non-resident semester study projects.**

Residencies include classes, readings, conferences and small workshops led by two faculty. Immersed with other developing writers in a stimulating environment, students forge working relationships with each other and with experienced practitioners of poetry and fiction.

Under the careful guidance of the faculty, students focus on their own writing for the semester study project. A low student-faculty ratio (5-1) ensures close personal attention.

We also offer **Post-Graduate Semesters** and **One-Year Intensives** for those who have completed a graduate degree in creative writing.

Scholarships, minority scholarships and financial aid available.

Vermont College admits students regardless of race, creed, sex or ethnic origin.

Residencies catered by the New England Culinary Institute.

Poetry Faculty

Robin Behn
Mark Cox
Deborah Digges
Nancy Eimers
Mark Halliday
Richard Jackson
Jack Myers
William Olsen
David Rivard
J. Allyn Rosser
Mary Ruefle
Betsy Sholl
Leslie Ullman
Roger Weingarten
David Wojahn

Fiction Faculty

Carol Anshaw
Phyllis Barber
Francois Camoin
Abby Frucht
Douglas Glover
Sydney Lea
Diane Lefer
Ellen Lesser
Bret Lott
Sena Jeter Naslund
Christopher Noel
Pamela Painter
Sharon Sheehe Stark
Gladys Swan
W. D. Wetherell

For more information contact:
Roger Weingarten, Director
MFA in Writing
Vermont College
Montpelier, VT 05602
Tel: (802) 828-8840 Fax: (802) 828-8649

Vermont College of Norwich University

Ploughshares

a literary adventure

Known for its compelling fiction and poetry, *Ploughshares* is widely regarded as one of America's most influential literary journals. Each issue is guest-edited by a different writer for a fresh, provocative slant— exploring personal visions, aesthetics, and literary circles—and contributors include both well-known and emerging writers. In fact, *Ploughshares* has become a premier proving ground for new talent, showcasing the early works of Sue Miller, Mona Simpson, Robert Pinsky, and countless others. Past guest editors include Richard Ford, Derek Walcott, Tobias Wolff, Carolyn Forché, and Rosellen Brown. This unique editorial format has made *Ploughshares*, in effect, into a dynamic anthology series—one that has established a tradition of quality and prescience. *Ploughshares* is published in quality trade paperback in April, August, and December: usually a fiction issue in the Fall and mixed issues of poetry and fiction in the Spring and Winter. Inside each issue, you'll find not only great new stories and poems, but also a profile on the guest editor, book reviews, and miscellaneous notes about *Ploughshares*, its writers, and the literary world. Subscribe today.

Sample *Ploughshares* on the Web: http://www.emerson.edu/ploughshares

----